636.7 T46
Thomas, S
The new P

90 00888

D1047261

KALAMAZOO PUBLIC LIBRARY

JUN   1990

DEMCO

THE NEW
pug

Envy, Hatred, Malice, by Buton Rivière, in Haussner's Restaurant, Baltimore, Maryland. *Photo courtesy Helen Pittinger*

THE NEW
pug

by
Shirley Thomas

HOWELL
BOOK HOUSE
New York

KALAMAZOO PUBLIC LIBRARY

Copyright © 1990 by Howell Book House, Inc.

All rights reserved. No part of this book may be reproduced or transmitted in any form or by any means, electronic or mechanical, including photocopying, recording, or by any information storage and retrieval system, without permission in writing from the Publisher.

Howell Book House
Macmillan Publishing Company
866 Third Avenue, New York, NY 10022
Collier Macmillan Canada, Inc.

Library of Congress Cataloging-in-Publication Data

Thomas, Shirley, 1926–
    The new Pug/by Shirley Thomas.
      p.   cm.
    ISBN 0-87605-264-2
    1. Pug. I. Title.
SF429.P9T48   1990   89-11160   CIP
636.7'6—dc20

Macmillan books are available at special discounts for bulk purchases for sales promotions, premiums, fund-raising, or educational use. For details contact:
                    Special Sales Director
                    Macmillan Publishing Company
                    866 Third Avenue
                    New York, NY 10022

10 9 8 7 6 5 4 3 2 1

Printed in the United States of America

This book is for

CH. BITTERWELL BROTH OF A BOY

*my adored Pug dog, who influenced my life,
and for my children*

PAMELA, BRADLEY AND GAIL

*who encouraged me to write this book,
and for my devoted husband*

RAYNE A. THOMAS

90 09888

Contents

Acknowledgments

IN WRITING this book I have drawn upon my experience as a breeder, exhibitor and judge over a period of fifty years. I have used this knowledge in the hope that this book will become an educational tool to further the advancement of the Pug breed.

I wish to thank the following individuals for their inestimable assistance in the preparation of this book. A special thank-you goes to Cecilia A. Geary, whose able help made my task easier, and to E. Ruth Terry, who provided the skeleton drawing of the Pug. I am grateful to Pauline Thomas, who contributed the fine artwork used in this book to illustrate the breed. I wish to thank Ann R. Weitz and Pamela A. Weaver, who contributed to the obedience portion of this book, and Dr. Richard Lange, Queens Village Animal Hospital, for his invaluable help with the medical correlation. I especially wish to thank all the contributors collectively for their autobiographies and pictures. They have made this book possible.

THE NEW
pug

謝翠霞

Noted Chinese artist Hsi Tsui-Hsia from Taiwan sketched this impressive artifact of a *Loong Chau*, Lo-Sze dragon claw Pug found in the *Imperial Dog Book*.

1

Origin and History of the Pug

T HE PUG HAS HAD many names attached to him in the course of history, and no one knows for sure where the name comes from. The word "pug" was commonly used in England in the second half of the sixteenth century. The first clear identification of the word with a dog occurred in the *M. Bailey Dictionary* in 1731, when the author wrote: "*Pug,* a nickname for a Monkey or Dog." Some felt the word "pug" was applied to the Pug dog because of his early appearance—a flattened face resembling that of a monkey.

Reverend Pearce, who wrote under the name of Idstone, and Rev. G. Ash both echo Stonehenge (I. H. Walsh) in his belief, stating that "pug" is derived from the Latin word *pugnus,* meaning the human fist, because the dog's profile resembled the shadow of a clenched fist. It is unlikely, however, that the word is derived from either Latin or Greek.

Milo E. Denlinger, in his book *The Complete Pug,* writes: "A far better hypothesis, probably the correct one, is that *Pug* is a corruption of *Puck,* the mischievous fairy of Shakespeare's *A Midsummer Night's Dream* and other early romances. Puck was sometimes known as Robin Goodfellow or Friar Rush." This derivation is suggested by *Century Dictionary,* the ethnologies of which are usually trustworthy. The puckish disposition of the Pug is undeniable. Further evidence that this derivation is correct is offered by the employment of the term "pucked up" by some of the nineteenth-century authorities to describe the Pug's wrinkled face.

The Chinese, as we shall see in more detail later on, were known to call

Pugs by several names, among them *Foo* or *Fu* dog, Lo-Chaing-Sze, Lo-Chaing and Pia dog. When the Pug was sent from Korea to Japan, it was referred to as Ssuchuan Pai. (Some writers assert that Dutch traders might have found this name difficult to translate and misinterpreted the Chinese language, since *pai* could have sounded like "pug.") And in Tibet the Pug was known as the Hand dog.

The Origin and Early History of the Pug

The short-faced common ancestors of the Pug dog—the Pekingese and the Lion dog—developed in the Orient. During the Shang dynasty (1751 to 1111 B.C.), the first dog judge, a dog feeder—or *chancien*—appeared, his official post dating back to 1115 B.C. He judged breed type, quality and characteristics of different dogs, and it was during this period that Pugs were considered hunting dogs rather than Toys. (Later, in the Chou dynasty [800 B.C.], *The Book of Rites* divided dogs into three classes: hunting dogs, water dogs—and edible dogs!)

We first hear of the short-mouthed dogs in 600 B.C.—and they were pampered right away. The emperor's servants designed specially built carriages for the Pugs. They rode comfortably to the hunting place while the other dogs would walk behind the carriages. The purpose of the carriage was to save the Pugs' energy and conceal them from the populace before arriving at the hunting place.

Though his dynasty lasted only a short while (255 to 205 B.C.), Emperor Chin Shih managed in that time to destroy all the scrolls, records, art and materials pertaining to the Pug. These works, which provided important historical information, can never be replaced.

The Major Han dynasty (206 B.C. to A.D. 220) was marked by trade in silk, spices, Pugs and Pekingese to Western countries. The small dogs, now considered sporting dogs, were bred by the eunuchs and court officials for the emperor and other high officials. All were carefully guarded and had servants to care for their needs.

In the Tang dynasty, during the period of Tien Wu Ti (A.D. 673 to 686) and Ch'ih T'ung Ti (A.D. 690 to 696), Pugs, called Ssuchuan Pai (pronounced *bai*) dogs were frequently sent as presents, first to Korea and then on to Japan. Records show that Tien Ping of Shen Wu Ti (A.D. 732), the prince of the eastern Hsim Lo state, sent his envoy Chin Chang Hsun with forty attendants to Japan for an audience. They brought with them as a tribute one parrot, one thrush, one ass, two mules, one hunting dog and one Ssuchuan Pai dog. The Pai dog appears to have remained in fashion and became very famous. There is no doubt that the small dogs of Japan were procured from China.

In the reign of Hsi Tsoong, still during the Tang dynasty, a member of the Council of State named Wang To owned a short-legged Pai dog named Hua-Ya, meaning flowery duck. One night an assassin broke into the house through the roof but, upon being discovered by the Pug, was frustrated in his mission.

One of the most famous references to small, short-faced dogs in Chinese history concerns Emperor Ming of the Tang dynasty and his favorite wife, Yang Kwei Fei, whose beauty is widely acknowledged. One day the emperor was playing chess with a certain prince. Emperor Ming was losing. His wife, who was an interested spectator, dropped her pet Pug upon the board so that the pieces were upset and the game ruined, to the great delight of the emperor. This dog, white in color and named Wo (pronounced *Waugh*), came from the Kang country, one of nine kingdoms founded by Emperor Wen in the Pamirs. The famous poet Yuan Wei Ch'ih of this period was referring to this Pug when he wrote in Kang Hsi's dictionary:

> How fierce is proud Wo,
> Though still in his slumbers

Emperor Kang Hsi's dictionary refers to the character wo and states that this name was applied to a race of small dogs. The name was used toward the close of the Tang dynasty. The famous dictionary compiled under Emperor Kang Hsi quotes two old encyclopedias as considering the word *pai* to refer to: (1) a dog with short legs (quoted from *Shu Wen: Han Dynasty*); (2) a dog with a short head (quoted from *Kwang Yun: Sung Dynasty*. This authority states that the above character was also pronounced *p'ia—pie* in English); or (3) an under-table dog (quoted from *Kwang Yun: Sung Dynasty*).

The most important town in the province of Ssuchuan is Lo-Chaing. The Ssuchuan Pai dog from A.D. 950 was called Lo-Chaing-Sze, Lo-Chaing or Lo-Sze. At that time existed the epoch of the five dynasties (Posterior Liang, Posterior Tang, Posterior Tsein, Posterior Han and Posterior Chou), the emperors of which were heavily involved in cultivating the true blood and breed type of the Lo-Sze dog.

History records that Emperor Kang Hsi's study at Peking was ornamented by three pictures cataloged as "Rocks, Cat and Dog," "Dogs in Play" and "Cat and Dogs." They represented small pet dogs of the Lo-Chaing breed. The captions on these paintings, "Yuan Chien Lei Han," cannot be accurately translated. They were painted by a native of Ssuchuan for the emperor reigning at Chengtu during this period.

Also during this period, so careful was the breeding of the palace dogs that eight distinct primary species of the small, short-legged dog evolved, their differences appearing to be a matter of color and length of coat. The Yellow City was the home of thousands of dogs. Four thousand eunuchs, living in forty-eight sections of the palace, competed in producing remarkable specimens.

The number of Lo-Sze increased incredibly during the period of the Great Sung dynasties (A.D. 960 to 1279).

One of the most famous Lo-Sze dogs was named Tao Hua, or Peach Flower. Emperor T'ai Tsung received Tao Hua as a gift from a Ssuchuan official from Ho-Chow, which is about fifty miles north of Chungking.

Peach Flower, regarded by the emperor with the utmost esteem, followed him everywhere. This intelligent little Pug informed everyone of the emperor's arrival by his bark. When Emperor T'ai Tsung passed away, the heart-broken Peach Flower would not accept the new emperor, Chin Tsung. As a sign of mourning, the emperor commanded that an iron cage with soft, white cushions be made for Peach Flower. This cage, containing Peach Flower and the imperial chair, was carried to Emperor T'ai Tsung's tomb. There Peach Flower died. Emperor Chin Tsung, firmly adhering to the doctrine of Confucianism, issued a decree. It was ordered that Peach Flower be wrapped in the cloth of an imperial umbrella and buried beside Emperor T'ai Tsung.

From this period onward numerous emperors showed a deep interest in the Pekingese, Japanese Spaniel and the Pug. Emperor Lung-Tu had such a tender regard for his Lo-Sze dog that he presented him with the official hat and belt of the literary Hosien grade—considered the highest literary honor of all time.

This emperor, in fact, raised quite a few Pugs. Male Pug dogs were given the rank of Kai-Fu (viceroy; ruling in the name of the king or queen with regal authority). The bitches equaled the ranks of the wives of high officials.

After the end of the great Sung dynasty, Pugs, Pekingese and other breeds became all but a memory. The Tartar dynasties from A.D. 916 to 1125 did not have much interest in dogs.

In the Ming dynasty (A.D. 1368 to 1644) cat breeding flourished, some of the Chinese emperors carrying their enthusiasm for cats to remarkable excess. The eunuch Liu Jou Yu said that there were three or four men, body servants of the emperor, whose special business was the feeding of those cats that had official rank or fame. Cats appear to have continued to be the favorite pets of the Chinese court ladies until the end of the Ming period, when they were replaced by small breeds of dogs.

It was during the Ming period that modern European traders first entered into trade relations with the Chinese empire. The Portuguese began trading in Canton in the year 1516, Spain opened trading in 1575, the Dutch in 1604 and England in 1634. The Spanish permitted the Chinese to trade with them at Manila, and the Dutch and English traded first at Amoy and then in Formosa.

From as early as the Sung dynasty, direct foreign trade with the Chinese capitals had been slight. Merchant caravans from the western frontier of China were allowed through, under the pretense of being ambassadors offering bribes to the Chinese emperors. They brought jade, diamonds and suitable merchandise for such an overland trip. In exchange they received lavish entertainment and presents far exceeding the value of their own. The Pug brought to Europe during this time became the root of European Pugs.

By the start of the sixteenth century, references to dogs in Chinese scrolls and literature were becoming frequent. Simultaneously, Japanese Spaniels and Pugs, which appeared in Italian paintings, were in big demand.

The printing of *The First Imperial Dog Book* was completed at the end of the seventeenth century. This book, and the others that followed, were intended to set the standards for all breeds of dogs. The illustrations, however, done by Chinese court artists, are not realistic, so we cannot regard them as authoritative records of exact breed type.

During this period, breeding small Pugs became the fashion and breeders were guided by "sleeve dog specifications." The dogs of the Royal Palace of the Forbidden City in Peking were never allowed to be seen by the people of China. But because the emperors and their ladies still wanted a tiny dog to pamper, play with and pet, dogs were carefully bred to such a size that they could be carried inside the wide sleeves of the robes of the ladies and the highest officials. This is how the term "sleeve dog" came about.

The average measurements of the Pug at this time, as converted from the Chinese, were: body, 7.8 inches; height of body, 1.8 or 3.5 inches; length of leg, 1.6 or 1.8 inches; tail, about 3 inches. The only dog described as a sleeve dog in some of the imperial dog books was a short-coated Pia dog of very small size.

The late Empress Dowager Tzu Hsi, who was known as Old Buddha, objected to artificial dwarfing of such small dogs. The empress, being an artist, was chiefly interested in breeding for color and in developing symmetrical markings on her dogs. Strongly deploring the development of abnormalities such as bowed legs or a protruding tongue, she bred for the white spot on the forehead and the saddlemark on the dogs' backs. Until her death in 1911, the empress was a brilliant breeder who was faithful in maintaining pure breed type throughout her whole kennel, and that kennel consisted of over a hundred dogs. She favored the Pekingese breed.

In 1860 British soldiers attacked the Imperial Palace, and during the occupation of the city many dogs were forcibly taken from their owners. In Peking, Pugs and Pekingese were sought after by dog fanciers from the west but not many of the palace specimens were imported to England until after the death of the empress dowager.

The imperial breeding of dogs had been made the sport of Chinese fashion. The Chinese occasionally crossed the breeds of the three races of dogs: the Lion, the Pug and the Pekingese. The lines varied because of the importation of new blood from various parts of the vast Chinese empire. For several generations breeders would find throwbacks, to a long-haired type or a short-haired Pug ancestor. Some of the dogs presented to emperors by officials and eunuchs in the palace were obtained by cross-breeding. At the end of the Manchu dynasty there were hundreds of dogs in the palace. Only a few were under the eye of their imperial masters; the rest were bred by eunuchs. The eunuchs bought or sold many among themselves, and they occasionally sold their best specimens to Chinese officials.

Collier, who wrote the great book *Dogs in China and Japan,* obtained important information from keeper of dogs Wang Hou Chun, who had seventy-five years experience in the palace of Wu Yeh. This is his opinion of the difference between the Pug and the Pekingese:

One of the most important characteristics of the Chinese Lo-Sze dog is, in addition to universal shortness of coat, elasticity of skin existing in far better degree than with the Pekingese. The point much sought after by the Chinese breeders was the *Prince Mark,* formed by three wrinkles on the forehead with vertical bar in imitation of the Chinese character for *Prince.* This same character is distinguished by the Chinese in the stripes on the forehead of the Tiger, which, in consequence, is the object of superstitious veneration among the ignorant. The button, or white blaze on the forehead, was also encouraged in the Lo-Sze dog but was not of the same importance as the wrinkles. Other points, such as compactness of body, flatness of face, squareness of jaw and soundness of bone, are similar to those of the Pekingese, except as regards to the ears, which were small and likened to a dried half apricot, set with the outer face on the side of the head and pointing slightly backwards. The *Chiao-tzu,* or Horn-ear, is also admissible. The legs are slightly bent at the elbow. The tail is docked by the Chinese, with a view to symmetrical form. The curly tail, however, is known to have existed *Sze Kuo chu-erh* and the double curl was also known.

The most admired and rarest of the breed was the Loong Chua Lo-Sze (Dragon-Claw Pug), which was short-coated except for the ears, the toes, behind the legs and the chrysanthemum flower tail, all of which were very well feathered. This appears to have been a race that became extinct about fifty years ago. This Pug occurred in many colors and was bred as small as possible.

The Buddhist monasteries in Tibet are said to have favored the Pug as pets. This raises many unanswered questions that I am still trying to resolve. In the past few years I have received information from a source formerly of Taiwan concerning a secretly guarded Pug colony stolen out of China during the time of the Ming dynasty. This colony, which is still being raised after all these years, is thought to be located in Taiwan. They are supposed to be original lines and are still called Pia dogs. It is said that the pure lines have never been crossed, not even with the new blood introduced into Taiwan in the last few years.

I have also heard that some of the early writings on the Pia dog still remain in China and cannot be translated. These writings go back to the Hsia dynasty (2183 to 1752 B.C.). Many of these dialects are unknown to us and to the Chinese and cannot be accurately transcribed, since the same word can have many meanings. Some subsequent material was also found in Tibet and is in safekeeping with the Pug colony. My source claims and believes that the Pia dog was sent from the monasteries in Tibet to Lo Chaing and Japan.

To date, the Pia dog remains small and varied in color. The Pia dogs with the white "prince mark" on the forehead are still the most valuable and are greatly prized.

History of the Pug in Europe

Many canine varieties represent distinct breeds that are manmade and traceable. The Pug's history, however, reaches so far back that the earliest chapters are lost. The mystery of the origin of the Pug has not been solved. And after much research, I have learned that nobody really knows how the breed came to Europe.

Pugs in Holland

It is said that Holland was the first European country to see the Pug. It may be that the Dutch East India Company, which thrived on trading all over the Orient and Europe, was the first to bring this wonderful little dog called the *Mopshond* back.

We do know that William III and Mary II came from Holland to England in 1688 to ascend the throne of Great Britain, and they had Pugs with them. How many we do not know. When William landed, the Dutch Pugs came ashore with him with orange ribbons attached to their collars, as symbols of the House of Orange. These Pugs won the hearts of the royal patronage in court, and their popularity increased rapidly. They appealed greatly to the British, who at that time called them Dutch Mastiffs.

The Pug's association with the House of Orange goes further back than King William. Sir Roger William's *Action in the Low Countries,* published in 1618, refers to an incident that took place around 1572. This classic story is about a Pug who saved the life of William the Silent at Hermigny and altered the history of Europe. The story recounts a surprise attack on Dutch camp by Spanish troops led by Julian Romero under the command of the Duc d'Alva:

> For I hear the Prince say often, that as he thought, but for a dog he had been taken. The Camisado was given with such resolution, that the place of arms took no alarme until these fellowes were running in with the enemies in their tails. Whereupon the dogge, hearing a great noyse, fell to scratching and crying and withall leapt on the Prince's face, awaking him being asleep, before any of his men. And Albeit the Prince lay in his armes, with a lackey alwaies holding one of his horses ready bridled; yet at the going out of his tent, with much adoe he recovered his horse before the enemie arrived. Nevertheless one of the quiries was slaine taking horse presently after him; and divers of his servants were forced to escape amongst the guards of foote, which could not recover their horses. For truth ever since, until the Prince's dying day, he kept one of that dog's races; so did many of his friends and followers. The most of all of these dogs were white little houndes, with crooked nose, called *Camuses* [a French word meaning snub-nosed]. The Prince himself said afterwards, but for my little dog I should have been killed.

The little dog in question was named Pompey. It is said that he survived the battle and remained fiercely loyal and protective of his master's life. When the Prince eventually died, the dog defied the undertaker's men as they placed the prince in his coffin. Due to this dog's heroism, Pugs became the official dog of the House of Orange.

Quite a few remarks have been made about how "white little houndes" could be identified as Pugs. The Lo-Sze dogs in China were heavily marked with white. Dalziel, in 1888 in his book *British Dogs,* writes that he saw almost white Pugs, and that a lady in London described one to him. He has also stated that he was informed that Mrs. Beswicke Royd's family for many generations owned a fine breed of Pugs, now lost. They had a pair that invariably threw one pure white pup in each litter. The eminent veterinarian Blaine records a

The imagery found in Chinese art was probably strongly affected by the animals craftsmen commonly observed. These lions guarding part of the imperial compound in Beijing could more closely resemble some of the native dog breeds than the "king of beasts."

China, the ancient birthplace of the Pug, has held fascination for the West for many centuries. This vista is located in Guilin, north of Canton.

similar instance in a Pug bitch of his own, which in three consecutive litters had one pure white pup.

It was fashionable to see the wealthy ladies strutting around the courts with their Pugs. William Hogarth's 1730 painting *House of Cards* shows a black Pug in the left-hand corner. Hogarth also owned a Pug named Trump; his *Self-Portrait,* showing him with a Pug, hangs in the Tate Gallery in England, and he used Pugs in other portraits. One is in the possession of the Kennel Club in England. This great artist was born in 1697, and from his portraits we are able to know what the Pug breed looked like in the reign of William and Mary.

The wife of George III, Queen Charlotte Mecklenburg-Strelitz, fell in love with the breed during his reign (1760 to 1820). It is said that she maintained a large kennel of Pugs. The royal Pugs had a great effect on the future of the breed. One of Charlotte's Pugs appears in the famous painting of George III, at Hampton Court, England.

There were reports that George IV kept a Pug, and others claimed he had several specimens of the breed, but not much was heard about Pugs at the end of George's IV's reign.

In his book of 1867, *Dogs of the British Islands,* the aforementioned Stonehenge commented on the cross-breeding of Pugs:

> Due to strong and established lines of the Dutch, and to the dedicated people like Lord and Lady Willoughby, d'Eresby of Grimsthorpe, Mr. C. Morrison and Mrs. Laura Mayhew they were able to save the Pug breed and again increase its popularity.

Pugs in Russia

Reports and rumors referring to the presence of Pugs in Moscow as early as the sixteenth century have never been confirmed, although it is known that Emperor King Hsi sent a Chinese envoy to welcome a Russian ambassador who was interested in dogs; the emperor gave the ambassador one or two Pugs as gifts. There is also a story about Princess Provos Hedwig Sophia Augusta, aunt of Catherine the Great, who loved and kept parrots. The princess supposedly had twenty Pugs and her parrots housed in a single room at Quedleberg Abbey. Near the abbey stood a large marketplace. Pugs were plentiful there, and could be purchased for the equivalent of ten cents each.

Around 1804, Taplin, writing in *Sportsman's Cabinet,* theorized that the Pug came to Europe from Russia. This book was subtitled: *A Correct Delineation of the Canine Race.* Taplin, an arrogant man, failed terribly in giving his account of the Pug. Amusingly, he suggested that Pugs were produced by crossing the English Bulldog and the Great Dane. He wrote very disparagingly about the Pug, and widespread circulation of his book did much to hurt the popularity of the breed.

The Prince Mark: In China, this mark, formed by the wrinkles on the Pug's forehead, is held in the highest esteem.

A picturesque view in Hunan Province

The Pug was well known in the seventeenth century in France, but the breed had been seriously affected by cross-breeding.

The French name for the Pug is *Carlin,* taken from the play *Harlequin of Carlin.* The play's main character wore a black mask during the performance. The black mask on the Pug was a characteristic feature of the breed at this time, and the dogs' facial markings were said to resemble Carlin's black mask.

Josephine Bonaparte played an important part in Pug history. On her wedding night, when Napoleon tried to get into bed, her Pug, named Fortune, bit him on the leg. Later Fortune, while playing in the garden at Montabella, challenged the cook's English Bulldog and was found dead.

Napoleon replaced him with another Pug, also named Fortune, who idolized Josephine—to the point where friends and visitors wished he could be more friendly to them. Later, when Josephine was imprisoned at Les Carmes, Napoleon hid love notes under Fortune's collar and the dog carried them to her.

Napoleon's brother, Prince Lucien Bonaparte, also had a large kennel of Pugs, in Canino.

Pugs in Portugal

The Portuguese theory on how the Pug arrived West may be a feasible one. The claim is that the Portuguese traders brought Pugs around the Cape of Good Hope from China and sold the dogs to the Dutch. Facts do prove that Portuguese traders were among the first to reopen commerce with China.

Pugs in the Netherlands

Many people feel that the Pug originated in Holland, due to the abundance of Pugs found there. It is certainly evident that the Netherlands contributed to and had a big influence on the development of the breed in that country and in England.

After weighing the facts, I, along with other authorities, have come to the conclusion that the Dutch East India Company preceded the Portuguese and brought the Pugs to Holland from China. They were successful, knowledgeable traders, and they knew that Pugs, Pekingese and Japanese Spaniels would be in great demand in Europe.

Pugs in Spain

A magnificent painting by Goya places the *Dogullo,* or Pug, in Spain in 1785. The painting of the Marquesa de Pontejas features a well-put-together Pug with cropped ears, wearing his campanula collar (*campanula* refers to a genus of plants bearing bell-shaped flowers). The original painting is on display in the Andrew Mellon Collection at the National Gallery of Arts, Washington, D.C.

Within this same period, at the court of Ferdinand and Isabella, Isabella, the daughter of Phillip II of Spain, made a famous pledge during the Siege of Ostend. She said that she would not change her linen until the fort was taken. The siege lasted three years, and after all that time her linen was a brownish-yellow color. In France, because of her pledge, the coat color of the Pug came to be called "Isabellan." Also, Belle or Bella became popular names for Pugs during this period.

Pugs in Italy

The *Caganlino* or *Camuso,* meaning "Pug dog," became popular in the eighteenth century in Italy. Not much documentation is available, however, except for the writings of Mrs. Thrale, an intelligent and cleverly amusing lady who wrote under the nom de plume Signora Pignora when she remarried. She recorded her travels in *A Journey through France, Italy and Germany,* published in 1789. In her book she mentions seeing the Pug in Italy a few times. She had to be well informed about the breed, as she refers to them as "a transplanted Hollander, carried thither originally from China. . . . They seem to thrive particularly well in this part of the world, the little Pugs or Dutch Mastiffs." Mrs. Thrale also tells the story of a countess's Pug who was run over. An Italian man told Mrs. Thrale that his wife had nursed this dog like her own child and that she was heartbroken over its demise. He told her this was a common practice, and that ladies of quality paid his wife for her milk. Mrs. Thrale thought this to be highly offensive.

In Italy, the social set had their Pugs, dressed in colorful little jackets and matching pantaloons, sit next to the coachman on the front seat of their carriages.

Pugs in Germany

During the early eighteenth century the *Mopshond, Mops* or Pug became popular in Germany. Meissen porcelain figurines give us an example of the Pug during that period, showing his cropped ears and bell collar. The managing director of the Meissen factory, Count Bruhl, himself had many Pugs, and those very dogs served as models for the figurines—now expensive collectors' items. Meissen's best customer was the Elector of Saxony, a Grand Master of Freemasons. In 1736, the Pope excommunicated the Masons in Germany, and they continued as the *Mopsorden* (the order of the Pug). The Pug became their secret symbol.

Breeders in Germany tried cross-breeding the Pug and the Miniature Pinscher during this period in an attempt to shorten the muzzles of other canine types.

A copy of an old painting of two Pugs (Mops) in Germany. *Photo courtesy Blanche Roberts.*

ffir, owned by Lily Burden, England, was tured on a postcard dated June 1907.

15

In 1790 the fad of cross-breeding slowed down. Due to a few dedicated Pug fanciers, Pugs remained pure.

Cropped ears were in style at this time. In addition, some idiot came up with the idea of pulling the Pugs' ears out by the roots, thinking the cruel procedure would improve the dogs' expressions and give them more wrinkles. Thankfully, the phase quickly passed and this inhumane practice was eliminated. Queen Victoria was instrumental in getting ear cropping itself banned in England. The Pug was one of her favorite breeds.

In 1860 the first show for sporting dogs was held in Birmingham. Pugs were permitted to be shown, but none were entered. At the second show, held at Leeds in 1861, a special class was arranged for Pugs. The Kennel Club was officially established in 1871, and its first stud book listed sixty-six Pugs. Bloom, a Pug owned by a Mr. Brown, was the first to win at a dog show, but there is no indication that this dog was ever shown again.

Two important types of Pugs, the Willoughby and Morrison strains, had been developed, and were rivals for many years.

Although few considered the Willoughby-type Pugs, developed by Lord Willoughby d'Eresby from Gernsthorpe, an asset to the breed, those who did boasted about them, and Victorian judges actually were instrumental in promoting the line. The Willoughby Pugs, stone fawn in color, were sometimes called pepper and salt because of their smutty coats.

In an attempt to improve the breed, Lord Willoughby went to St. Petersburg and contacted a Mrs. Blonden, a lady tight-rope walker, who sold him two Russian Pugs. (Others claim he obtained a Pug from Vienna that belonged to a Hungarian countess. One of the dogs purchased from Mrs. Blonden, Mops, was bred to a fawn bitch, Nell, from Holland that had a shorter face and heavier jowl. Nell's attributes were just what was needed to improve the line, and the crossing of the two dogs produced a line of Pugs noted for their smutty, cold-stone fawn color with entire, or nearly entire, black heads. They had wide saddle marks or wide traces, and were tall, thin, and small in eye. These characteristics still appear in litters today, indicating that Pugs are not yet free of the negative aspects of the Willoughby influence.

The Morrison line developed from a pure Dutch Pug. It is said that this strain descended from Pugs of Queen Charlotte and George III, who obtained their original stock from the continent. From this line Charles Morrison, a tavern owner from Walham Green, developed the Morrison Pug. The Morrison breeding program produced cobby bodies, rich apricot-fawn coats and lovely heads. Morrison and his two Pugs, Punch and Tetty, are responsible for the improvement of the Pug breed.

After much selective breeding, the Morrison lines and the Willoughby lines were crossed and recrossed. Thereby, these lines became fused together as one, but breeders today can still recognize the individual characteristics of the two types of Pugs.

Another important development of the Pug breed came about in 1860.

A photographic reproduction of an old Victorian painting

An old postcard printed in France featuring a mother Pug and her puppies

17

Two Pugs were stolen from the palace of the emperor of China during the siege of Peking, and soldiers or members of the embassy are thought to have brought them back to England. In any case, a Mrs. St. John received these pure Chinese Pugs as a gift. Laura Mayhew, a distinguished breeder and a friend of Mrs. St. John, was thrilled about the arrival of these Pugs from China, and had Mrs. St. John bring them to her home in Twickenham. The two Pugs, Lamb and Moss, looked like twins—clear apricot fawn, no white and beautiful heads. They were lovely dogs, although they needed a bit more leg and shorter backs.

Lamb and Moss produced a son, Click, and Mrs. Mayhew became his owner. Click, bred to many bitches, produced top-quality Pugs, especially valuable bitches. The fresh Oriental blood interbred into the Willoughby and Morrison lines made their strains stronger. Click's lines were the finest produced in the nineteenth century and strengthened the Pug breed. In fact, in both England and America the majority of modern Pug dogs trace back to Click.

The first club for Pugs, the Pug Dog Club, in England was founded on January 26, 1883, with Miss M. A. E. Holdsworth as secretary. A few years later Charles Cruft became the club's secretary. From the knowledge he gained running the shows for the club, he organized the greatest dog show in the world, which is Cruft's. Shortly after the Pug Dog Club was formed, the standard of points for the breed, which Hugh Dalziel drew up, was adopted by the club. A few years later the London and Provincial Pug Club was formed. This society tried to draw up their own standard of points, but were unsuccessful in getting it adopted. Later Pug clubs included the Northern Pug Dog Club and the Scottish Pug Dog Club.

British Dogs, by Hugh Dalziel, second edition 1888, gives the actual weights and measurements of some of the top dogs:

> *Owner:* Mr. S. B. Witchell—Young Friday: Weight, 14¾ pounds; length of leg, 6 inches; height at shoulder, 12 inches; length from forechest to stern, 12 inches; girth of chest, 20 inches; girth of loin, 16 inches; girth of skull 14½ inches; length of nose, 1⅛ inches; girth of muzzle, 8 inches; width between ears, 4½ inches.
> *Owner:* Mr. Hobson Key—Jumbo: Weight, 15 pounds; length of body, 12½ inches; height at shoulder, 12 inches; from ground to elbow, 6¼ inches; girth of skull, 12¼ inches; girth of chest, 19 inches.
> *Owner:* Mrs. P.R. Pigott—Judy: K.C.S.B. 5686 (registration number in the Kennel Club Stud Book); age, 5½ years; weight, 16½ pounds; height at shoulder, 11½ inches; length of nose to set on tail, 23½ inches; length of tail, 7 inches; girth of chest, 19½ inches; girth of loin, 16 inches; girth of head, 13 inches; girth of arm 1 inch above the elbow, 5 inches; girth of leg 1 inch below the elbow, 3½ inches; length of head from occiput to tip of nose, 4½ inches; girth of muzzle midway between eyes and tip of nose, 6½ inches; color and markings, light fawn.

eneral Black Beira collected £65 for the
lief of the widows and orphans of soldiers
led in South Africa during the Boer War.
r this he was awarded the military rank
Inspector General of Fortifications in the
ogs' Collecting Brigade" and presented
th a Silver Cup at Earl's Court.

liss L. J. E. Pughe's prize Pugs—
assiope, by Eng. Ch. Black Sprite,
nd her son, Bobbie Burns Secundus,
y Eng. Ch. Bobbie Burns, 1905

19

Owner: Mrs. Foster—Banjo: Age, 2 years; weight, 12 pounds; height at shoulder, 10½ inches; length of nose to set on tail, 19½ inches; length of tail, 5½ inches; girth of chest, 17 inches; girth of loin, 14 inches; girth of head, 12½ inches; girth of arm 1 inch above elbow, 5½ inches; girth of leg 1 inch below elbow, 4½ inches; length of occiput to tip of nose, 4¾ inches; girth of muzzle midway between eyes and tip of nose, 6⅜ inches; color and markings, cold-stone fawn with black ears and good trace.

Owner: Mr. E. Weekly—Vic: Age, 3 years 11 months; weight, 20 pounds; height at shoulder, 12 inches; length from nose to set on tail, 21 inches; length of tail, 8 inches; girth of chest, 22½ inches; girth of loin, 16¾ inches; girth of head, 12¾ inches; girth of arm 1 inch above elbow, 5 inches; girth of leg 1 inch below elbow, 4½ inches; length of head from occiput to tip of nose, 5 inches; girth of muzzle midway between eyes and tip of nose, 6 inches; color and markings, apricot fawn.

With this information we can make a comparison study between the Pugs of 1888 and modern Pugs. Measure and weigh your own dog, using the same format. This will help you understand what all the parts of the Pug are about and how they fit together.

Many new breeders today do not know how to measure the Pug. The Pug must be a square dog. Let's take a look at Mr. S. B. Witchell's dog Young Friday. Please note carefully: "height at shoulder, 12 inches" (measuring from the withers to the ground); "length from forechest to stern, 12 inches." Yes, Young Friday was a perfectly square dog. This is the correct way to measure a Pug to find out if he is square.

What does all this tell us? At a fast glance we can see that Jumbo is ½ inch too long in body. All the dogs' girths of arms and legs are 1 inch. This tells us they were all too fine in bone compared to Pugs today.

Black Pugs

Around 1886 Pug breeders started to take the breeding of black Pugs seriously. *The Tailor's Shop,* painted by the famous Dutch artist Q. Brekelen-ham, proves that black Pugs were around as early as 1653, and *The House of Cards,* painted by William Hogarth, 1730, also included a black Pug. But the black Pug, born into a fawn litter,* was not valued by the early breeder; black Pugs would be culled as soon as they were born.

Laura Mayhew's son, who wrote about his mother's Pugs, mentioned seeing a lot of black Pugs born, and that his mother bucketed the puppies immediately.

Due to the lack of recorded information on the black Pug, many writers

---

*Two fawns have also produced all-white puppies. Some breeders claim that this is due to the breed's Oriental ancestry, and that producing black or all-white puppies is a common occurrence. In fact, Pug breeders today should take heed, because it can happen again.

Eng. Ch. Cedarwood Blunshills Nimrod,
owned by Mrs. Pauline Thorp

Horatio of Elmsleigh, owned by the
Gibsons

said that Lady Brassey, a world traveler, brought the first two black Pugs into England when, in 1877, she returned in her yacht *Sunbeam* from China. Since authorities realized that there were black Pugs in England before her trip, few people believe she actually did introduce them into England. However, she certainly created interest in them. At the Madison show in 1886, Lady Brassey entered four black Pugs—Jacopo, Nap, Jack Spratt and Bessie Spratt—and they won, starting with Jacopo going first in his class. This dog show was very influential both in generating interest in black Pugs and in starting several kennels specializing in them.

It is said that the original variety of black Pugs stem from Lady Brassey's lines, since they were the first black Pugs on record in England. The Brassey Pugs Nap II, Jack Spratt and his daughter Bessie Spratt have gone down in the record book as the foundation stock of all black Pugs.

Also, interbreeding took place between the fawn and black, and it is no longer possible to have a pure black line of Pugs.

In 1905 Mrs. L. J. E. Pughe stated, "I have been frequently asked to tell the history of the black Pug. Briefly I may say that they were first introduced into this country, England, by the late Lady Brassey and are supposed to have derived from a cross between a fawn and a Japan Pug."

Pugs in the Twentieth Century

In the closing years of the nineteenth century the popularity of Pomeranians, and then Pekingese, grew and the Pug took a back seat for a while. But in the early decades of the twentieth century, several prominent Pug fanciers came along to promote the breed. They included Miss Neish, Mrs. Raleigh Grey, Mrs. F. Howell, Miss Rosa Little, Mrs. Prowett Ferdinand, Mrs. Benson, Mrs. Hampden Shaw, Miss Spurling, Miss C. Smart, Miss Blanche Thompson, Mrs. C. C. Meese and Miss H. C. Cooper.

On my first trip to England I met Mrs. Blunsdem, a charming lady eighty-five years of age. I enjoyed the day at her home seeing all her wonderful Pugs. She showed me pictures and told me about the litter of *blue* Pugs that had been bred by Miss Bellamy in 1913, one of which is in the Natural History Museum. Mrs. Blunsdem also had a litter of three thirteen-week-old Pug puppies sired by a fawn dog and a fawn bitch. The bitch and one male were fawn and the other male was black. Her kennel consisted of fawns only.

I spent a few days with Mrs. Pauline Thorp, Cedarwood Pugs, and fell in love with Ch. Justatwerp of Cedarwood. I had the pleasure of having tea with Susan Graham Weall and her famous Phidgity Pugs. I also spent some time with Major and Mrs. Gibson and their Elmsleigh Pugs, and Mr. and Mrs. Elbourne and their Bournle Pugs. I met Nancy Gifford and fell in love with the Martlesham Pugs' heads. I was also lucky enough to meet with Mrs. Young, Rydens Pugs; Mrs. Coleman, Cerne Pugs; Mrs. Spencer, Pyebeta Pugs; Mr. Quinney, Adoram Pugs; and Margo Raisin, Paramin Pugs.

All are dedicated to the Pug breed and are doing everything in their power to try to breed quality Pugs and maintain true breed type.

2

The Pug Comes to America

THE PUG BREED arrived in America from England and China. Pugs were accepted by the American Kennel Club in 1885.

One of the foremost breeders of Pugs during the first quarter of the century was the late A. G. Eberhart. His book, *Everything About the Dog,* was published in 1887. It contained prescriptions, diseases and causes. He had over thirty-five years of experience breeding and treating sick dogs, but he was not a veterinarian. At the Eberhart Kennels, located in Camp Bennison, Cincinnati, Ohio, he raised Bulldogs, Toy Poodles, Maltese, Toy Manchester Terriers and Pugs. One of his advertisements in his book states, "We are the oldest and at the present time the only breeders of Pugs in America, fifty in the kennel." Through the years the Eberharts purchased quite a few Pugs from England and throughout the United States to help improve the development of the breed. For example, they imported Ch. (Champion) Loki, Ch. Bessie Pentice, Rexford Drummer Lad, Ch. Gold Coin and Ch. Wallace, all from England, and in 1888 the Eberharts purchased East Lake Virgie, bred by East Lake Kennels, Jefferson, Ohio, in order to improve the fronts within their lines. Virgie, whelped April 6, 1888, was a silver fawn with black markings; by Bradford Ruby, out of Puss B. (litter sister to Colonel T.). Also, Boycott, owned and bred by the Eberharts, whelped January 5, 1886, was an apricot fawn with black points; by the imported Duke, out of Bonnie.

Eberhart Kennels were also active in showing and breeding. Their dogs were known throughout America and around the world.

Ch. Loki, owned by A. G. Eberhart, as featured the advertisement in Eberhart's book, *Everything About the Dog,* published in 1887

Advertisements showing some of the Eberhart Pugs, from Eberhart's *Everything About the Dog*

ENGLISH PUGS.

CHAMPION LOKI.

Champ GOLD COIN.

AT STUD.

Champ. LOKI	Fee,	$15
Champ. GOLD COIN	"	$15
Champ. WALLACE	"	$15
Rexford Drummer Lad,	"	$10
SATAN II	"	$10
SOBER LAD	"	$10

Handsomest small Pug living.
Winner of 100 prizes. Has
defeated all comers.
No money can buy him.
Loki knows he is handsome—
shows it in his face.

BROOD MATRONS—

Champ. BESSIE
PENRICE.
MARY HOOKER.
LADY BRADLEY.
JEAN GIRL.
BECKY SHARP.
HAZEL KIRK.
NORA HOOKER.
QUEEN LOIE.

We can generally furnish a pup at from **$15 to $25.**
All eligible to registry. Full pedigrees furnished, and all
pups treated for worms before shipping
We are the **OLDEST** and at present the **ONLY**
BREEDERS of Pugs in America, fifty in kennel.

A wonderfully
INTELLIGENT
and loving pet is a Pug.
A great house dog.

The
Eberhart
Kennels,

Camp Dennison, Ohio.

REXFORD DRUMMER LAD.
Best headed, shortest face Pug living.

Champ. BESSIE PENRICE.

The Mohawk Kennels from Auburn Junction, Illinois, imported two Pugs from England: Royal Dandy and Judy II. They produced Judy III, a fawn, in March 1880. Judy III received numerous bench show wins during her career. The pedigrees of many early American Pugs trace back to Judy II.

The Chequasset Kennels, Lancaster, Massachusetts, purchased Young Toby from Col. Buchanan of Scotland. Young Toby, whelped March 10, 1882, was an apricot fawn with black points; by Ch. Toby (by Click, out of Hebe), out of Topsy (by Ch. Comedy, out of Fussie). Toby's sire, Click, was by Lamb, out of Moss; Toby's dam, Hebe, was by Crusoe, out of Phillis.

What is interesting about this pedigree is that it goes back to Lamb and Moss, owned by Mrs. St. John of England. This is one of the first pedigrees out of Lamb and Moss, who, as we noted earlier, were imported from China. Young Toby went on to many notable bench show wins.

Another English import, named Roderick, was disqualified at the Kennel Club of Philadelphia show in 1879 because the judge felt his tail should have been on the left side. The English believed that the sex of the dog should be denoted by which side the tail curled. The winner was another English import, a Pug named Pinko, who did carry his tail on the left side. Whether or not the judge was English, we do not know. Roderick, owned by Dr. M. H. Cryer, did, however, go on to do a lot of winning after the Philadelphia show.

In 1886 Cryer of Philadelphia imported black, chestnut and white Pugs from China to America. The Chinese strain of black Pugs all showed traces of white on the head, chest and paws. The black Pugs that Lady Brassey brought back to England from China were all marked in the same manner, a fault still recurring in both the fawn and black Pug today. Dr. Cryer and his wife, Eva B. Cryer, of Philadelphia were determined to promote the advancement of the Pug breed. They tried to breed quality Pugs. In 1888 the first listing of Dr. and Mrs. Cryer's Pugs were in the *American Kennel Stud Book:*

Max—M. H. Cryer, Philadelphia, Pa. Breeder, owner. Whelped July 6, 1888; fawn, by *Roderick,* out of *Dolly. Bessie*—M. H. Cryer, Philadelphia, Pa. Breeder, owner. Whelped April 6, 1885; fawn, by *Othello,* out of *Dolly.*

The following information, contained in Dr. M. H. Cryer's book, *The Prize Pugs of America and England,* gives evidence of his deep knowledge.

Ch. George (A.K.C.#3286, *American Kennel Club Stud Book,* 1885). *George* (Champion). Owned by Mrs. A. E. Pue, 126 South Twenty Six Street, Philadelphia. Breeder: Miss Lelia Tegvan, South Carolina; imported in utero; born November 1, 1878. Sire *Muggins,* pedigree unknown; dam *Coquette,* pedigree unknown. This Pug had but a few good dogs to compete with and was exhibited in the early days of shows when judges were apt to be swayed more by popular opinion and less by the standard held to the fancy. Naturally a lady exhibiting a dog under these circumstances had a great advantage. *George* always appeared at his best, as he was kept in fine condition and was never afraid in the ring. His color, condition, body, legs, feet, tail, nails and symmetry were very good; in head, mask, wrinkles, coat and neck he was fair. His eyes were large and expres-

Ch. Dude, bred by Dr. M. H. Cryer

Haughty Madge, photographed on February 6, 1894, is one of the oldest recorded American Pug bitches. Born March 15, 1891, she was bred by Mrs. C. Houlkert and owned by Rookery Kennels. (Bently ex Seagull) Madge's offspring Queen Madge and Countess Madge were winners at Westminster, 1897–98. *Photo courtesy Helen Pittinger.*

sive, but too light in color. His ears were good in shape nor well carried, and he was over sized (nearly twenty-five pounds).

George was the first Pug in this country to be registered by the American Kennel Club. He appears in volume two of the *American Kennel Club Stud Book,* on page 233:

#3286 *George* (Dog). Mrs. E. A. Pue, Philadelphia, Pa. Whelped Dec. 1878. Fawn and black; by *Muggins,* out of *Coquette.* Bench Show: 2d New York, 1881; 1st Pittsburgh, 1882; Champion New York, 1882.

Around 1883 the Wagstaff family from Babylon, Long Island, New York, became involved in the Pug breed. Their first Pug, Jim Crow, was owned by Mollie Wagstaff and bred by C. Du Bois Wagstaff. Whelped July 1884, Jim Crow was a stone fawn, by Sambo (by Toby, out of Topsey), out of Topsey (out of a pair imported by Charles Lincoln).

Years later Dorothy Frothingham married into the Wagstaff family and became heavily involved in Pugs in the early 1930s. Dorothy owned the Torch of Redgate. Ch. Udalia's Mei-Ling, owned and handled by Dorothy, was only eight months old at the time she won the Toy Group at the Westminster Dog Show in 1945. Mei-Ling had a lovely head, correct front and strong rear, but she could have been shorter in back, with a higher tail set.

Dorothy was asked to judge the first specialty show of the Pug Dog Club of America, Inc., which was held on February 10, 1957.

In 1889 F. C. Nims, of Painesville, Ohio, began his Pug kennel with a bitch born on April 22, 1888, purchased from C. F. Wilson, Palmyra, Ohio. This bitch (by Nellie, out of Zango), goes back to Punch, who was the foundation dog of the Morrison line in England. Nims bred Fair Inez to Kash and she produced four puppies on July 27, 1889: Mons Dotsero, a silver fawn; Romany Rye, a stone fawn; Sir Kashmere, a stone fawn; and Lady Merino, a pearl fawn. He repeated the breeding, and on March 9, 1880, Inez whelped two puppies: Dave Day, a silver fawn, and La Chipeta, cream fawn. He bred Fair Inez to Max and on May 3, 1897, she produced Merry Max, a stone fawn.

In Nims' ad in the April 3, 1897, issue of the *American Stock Keeper,* he claimed: "The strongest kennel of sires in America." In the ad some imports are listed: Finsbury Dong, Finsbury Ding, Ch. Drummer, Finsbury Duke, challenge certificate winner Robin Hood, Merry Max and Dave Day. It is amusing to note that Merry Max and Dave Day were actually born in America. This was when F. C. Nims became known as the "Rookery Kennels."

In the *American Stock Keeper* report on the 1897 Baltimore Show, Judge Brett's classes, it was stated: "A small entry, but some of our best were in it. In challenge dogs it was most close between Robin Hood and Otterburn Treasure; the former has the best head and ear, the other better in legs and color."

At the same show the Miscellaneous Class judge, Mr. T. W. Turner, wrote: ". . . and Nellie, a big rough-coated Pug, with a straight-haired curl, was third. This was a Russian Pug." That's right—a long-coated Pug. This is why it could not be shown in the regular classes.

The *American Book of the Dog*, published in 1891, has an interesting article by George W. Fisher which states:

> There is no breed that has been bred more carefully and that has been improved so much in the last ten years as has a Pug. The long legged and muzzled Pug is now replaced by the handsome little cobby fellow of an entirely different type. I am perfectly safe in saying that the Pug requires more care in breeding than any other dog. So many of the Pugs have rose ears, are undershot, out at elbows. and some have black breasts with white legs and feet.

This is still a big problem in the Pug breed. Breeders must breed carefully to keep coat color clean.

The first Pug of George W. Fisher to be listed in the *American Kennel Stud Book* is Tom Thumb, in 1886. Also listed was Black Knight, born January 21, 1898, color black, owned by Mrs. Howard Gould, Port Washington, New York, and bred by Mrs. A. A. Kingdom. This dog, Black Knight, goes back to the great General Black Beira, owned by Mrs. L. E. Pughe, who is the author of *Hints on the Management of Black Pugs*, from Blackburn, England. In her book General Black Beira tells the tale of his own and his companions' lives. This is the first paragraph of his story:

> I am a black Pug, rather a good-looking fellow, I hear folks say; and the proud grandson of the great Champion Duke Beira. I am called Beira after him.

Ch. Duke Beira, owned by a Miss Jenkinson, was the first good black in England to hold his own with the fawn Pugs.

Mrs. Pughe bred quality black Pugs. Through Black Knight we are able to perpetuate his ancestor's qualities in the development of black Pugs in this country.

A few years later Mrs. L. C. Smith, of Long Beach, California, who later moved to Arizona, raised quality Pugs under the prefix "Cupid." Her friends called her "Pug" Smith. Mrs. Smith worked hard to keep the breed alive in America. Her dogs were published in the *American Kennel Club Stud Book* in 1914.

In 1914 Winnie and Edwin Killip arrived in the United States from the Isle of Man and settled in Miami, Arizona, and started raising Pugs under the suffix "of Man." Winnie's father, Alfred Roninson, was superintendent of the Isle of Man Kennel for many years and started breeding Pugs in 1905. The Killips had many Pugs shipped to them from their home town. In 1925 they moved to Los Angeles, California, and in 1930 they went home to the Isle of Man for a few months and brought back a lovely bitch, Manx Fairy, which her father had raised. Manx Fairy was the first Pug bitch that went from the Isle of Man to the Crufts show and won a blue ribbon. She was shown by Edwin in an Isle of Man show, where she was Best Pug and Best Toy in Show. Manx Fairy's trip to her new home in Los Angeles was uneventful until she was shown in Los Angeles and San Francisco. She became the first champion

Pug on the West Coast and never lost a show. Some of the Killips' top dogs were Manx Fairy, The Dreamster, The Prodigal Son, Lady of Man and Lord Derby. It was interesting to note that they were all named after a book written by Sir Hall Cain, the great Manx author.

During the years, the Killips imported many dogs from England, one of which was Goldengleam Snuff Box, who finished his championship in four shows and, being a dominate sire, produced some notable Pugs. He sired Ch. Lord Blears, who in turn sired several lovely Pugs. The Killips also imported an English champion, Lord Tom of Broadway, which Edwin considered his best Pug.

Gordon Phillips' mother started raising Pugs in 1891, when she was a girl of sixteen, under the prefix of "Anidee's." Many years later in 1939, Gordon and his wife started to get involved in Pugs and purchased one from Rose Baldwin's line. Two years later they purchased from Mrs. Edwin C. Killip another Pug, Duchess Anidee of Man, who became their foundation bitch. Their first big winner was a bitch, Ch. Anidee's Curlie Cutie, who won Best of Breed over many of the top special dogs of her day.

From Earl Simons they purchased Ch. Glenray's It's a Wonder, a black dog, who became an American, Canadian, and Mexican champion—the only triple champion at that time. Mrs. Blanche McGee sold them a black bitch, McGee's Darklu Sapphire, who goes back to Al Brown's stock. In 1970 Ch. Anidee's Star Sapphire won the City of Angels Pug Club Specialty Show.

Winnifred May Steggall, originally born in England, founded the Winna Kennels in 1928 while living in Montreal, Canada. In 1952 Winnifred finally achieved recognition in the Pug breed when she finished her seventh generation of international champions in Canada and the United States. Quite a few of the Winna Pugs can be found in many bloodlines. Her Ch. Winna Prince Charmer, a top show dog, had more Bests of Breed and Group placements than any other Pug, making him the number one Pug in the country at that time. Ch. Winna John Bull and Ch. Winna John Peel will be remembered best. Mrs. Steggall devoted her whole life to Pugs until her death on January 29, 1968.

The popularity of the Pugs was at an all-time low during the war years. We can thank the Sigvale Kennels of Sarah Given Waller, in Libertyville, Illinois, for sustaining the breed. She housed over one hundred Pugs and entered at least fifteen to twenty at a given show to help establish it. Some of her dogs were Ch. Silver King of Broadway, Ch. Major Domo of Broadway and Ch. Rose Marie of Broadway.

In 1940 Florence Bartels decided to perpetuate black Pugs. Dr. Nancy Riser, Fred Greenly and a few others entered into this project with her. Dr. Riser's beautiful black Pug dog Ch. Vikiri Little Black Sambo is a memorable specimen.

Ch. Diamond Jim and Pugville's Butcher Boy were owned by James Trullinger, who lived in Forest Hills, New York. Diamond Jim—thirty-eight pounds of Pug—went Best of Breed at the Westminster Kennel Club show in 1940. Jimmy Trullinger had been active in the Pug Dog Club of America for many years. He started to judge at the age of twenty-one and became the youngest all-breed judge of the time.

Even So Kennels were established in 1946 by Agnes Miner. Her foundation stock of Ch. Melcroft Moonbeam and the black daughter of Winna Canadian Capers started her kennels off with a bang. She also owned Ch. Blondo Hill-Happy Birthday and Ch. Judge Hawkins of Even So, who was the son of Mar-Ma-Duke. Her first Best in Show winner was Ch. Short Snort of Even So.

In 1947 Clinton Allen of Marysville, Missouri, initiated the Allen line of Pugs. Clint had purchased two bitches, Mima Bella of Swainston and Swainston's Tumbelina, and one dog, Ch. Philwil Cherub of Glenva, from England. Philwil Cherub, who was considered a great sire of his day, can be traced to most modern-day pedigrees. Clint Allen's lines produced Ch. Allen's Mighty Mo, Ch. Allen's War Cloud and Ch. Allen's Glory Spring, who was a winner of thirty-five Groups. Swainston's Tumbelina had a poor head, up-faced, narrow underjaw, long thick ears and too much white around her eyes. We are still seeing some of these bad heads today.

In 1950 the Pug breed exploded. Walter Foster of Fostoria Kennels, in Old Westbury, New York, handled for Filomena Doherty's noted Pugville Kennels in Bernardsville, New Jersey.

During this time I apprenticed under Walter Foster for my professional handlers' all-breed license. Walter showed Am., Can., Cuban & Bda. Ch. Pugville's Mighty Jim to his fullest potential. Mighty Jim's record stood at 8 Bests in Show, 2 American-bred Bests in Show, 65 Group firsts and 172 Bests of Breed.

At the same time Mighty Jim was being shown, another noteworthy dog, Ch. Pugholm's Peter Punkin Eater, owned by Elizabeth and Frederic Soderberg, of Albany, New York, and shown by Thomas Gately. A Best-in-Show winner, he also accumulated fifteen Group placements, and in 1958 Punkin won the Toy Group at Westminster. To his show ring successes, Punkin was a strong producer, siring eighteen champions.

Punkin, being a prepotent sire, transmitted excellent toplines to most of his offspring. A shorter back and a longer upper arm would have enhanced his breed type.

The Soderbergs purchased an attractive dog, Ch. We-Hu Spunk, from a Mrs. Meek in New Jersey. Within thirty-six days he was a champion and went unbeaten in the breed in 1954. Spunk, though a well-balanced dog, could have had a better topline and a higher tail set.

The Soderbergs bought Ch. Allen's Golden Dawn from Pearl Cassler; she became part of their foundation stock and a line was born.

Mrs. Northrup Bellinger, a breeder of Irish Setters and Kerry Blue Terriers in Scotia, New York, established the Belcrest Kennels in 1935. Her daughter Suzanne introduced Pugs into their kennel in 1950. Some of their earlier Pugs were Ch. Tarralong Phillip and Ch. Belcrest Jim Dandy. I remember seeing Jim Dandy at many shows and commented on his correct breed type, proper size and good balance. Suzanne's Belcrest Barney Google II was

Ch. Heisler's Roberta, shown by Luther Heisler

Ch. Bonjor's Reluctant Tiger pictured winning Best of Winners at the 1973 Pug Dog Club of America Specialty show under judge Gordon Winders; John Marsh, handler. Club President Filomena Doherty presents the trophy. In 1974 Tiger was #1 Pug all ratings. He was owned by June and John Benson.

Ch. Pugholm's Peter Punkin Eater, owned by Elizabeth and Frederic Soderberg

Ch. Belcrest's Aristocratic, owned by Suzanne and Joseph Rowe

the sire of Ch. Millers's Imperial Drum Major, the first Pug to win a Best in Show on the West Coast. Drum Major was bred by David Miller, who later sold him to Hazel Martin.

Joe Rowe was a bartender who bred Chihuahuas. He met Suzanne Bellinger, they married—and Joe also got hooked on Pugs. Suzanne and Joe, both retired now, have relocated to Florida and have been actively judging for some time.

The Gores' Pug Ranch began in 1951. Herman and Louise Gore of Louisville, Kentucky, started their lines from a combination of many lines: Velvet, Allen, Winna and Melcroft. Ch. Gore's Swaps, the litter brother of Mar-Ma-Duke, was their foundation male.

Ch. Gore's Sir Flip, a terrier-type Pug, was dominant in transmitting his straight front, good head and nice topline to his offspring. Flip also passed on his low tail set and straight rear, which is a weak spot in their line. I remember judging Ch. Gore's Jack Tarr, a good-looking black dog, breed type, what I would consider an honest dog, owned by Russell Hicks. Ch. Heritage Tom Cat of Gore, owned by Barbara Minella, was breed type. He was a hard dog to fault but had a straight rear. It is regrettable that Louise Gore sold Ch. Gore's Jolly Joker to Japan. Jolly, a sound, typical Pug of correct size, could have been an asset to the Pug breed.

Louise Gore is a wonderfully giving person, always ready to help the beginner or breeder in the development of the Pug breed. She is truly a devoted Pug lady and has never been given enough credit for all she has done.

The Sabbaday Kennels were established in 1952 by Mary and Ed Pickhardt, Washington, Connecticut. They purchased all of Elaine Brewster Sewall's Pugs from the Tarralong Kennels. This was a strong head line. They also bought from Helen Smith Ch. Star Jade of Northboro, who went back to the Tarralong lines. Jade was dominant in producing dogs that were lame on their left front leg. (Today this is called shoulder and elbow dysplasia.) This was a major problem in the Tarralong lines. The Pickhardts also obtained Allen's Susie Q from Clinton stock. The combination of these lines produced the foundation stock of the Sabbaday Kennels.

Ch. Star Jade of Northboro and Ch. Sabbaday Opus are in the majority of modern-day lines. Opus had a correct front and good head; he was a little too long in the loin area and carried the Sabbaday trait of turning the toes of the right paw outward. I could always spot a Sabbaday dog by looking at their feet. Even though he was larger than preferable, this dog did a lot to improve the Pug breed.

Ed Pickhardt was quite a dog man, and the backbone of the Sabbaday Kennels. He and Mary were both devoted to Pugs and gave a great deal of time and energy in trying to improve the breed. They both judged for many years. Some of their best-remembered dogs are Am. & Bda. Ch. Sabbaday Bonanza, Ch. Sabbaday Heir Apparent and Ch. Sabbaday by Request.

The Blaylock Kennels, owned by Mr. and Mrs. Rolla Blaylock of St. Louis, Missouri, had a big influence on the Pug breed. Their first bitch, purchased in 1953 from Dr. P. H. Gregory of the "Velvet" prefix, was Toi-Len.

Ch. Gore's Jack Tarr pictured winning the Veteran Dog Class at the Blue Bonnet Pug Dog Club Specialty under the author as judge. Owner: Russell Hicks.

Ch. Reinitz Frantic Joy of Gore, owned by Dr. and Mrs. Arthur Reinitz, was Best of Opposite Sex at the Pug Dog Club of America's 1970 Specialty show under judge James W. Trullinger. The handler was Louise Gore.

Their foundation stock was a blend of the Winna and Melcroft lines, and they purchased the Streeter and Harloo lines from England for blacks; included were some of the Car-Mac lines. We will always remember the Blaylock lines for Ch. Blaylock's Cheata, Ch. Blaylock's Madame Ko-Ko, Ch. Velvet Bennie, Ch. Cerene Shamus, Ch. Raven of Tydens, Ch. Blaylock's Bold Ruler, Ch. Blaylock's Rick-O-Shay, Ch. Kropp's Stande Burt and most of all Ch. Blaylock's Cushia and Ch. Blaylock's Goliath. The Blaylock line is being carried on by close friends. Most of the big Pugs and ones with long bodies descend from these lines.

On November 10, 1957, Gus and Lottie Buttons' seventeen-year-old son Nickey handled Ch. Buttons Zipper to Best in Show at the Minneapolis Kennel Club show, *from the classes*. The Buttons (from Adel, Ohio) formed the basis of their kennel in 1953 when Zipper was paired with a bitch out of Allen's Blondo Hill Fancy Dan by Trisdale's Bouncing Bet.

A dog I feel played an important role in the development of present-day Pug is Ch. Blaylock's Mar-Ma-Duke, sire of twenty-six champions. Gordon Winders of Rochelle, Illinois, owned Mar-Ma-Duke. Bred by Mrs. Rolla Blaylock, he was handled throughout his show career by Jack Funk. His show wins included 13 all-breed Bests in Show, three Best American-bred Bests in Show, four Pug Specialty Bests of Breed, 71 Toy Group Ones, and 175 Bests of Breed. He is the sire of thirty champions. Mar-Ma-Duke, whose front and topline could have been better, excelled in his head. (He also carried a light eye gene.) He will always be remembered for the legacy of admirable Pugs and for being a major contributor to the splendid heads we see today.

Dr. and Mrs. Franklin Heisley established the Carol-Mar Kennels in the Northwest. They bred Ch. Bon Top of Eloise of Carol-Mar. Eloise became the first Pug bitch to go Best in Show in the United States.

Fred Jacobberger, from Omaha, Nebraska, a member of the American Kennel Club Board of Directors, was an active breeder of Pug for many years. His kennel prefix was "Blondo Hill," and he used a combination of Winna, Melcroft and Philwil (which go back to Allen) lines. A few of his top dogs were Ch. Allen's War Cloud, Ch. Blondo Hill Rose Marie, Ch. Blondo Hill Fancy Dan, Ch. Blondo Hill Tom Fool and Ch. Winna the Drum Majorette.

Ch. Phidgity Phircone, the 1968 Sire of the Year, had been imported from England by Dick Paisley of Alexandria, Virginia. Phidgity was an impressive little dog of about seventeen and a half pounds and correct breed type. He was square, balanced, with a sound rear, a lovely head, level topline and excellent bone, although his ears could have been a bit smaller, his upper arm longer and he could have had a little more neck. He was one of the few Pug that moved correctly. Phidgity, a first-class Pug, perpetuated all of his qualities in his offspring. Paisley also imported the following dogs from England: Ch. Satan of Rydens, black; Ch. Tick Tock of Le Tasyll, black; Ch. Neubraa Papageno, fawn; and Ch. Martlesham Galahad of Bournle, fawn. Satan sired Ch. Baronrath Travilah, the first black bitch to achieve a Best in Show. Ch. Martlesham Galahad of Bournle (Laddie, as we all called him) had a gorgeous Martlesham head. It was rumored that Laddie was sterile.

English import Ch. Martlesham Galahad of Bournie, owned and handled by Richard Paisley

English import Ch. Tick Tock of Le Tasy owned and handled by Richard Paisley

Dick Paisley loved and cherished his Pug and tried his best to import Pug from England to improve the breed. He was always around to give someone a helping hand. Dick was an American Kennel Club approved judge and served for many years on the board of the Pug Dog Club of America.

Esther and Gus Wolf, of Omaha, Nebraska, have been in Pugs for many years. They got started in obedience, then bought a female Pug from Fred Jacobberger, Eadie's Betti-Win. She was bred five times to Ch. Tom Fool. Gus and Esther judged for over thirty years until Gus's death in October 1985, but Esther still judges on occasion.

All the Wolf champions were also obedience titlists. Ch. Hondo Sahib; Ming Toy, CDX; Ch. Wolf's Li'l Short Snort, CDX; and Ch. Kauffee Royal Rose, CD, as well as having their share of conformation wins, were the top obedience dogs. Only Joe was going too great to take time out for obedience.

Ch. Wolf's Li'l Joe was Esther and Gus's real claim to fame. He was home-bred, home-raised and owner-handled. Esther and Gus showed Joe to 6 Bests in Show, 122 Bests of Breed and 41 Toy Group wins. For four years Joe won almost every top award the Pug Dog Club of America had to offer. For two years he was undefeated in the breed. Joe sired eighty-four champions and was the top producer for eight consecutive years. He is the top stud dog in the breed world.

Joe had strong breed type. He was square, with a short back, level topline, lovely head, excellent bone, correct spring of rib, correct size and color, and balance—and he was a good showman. As you know, there is no perfect Pug. Joe's right ear was button and his left ear was rose, his right leg had a slight bow and his left leg was straight and he was a little straight in the shoulder. It wouldn't have taken much to make Joe a perfect Pug, however. Joe passed to his offspring his excellent bone, short back and head. At times in his get the white Chinese traits would come through, and he would occasionally throw a bowed front. He was quite a terrific dog.

Pug O' My Heart's Kennels had its start in San Francisco in 1960 when the late Patricia Neidig and Jean G. Prendercast saw Ch. Doc at the Golden Gate Kennel Club benched winter show. They contacted Doc's owner and subsequently acquired the dog's son, Ch. Velvet Beads, then four months old. Shortly after they also acquired a grandson of Doc's, Ch. Duffy's Happy Ways.

These dogs were the foundation of Pug O' My Heart's Pug line. You will note many of the Pug greats in their pedigrees: Ch. Abbyville Personality, Ch. Pugville's Mighty Jim, Ch. Melcroft's Music Maker and Ch. Winna John Bull.

When their home in San Francisco became too small for their breeding program the women retired and moved to a ranch seventy-five miles north of San Francisco in the "wine country." The ranch, called Pug Power Ranch, was featured in the 1978 winter edition of *Gaines Progress*. Here they bred two City of Angels Pug Club Specialty winners. In 1967, with the largest-ever entry of 132 Pugs, Ch. Pug O' My Heart's Vandal was the winner. In 1971, his son, Ch. Pug O' My Heart's Hullabaloo, won the Specialty. For both sire and son to take this honor was a first.

Ch. Vandal won the City of Angels Club "High Win of the Year" award

A lovely head study of Ch. Wolf's Li'l Joe. Owners: Esther and Gus Wolf.

Ch. Pug O' My Heart's Vandal

in 1965, 1966 and 1967, and retired that trophy. He was the third and fourth ranked Pug in the United States for those years by the Phillips Rating System.

As Jean and Patricia put it, "We are not breeding Pugs for profit, but rather the perfect Pug." They both felt that linebreeding is the most reliable method, since one can be more confident of the results. Jean and Patricia both worked hard at trying to improve the Pug breed.

The Breed Today

Since Pugs arrived in America, dedicated breeders have all been striving to correct the problems that keep turning up in all the Pug lines. We are all still seeing the same problems—toplines, color, fronts, rears, size, heads, ears and tails—that have been with us since the Pug arrived from China.

Unless you know what faults and virtues lie behind your lines, there is no way that you can begin to breed a quality Pug. The problems can never be totally eradicated, but we must do everything within our power to keep them under control. All breeders are working basically out of the same gene pool, but selectively must be utilized to identify the more dominant or more recessive problems in our lines. Only in this way can we effectively reduce the negative characteristics in the breed.

You will note that I have commented on the size of the Pug. My reason for this is to show how the Pug reverts back to his ancestors. During the late 1930s into the mid-1960s, Pug size was a tremendous problem. Average weight ranged from twenty-five to forty-two pounds. Recently big Pugs are winning again. STOP. You must maintain size to control breed type. Judges should never consider giving ribbons or points to a Pug over twenty-two pounds.

I have also commented on tails, toplines and straight rears, which are a greater problem today. On the whole, fronts were very good, but today we are seeing a serious problem develop. An unacceptably large percentage of Pugs have terrier-type fronts, their upper arms are too short and they are too straight in the shoulder. I remember when we went through a phase of bowed fronts during the 1960s and 1970s; this reverted back to the Pug's Chinese ancestors. I am still seeing a few of these traits around.

If you honestly take a good look at one of your litters you may notice that one puppy may have a beautiful head, another a soft topline, another a weak rear and another ears that are too big. They can still mature into quality specimens that reflect breed type, but if any puppy does *not* show proper breed type on maturity, it should be eliminated from your breeding program.

Ch. August-Goblin of Gore and his daughter, Augustina-Goblin, owned by Armin and Jane Koring

Ch. Bonjor's Different Drummer, Best of Breed at the 1976 Pug Dog Club of Greater New York Specialty show, owned by Mr. and Mrs. H. L. Benninger

3

The Modern Pug
in America

OVER THE YEARS Pug breeders have worked hard to try to breed quality Pugs. We have come a long way, yet there are many other hurdles to overcome. The most important factor to maintain is breed type. Do you know the difference between the terrier-type Pug, the Bulldog-type Pug or the new addition to the Pug breed, the Chinese Shar-Pei-type Pug?

The Terrier-type Pug is elegant, stands out in the crowd. He has a long impressive neck that goes into perfectly straight shoulders, straight upper arms, straight legs and straight toes. He is usually about twenty-one to thirty-two pounds. It upsets me when I hear people say they prefer that type of dog; he is so attractive. This is not correct Pug breed type. We are seeing too many of these dogs winning today.

The Bulldog-type Pug is extra wide in front, with a lovely head stuck onto loaded shoulders. Occasionally you can throw in a bowed front or tied shoulders.

Most offensive of all—and we must put a stop to this new addition—is the Pug Shar-Pei. Because one or two agents and a few breeders are trying to make a name for themselves, we are seeing these overweight Pugs with rolls down their backs. They are not Pug breed type. They are gotten hog fat to try to hide their long back or incorrect toplines. Since they left China, went to Holland and England and came to America, Pugs *never had rolls down their backs, only shoulder rolls.* We must stop these agents who tell our judges and

An example of Terrier type Pug

An example of Bulldog type Pug

An example of Shar-Pei type Pug

new breeders and owners that a Pug can have rolls down their backs. Left unchecked, they will destroy correct Pug breed type.

I am going to try to tell you and show you through this chapter what Pug breed type is all about. Just picture that cobby, solid, square, well-sprung chest, short-backed little guy with a level topline and high-set, completely curled tail. His correctly balanced and wrinkled head is attached to a moderate arched neck that blends into well-laid-back shoulders and long upper arms, which set his heavy-boned front legs well under him. His front legs are straight and in many cases have a build up of muscle on the outside. His solid rear is strong, with well-muscled hams and a moderate bend of stifle. This is Pug type.

I cannot emphasize enough the importance of Pug breed type and how difficult it is to preserve breed type and soundness in today's Pugs. I hope that the following biographies help you understand how some of our dedicated breeders and a few of our new breeders became involved in Pugs; listen to their viewpoints on the breed.

Warjoy Pugs

Let's start off with Warren and Joyce Hudson of Warjoy Pugs from Bellevue, Washington. They started breeding and exhibiting Boxers in 1965 and bought their first Pug in 1974. The flat face and cobby body, together with pleasing, mellow disposition, are what originally attracted them to the breed. The Hudsons have been very active in the formation and continuance of the Puget Sound Pug Dog Club, and do all they can to promote the breed in Seattle and the Pacific Northwest. Warren is currently president and Joyce treasurer of this club.

The Hudsons have finished twenty Pugs as of late 1988. Following is a list of a few Pugs and a brief commentary on each:

Ch. *Warjoy's Impulse of Angel.* Their first Pug, from the bloodlines of Irene Heisley Green of Oregon and John and Evelyn DeYoung of California. She finished owner handled in five months of showing on September 19, 1976, and in February 1977 went Best of Breed over twenty-two Pugs at the Seattle Kennel Club show under breeder-judge James Moran.

Ch. *Warjoy's Freestyle.* Son of their first bitch, he was their first home-bred champion. He finished in 1979.

Ch. *Warjoy's Coal Crusher*—Register of Merit. The Hudson's first black champion, he finished in thirteen shows. His first major was at the Puget Sound Pug Dog Club specialty, where he also was Grand Sweepstakes Winner. He is a sire of merit, with eight American and four Canadian champions to date.

Ch. *Warjoy's Black Dragon.* This young black dog finished in slightly over a month of showing with five majors.

The Hudsons' opinion of the Pug as a breed is that breed type is fairly consistent. Pugs look like Pugs. Soundness is another thing, however; they feel

Ch. Warjoy's Black Dragon, with owner Warren Hudson

Ch. Warjoy's Penelope, owned by Warren and Joyce Hudson, is shown finishing her championship under judge Grace Stanton Moran; Mrs. Hudson is handling. *Bill Francis*

a great deal of effort needs to be made to keep Pugs sound. Straight-moving fronts and correct rears with level toplines need to be more consistent in the breed, they say; there are also far too many leggy Pugs with insufficient bone, and Pugs with long bodies.

The Hudsons have noticed a great improvement in the quality of Pugs being exhibited in the Northwest the last few years. Most bitches being shown now fall into the fourteen to eighteen pounds category, and the males usually do not go over twenty pounds. And while they say they are seeing much more thickness of bone in the breed than in past years, it is a constant battle to breed correct moving fronts and rears. Too frequently a typy Pug is observed in the ring with either a good front or a good rear, but seldom with both good front and rear.

There has been quite an increase in the apricot fawn in Northwest shows. This bright, warm, attractive color is quite a welcome change from the colder, grayer fawns of the past. Also, there has been a considerable increase in blacks. The quality of blacks has been quite good, conformation-wise, but the problem is that they are frequently not jet black in color. There is too much tendency to rustiness over the hips.

The Hudsons do not think the blacks and fawns should be separated into two breeds. This, they feel, would destroy the quality of the black Pug, as the gene pool would be too limited. It would also limit quantity; for example, in the western United States there would be an insufficient number of blacks shown to make majors and thus to make black champions. The Hudsons feel that separation would lead to two very different breeds, which would be undesirable, as there should be only one correct type of Pug. The one type should be as described in the standard.

"Hardness of developed muscle" is a problem in some lines of Pugs. Warren Hudson believes that this is hereditary as well as environmental. Some young Pugs take a very long time to harden up in maturity, and they usually never become as firmly developed as those individuals who were firmly muscled as young dogs.

All in all, Warren and Joyce feel the breed is progressing and that with constant vigilance and thoughtful, planned breeding programs the Pug dog will continue to be a viable, competitive member of the Toy Group.

Marilyn Brantley

Marilyn J. Brantley is a breeder-judge from Snohomish, Washington. She purchased her first Pug, a fawn female, about twenty-five years ago, after noticing some Pug puppies in a pet store window. Two weeks later she stopped back at the same pet store and purchased the black litter sister and has had both blacks and fawns since.

In 1977 Marilyn really became active as a breeder and exhibitor, starting with a black male, May's Blarney Stone, and a fawn female, Embee Robin of Tor. Both were shown to their championships, with Robin taking Best of Breed from the classes five times and also earning her Canadian championship.

Ch. May's Blarney Stone, bred only four times, sired a lovely black son who is one of the top producers in the Northwest today.

In 1979 Marilyn obtained Ch. Moe Joe the Mighty of Trinket and another black, Weston's Barbland Chik'n Jorge. Both were shown to their Canadian titles and Jorge later earned his American championship.

Marilyn Brantley was a cofounder of the Puget Sound Pug Dog Club and held most offices or was on the board of directors for several years. She is also a member of two other Pug clubs, one all-breed dog club, and the local Judges Education Association. She was approved to judge Pugs in 1983.

Marilyn feels very strongly that black Pugs should not become a variety. The blacks have improved greatly in the last few years, but are not ready for this drastic move. She believes that doing so at this time would result in quantity breeding in order to make majors, with the inevitable decrease in quality.

As a judge, Marilyn has the opportunity to go over many Pugs, and she finds that quite a few do not have the correct layback of shoulder, have too short upper arms and are too straight in stifle. She sees poor rear movement as also common, and feels many blacks lack heavy bone. These are areas that Marilyn feels breeders need to work on in their breeding programs.

Marilyn states no preference to the size of a Pug, and no preference of color, and will give equal consideration to a Pug that may a be somewhat smudgy fawn or off-color black, provided it is otherwise of high quality. She strongly believes that judges should excuse or withhold ribbons from poor-quality dogs.

Hallagan Pugs

Patricia Hallagan, of Hallagan Pugs, lives in Bloomington, Indiana, and her life with Pugs began in the early 1960s when, after an extensive search to find the "perfect" pet for their three little girls, she found "everything I was looking for in the Pug." She acquired a female puppy of pet quality from a local breeder and named her Gingersnap. Gingersnap enriched their lives and was a member of the family for many years. Patricia became interested in the breeding and showing of Pugs and began looking for a foundation bitch. Betty Weston helped her find a five-month fawn female that was out of a Fahey bitch and sired by an English import—Hallagan's Bit O Blarney. Bit O Blarney became the foundation bitch for Hallagan Pugs and is behind every Pug puppy they produced. By the time "Bitsy" was seventeen months old she had finished her championship (with four majors) and whelped her first litter. One month following her championship she was entered in the Cincinnati Specialty and, owner handled, she won Best of Opposite Sex under judge Hazel Martens.

In 1981 Patricia's husband's company transferred them to Taiwan for two years. Patricia purchased a male puppy from Dr. and Charlotte Patterson to take with them. When he matured he was sent home to Indiana to be shown by Tim Catterson and finished in five months. Ch. Ivanwold Beau of Hallagan has sired some very nice litters for the Hallagans. Bitsy and Beau are the only Pugs they have purchased.

Ch. West Ho Blue Banjo of Embee, owned by Marilyn Brantley

Am./Can. Ch. Paragon's Miss America pictured winning Best of Opposite Sex at the Puget Sound Specialty show under judge James Cavallaro; owner-handler, Marilyn Brantley.

Patricia's youngest daughter, Erin, trained many of their Pugs in obedience. She put CDs on Pugs and Shelties while she was still in grade school. During her high school years she became interested in conformation and began putting points on the Pugs from time to time. After college Erin married a young veterinarian, Doug Thieme, and moved to Florida. Doug and Erin have much to do with the success of Hallagan Pugs now and in the future.

Hallagan Pugs have bred several champions to date, and many more have their majors and will finish soon. Hallagan Pugs remains, however, a small operation, and the adult Pugs are limited to a very small number divided between Florida and Indiana. Many of their finished champions have been placed in excellent, loving pet homes, where they have their own people to love and grow old with.

Patricia Hallagan believes that the "modern" Pug is superior in many ways to the Pugs she saw in the ring twenty years ago. The bitches have more bone and better heads than many of the males had in the 1960s. One concern, however, is that the new emphasis on a smaller Pug may cause the loss of these desired features.

Patricia Mitchell

Patricia Mitchell lives in Apache Junction, Arizona, and has always had many different animals. She saw her first Pug while taking a Bulldog puppy to conformation classes. The Pug's name was Oliver and she was very taken by him. He was a nice fawn pet going to obedience classes. She recalls: "His beautiful big brown eyes could charm a treat from me every time he looked my way. I still see in my mind all the escapades he pulled while being obedience trained. His best trick was playing 'dead dog' while on the long down. It caused many a laugh from the trainers and the audience."

Patricia has been in Pugs since 1965. Her first "Pug experience" was a black named Mitchell's Black Bartholomew—Black Bart for short. He was a gorgeous black pet received as a Christmas present, after she couldn't stop talking about Oliver. Her next Pug was her first show Pug—Ch. Avona's San Juan Kutie, CD, Register of Merit ("Granny"). She finished her championship in thirteen shows, with back-to-back majors. She was retired early (three years of age) to begin a career as brood bitch. Her first litter produced three champions. Am. & Can. Ch. Ti Kas Incredible Hulk, a beautiful apricot male with many Group placements, earned his Canadian title at six years of age. Another of the pups was Ch. Ti Kas Lil Pistol Pete, male, also a multiple group placer. The last pup is a female, Ch. Ti Kas Tiffie Too.

"Granny" was bred with Ch. Ivanwold Pistol Pete of Rontu to produce these three winning pups. A repeat breeding produced Ch. Ti Kas Bohemien Rhapsody.

Patricia bought her next three show Pugs so she would not become too "line bound" with her breeding program: Ch. Ivanwold Lil Oscar, another Group placer; Can. Ch. Ti Kas Troubles Enough and Ch. Pepperridge Cap-N-

Ch. Hallagan's Chelsea O Candlewyk pictured winning Best of Opposite Sex at the January 1987 Tampa Bay Pug Club Specialty show under judge Kathleen Kolbert. Handler, Erin Hallagan Thieme; breeder-owner, Patricia M. Hallagan.

Ch. Hallagan's Paddy Wagon of Erin. Paddy won three majors in four days before his first birthday. He is pictured taking a five-point major from the Bred by Exhibitor class under judge Dr. Harry Smith at the St. Petersburg DFA show, handled by Erin Hallagan. Breeder-owners: Erin and Patricia M. Hallagan.

Crunch, who at ten months of age got his first Best of Breed and Group placement.

During this time Patricia decided to try her hand at obedience. She chose her "best listener" and oldest—Granny. She recounts the experience:

> Since she was conformation trained I figured she would be easy to train—wrong! The concept of 'sit' was *not* in her vocabulary. It took many sessions to convince her that sitting in the ring was okay. I am sure her age (ten years) had something to do with the many stunts she pulled at class. She definitely kept everyone in stitches and more than once I had to cover my face to keep from laughing out loud in the ring. Being a 'senior citizen,' I lavished her with a lot of snacks and tons of praise. It worked! She received a High in Specialty at the Central Indiana Pug Club show in late 1986. She obtained her Companion Dog title in March 1987 at ten years and seven months of age! To my knowledge she is the oldest Pug to obtain a CD title.

Patricia Mitchell feels that the assets of the modern Pug are size and bone, but that these two things are starting to go to extremes. The Pugs of yesteryear were more fragile in type and size. A bitch of thirty years ago could not look fit and trim two months after having pups like they do now; she sees improved diets as part of this. Also, modern Pugs lack good tails and the "trace"—the trace has almost become extinct, and tails are becoming extremely sloppy. It is rare to see a double curl tail today.

Pat's decision to show and breed Pugs was a rehabilitation idea after suffering a severe car accident nearly twenty years ago. She broke her neck and was told she'd probably be confined to a wheelchair. She needed a reason to walk, and the reason was her Pugs; you can't really show a Pug in conformation from a wheelchair.

Alcar's Pug Ranch

Carolyn and Albert Bradshaw of Burlingame, California, are the owners of Alcar's Pug Ranch. They were first attracted to Pugs because of how they look. In the late 1970s the Bradshaws were at an all-breed show in Tucson, where they lived, when they spotted a beautiful Pug. They raised and showed German Shepherds, and until then none of the Toys had caught their fancy. But this was different. One month later they bought a pet Pug, Choo Choo, and this little girl won their hearts: "She was kind of goofy, upjawed, a bit snaggle-toothed, and her tongue jutted out to one side. Choo Choo loved to jump in the backyard spa. She'd swim a few laps, then we would have to fish her out before she drowned."

In early 1981, the Bradshaws moved to San Francisco—to an apartment where no pets were allowed. The German Shepherds were sold, and Choo Choo was given to a friend. They were, they said, "dogless."

A short time later, however, while wandering around the Golden Gate benched show at the Cow Palace, they met Richard Mallory, who was showing his Ch. Aldaroy's Amazing Grace, a lovely Pug bitch. The next night he was

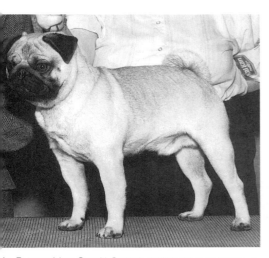

h. Pepperridge Cap-N-Crunch taking Best of Winners
the Muskogee Kennel Club under judge Dr. Leon
eligman; owned by Patricia Mitchell

Am./Can. Ch. Alcar's Frisco Bay Boy, owned by Carolyn and Albert Bradshaw. Frisco is a Specialty winner and a multiple Group winner.

Ch. Ti Kas Tiffie Too pictured winning
Best of Winners and Best of Opposite
Sex at the 1983 Lima Kennel Club
show, handled by Terese Worful for
owner Patricia Mitchell

leaving for the Westminster Show to breed Amazing Grace with Ch. Dhandy's Favorite Woodchuck. The Bradshaws acquired the pick-of-litter bitch, which became Ch. Aldaroy's Rose Wrinkles. There were six in the litter and five became champions.

Raising Wrinkles was done on the sly during her first year, since the Bradshaws were still living in their no-pets-allowed apartment. When she needed to go outside, Wrinkles would jump into a gym bag, and they would take her down in the elevator when it was empty or sneak her out the back stairway. When they finally purchased a home, the attached garage and back-yard became Alcar's Pug Ranch, the smallest ranch in the world.

After an exhaustive pedigree search and a series of interviews, they bred Wrinkles to Margery Shriver's Ch. Sheffield's Stuff 'N' Nonsense. The Stuff–Wrinkles breeding produced Am. & Can. Ch. Alcar's Frisco Bay Boy, the youngest Pug dog to win a Group One—at six and a half months of age!

The Bradshaws adopted a breeding objective to retain the strong traits evident in the larger Pugs within a smaller progeny. They select fine examples of a specific type of Pug with solid bone structure, good pigmentation, showy movement and outgoing personality. While avoiding strict linebreeding, their selections for breeding have been well-established, proven lines. As a result, the Alcars line has been influenced by the Sheffield line. Frisco was sired by Ch. Stuff 'N' Nonsense, and Frisco's littermate sister, Princess, was bred back to Ch. Sheffield's Little Red Wagon.

Frisco is an outstanding Pug, but he is larger than the standard calls for. Therefore, when breeding to Frisco, the Bradshaws acquired a small bitch from Paul and Elaine Lipka's Paulaine line. This has proven to be a nice combination, throwing Ch. Alcar's Lord Nelson, Ch. Alcar's Misbehavin and Ch. Alcar's Sluggo.

Most of the Bradshaws' offspring have a rich apricot color. However, the breeding of Princess to Red Wagon produced a beautiful clear fawn.

The Bradshaws believe it is important to breed only good sires to good dams, rather than putting a strong sire to a less than desirable dam—or vice versa—in an attempt to breed out faults. Pugs with serious obvious faults, they say, should not be bred.

To the Bradshaws, the modern Pug is a fine dog in terms of personality and other qualities of companionship. Since the larger Pugs possess more of what is desirable, the Bradshaws wish that size was not such a controversy. Regardless of the standard, they recommend trying to produce Pugs weighing about twenty pounds. In their words:

> Traits as judged by the Pug standard and a subjective approach to improve the breed beyond the standard should be more important to breeders than size alone. We feel that breeders should not consider a Pug with white toenails, small eyes, no discernible trace or thumb print, lack of deep head wrinkles, a tail with a weak curl or a lack of overall soundness as a good representative of the breed. The judges should be equally concerned when it comes to awarding a dog with some or all of the above-mentioned undesirable traits a ribbon.

Finally, the Bradshaws would like to see less effort by breeders in "matching" a Pug to a breed judge at American Kennel Club–sanctioned dog shows. Perhaps a goal for breeders should be to reduce criticism about inconsistent judging and reevaluate breeding practices compared to results. Good judges are the responsibility of the American Kennel Club in cooperation with the Pug Dog Club of America and the respective membership.

Cealyanne Pugs

New York City's famous Greenwich Village is home to an extraordinary lady and the Cealyanne Pugs. Cecilia Geary is the secretary of the Pug Dog Club of Greater New York and has been an active board member for many years. She recalls her start in Pugs:

> In 1963 I was leaving for a vacation. As I walked home from last-minute shopping I passed a pet shop and in their window saw a Pug puppy who had two Yorkie puppies up on a stool and wouldn't let them down. I hadn't seen a Pug in years and went into the shop to see this naughty little pup. I picked it up, made sure it was a bitch and asked the startled shopkeeper if she would take a deposit and hold the pup for me until I returned from vacation. I went off on my vacation and had a miserable time because all I wanted was to get back to my puppy. As soon as I returned, I brought my puppy home and loved her for the rest of her life. Patty wasn't show quality and I never bred her, but she introduced me to the joy of owning a Pug. Patty's portrait hangs in my apartment and she has a permanent special place in my heart.

In 1964 Cecilia joined the Pug Dog Club of America and met Shirley Thomas. Sometime later she and Mrs. Thomas co-owned Ch. Shirrayne's Cute Cookie, who became her first champion and the foundation bitch of her line. Cookie was bred to Ch. Wolf's Li'l Joe and from this litter came a bitch who became her first homebred champion, Cealyanne's Airy Gingersnap. Gingersnap finished her championship with four majors. Gingersnap's granddaughter, Ch. Cealyanne's Dazzling Daisy, has produced two lovely bitches, Cealyanne's Flaxen Fuschia and Cealyanne's Morning Glory.

Cecilia feels the hindquarters of many Pugs need improving. Watching the Pugs move in the show ring is disheartening—they are either cowhocked or hop along with little or no drive in the rear legs. She also feels that Pugs are getting too darned big. The Pug is a Toy dog and should be bred to the standard. It is desirable to have sufficient bone, but the size standard must be maintained.

Youngford Pugs

Virginia M. Warner of Youngford Pugs from Radnor, Pennsylvania, recalls her beginnings in Pugs:

> In 1967 I arrived from prep school to discover the newest addition to my family was not the German Shepherd I had expected, but a Pug. His name was Albert

Cealyanne's Pugs out for their daily stroll in Greenwich Village. Owned by Cecilia A. Geary.

Ch. Shirrayne's Cute Cookie winning a four-point major at the 1974 Bucks County Kennel Club. *From left:* Cecilia A. Geary, owner; judge, Mrs. Horace Wilson; and Cookie's breeder, co-owner and handler, Shirley Thomas.

and his arrival heralded the coming of a second Pug, Victoria, purchased from the late Pug breeder Carolyn Standish, Cappoquin Pugs. A subscription to *Pug Talk* was the next step. In its pages I saw my first black Pug. It was love at first sight; the love affair had begun.

In 1969, Ginni bought her first black, Bully, named after the black Pug Edward VII gave Princess Alexandra. Her second, Samantha, was purchased in 1974.

In September 1981, Bully was killed by a car, and Ginni had to have another black male to assuage her grief. Through the kind efforts of Carol Dederick, Stan and Pauline Hughes and Alan Harper, she acquired her first show-quality black Pug, V.I.P. Black Night. He had three majors when an untimely death cut short his career.

Again heartbroken, but beset with determination to make a mark, she acquired, from Norma and Alan Harper, Harper's Barnum Bailey, a Pug whose expressive head, short back, level topline and cobby body make him an asset to the breed. He finished his title at the prestigious Pug Dog Club of Greater New York Specialty Show in 1983.

From a breeding suggested by the author, Ginni acquired a lovely black bitch, Ch. Youngfords Sheerbliss Satina. Short of back, mischievous in personality with a sturdy athletic body, she embodies many of the qualities Ginni has striven to perpetuate in her blacks.

In 1984 at the American Kennel Club Centennial Dog Show Satina was awarded Winners Bitch and Best of Winners for a five-point major. On her way to her title, completed in only six shows, she was defeated only twice. She was Reserve Winners Bitch at the Pug Dog Club of America National and the Centennial Specialty that year.

At about this time Ginni began to envision in her mind's eye the type of black Pug she wanted to breed. To achieve this she added a new bloodline, acquiring from Doris Aldrich a black bitch sired by Ch. Sheffield's Stuff 'N' Nonsense. Structurally correct, with good bone and a nice length of leg, Kendoric's Lady Brassey was bred to Ch. Harper's Barnum Bailey. This mating produced Ch. Youngford's the Mahdi, Fuzzy, a Group winner who finished from the classes with a Best of Breed over specials. A combination of types, not as refined in head as his sire, but with good expression, he had the soundness and bone Ginni was looking for.

In choosing a mate for Satina, the lovely black dog Ch. Wisselwood Velvet Tubby was selected to double up on the well-known and much admired black Ch. Ebony's Marmaduke of Haven. This breeding produced Ch. Youngford's Black Bart, now owned by Jim and Phyllis Cobb. Bart finished his championship at the Westminster Kennel Club show in Madison Square Garden. Bart, a flashy little dog with good expression, sound movement, a short back and level topline, has several breed wins to his credit.

For Satina's second mate, the exemplary fawn dog Ch. Harpers Tommy Tune was chosen. From this mating, Ginni kept a black dog, Youngford's Hocus-pocus. He began his career by winning the very competitive Bred by

Ch. Harper's Barnum Bailey, owned by Virginia M. Warner

Ch. Youngford's the Madhi, owned by Virginia M. Warner

Exhibitor class at the National Specialty. In Hocus-pocus, Ginni has the size she's been looking to achieve, with a hint of coarseness. He has a lovely head with good length of neck. He is a sound mover with a level topline, and he has, she says, a very playful personality.

The success of these Pugs reflects the efforts of the many breeders who have worked long and hard on improving the black Pug. The long-legged, weedy, plain-headed blacks are nearly a creature of the past. Today's cobby, expressive-headed, balanced blacks are more the rule.

Still, there is work to be done. Ginni would like to see more bone in her black bitches. Height seems to have stabilized in the males, but many variations still exist in the females. Eye color is another area to monitor, and the width of underjaws could be improved. This seems more a problem in the blacks than with their fawn counterparts.

Kendoric Pugs

Doris Aldrich and the Kendoric Pugs reside in Pelham, Massachusetts. Doris's first encounter with Pugs was when she went to pick up a Poodle that had been clipped by a groomer who also raised Pugs. She saw Boh, who was nine months old at the time, and it was love at first sight. He came home with her. Determined that Boh be well behaved, Doris took him to obedience school. Although he wasn't turned on by obedience, he did everything properly because he wanted to please his master. Doris's parents loved Boh so much that Doris decided to get them a Pug for Christmas that year—Rupert. Both Boh and Rupert turned out to be grandsons of Ch. Wolf's Li'l Joe. With little effort on his part Boh got his CD title and also became a Canadian champion. Rupert was Doris's first American champion, and he went on to his Canadian championship and Group One wins in both the United States and Canada.

Boh was used at stud and Doris got the pick of the litter, who became the first Pug to carry the Kendoric prefix: Am. & Can. Ch. Kendoric's Li'l China Star, CD (Toffee). Then Doris discovered black Pugs—and had to have one. She purchased from Polly Lamarine, Silvertown Onyx (Amy), who has produced several champions both black and fawn.

Rupert's son, Ch. Ravencroft Kendoric Gambler (Chico), finished his championship by going Group One from the classes.

Over the years Doris Aldrich has bred twenty-five American champions, fifteen Canadian champions, nine Bermudan champions plus several foreign champions. She is the breeder of the most titled Pug in history, with twelve championship titles—Ch. Pelshire's Magic Phiddler, and she has four Pugs with a Register of Merit.

Doris spends many hours going over pedigrees and deciding on breeding partners. She feels that one of the biggest problems breeders have is "kennel blindness." Having started with two different lines she has gained a lot of knowledge by comparing one to the other and seeing the good and the bad points of each. She won't hesitate to go out and buy a dog that will improve her line.

Am./Can./Bda./Bah./P.R. Ch. Kendoric's Pipin' Hot, owned by Doris Aldrich

Am./Can./Bda. Ch. Kendoric's French Cuisine, Best of Breed at the 1986 Windham County Kennel Club, under judge Thomas Baldwin; owner, Doris Aldrich

Silvertown Pugs

The Silvertown Pugs are located in Meriden, Connecticut, where Polly J. and Jane R. Lamarine have been breeding Pugs since 1958. I remember when I first saw Polly showing—the Pug just idolized her. She still has the same rapport with her Pugs today.

Jane became interested in Pugs in 1958 when her mother purchased a Pug pup who later became Ch. Tri-Boro's Star Chief Mate, the first champion offspring of Ch. Star Jade of Northboro, who was purchased by Mary Pickhardt of Sabbaday Kennels. That same year Jane met Mary Pickhardt and they became not only client and handler but very dear friends, and Jane showed many of the Sabbaday Pugs to their championships.

In 1969 Polly acquired Sabbaday Sampler, who finished at the Westminster Kennel Club show, but this bitch was never bred. In 1971 Sabbaday Favor, owned by Sabbaday Kennels but bred by Dorothy Wagstaff of Litchfield, Connecticut, came to live with Jane and Polly and became their foundation bitch. Favor completed her American and Canadian championships and became the dam of four champions, three Register of Merit (ROM) daughters and a National Specialty Show winner, Ch. Sabbaday Kidd's Capricorn (owned by Sylvia Sidney).

Other Silvertown Pugs bred by Polly and Jane are Ch. Sabbaday Kidd's Capricorn, 1976 Pug Dog Club of America Best in Show winner and sire of one champion; Ch. Sabbaday Surprise Package, ROM, dam of eight champions; Am. & Can. Ch. Silvertown Grand Slam, sire of six champions, with 112 Bests of Breed, fourteen supported entries, 2 Specialty shows and 33 Group placements; Am. & Can. Ch. Silvertown Fringe Benefit, CD; Am. & Can. Ch. Silvertown Sequel, 40 Bests of Breed, 17 Group placements, 2 Specialty shows; Am. & Can. Ch. Silvertown Peter Piper, a Best in Show winner who finished at nine months of age with four majors.

Polly served for several years as secretary and board member of Pug Dog Club of America and is currently an officer of the Yankee Pug Club. Both Polly and Jane handle professionally and have finished many Pugs between them.

Jane believes that the size of bitches has become more stabilized, but that there are still too many large males, well over the desired size and weight. Toplines could also be better. She also notes seeing in some of the younger stock many loose tails (just lying over the back) and some Pugs that are too short-legged, which not only throws the dog out of balance but reflects in the movement.

Blaque's Pugs

Woodland Hills, California is the home of Blanche C. Roberts and her Blaque's Pugs. She received her first dog, a Pug, as a gift from her son in 1969. Although pet quality, Ginger sparked Blanche's interest in the breed.

Between 1969 and 1974 she bred a few litters and became involved with show Pugs. She bought from Paul Lipka a quality dog, Am. & Can. Ch. Blaque

Am./Can. Ch. Sabbaday Favor, ROM, and her daughter Ch. Sabbaday Surprise Package, ROM, shown winning one of their eight Best Brace in Show awards; owned by Polly Lamarine

Am./Can. Ch. Silvertown Peter Piper. Breede owners, Polly and Jane Lamarine. Peter is picture taking a Best in Show under Cyril Bernfeld at a fifteen months.

Am./Can. Ch. Silvertown No Foolin', Best of Breed at the Trap Falls KC under judge Iris de la Torre Bueno. "Hattie" finished her championship at eleven months of age with four majors. Handled by Jane Lamarine for owner Polly Lamarine.

Shahanshah of Paulaine. He became her first champion and the number-two Pug in the country for two years, winning 100 Bests of Breed and multiple Group placements. He sired twelve champions, including Ch. Jo Nol's Blaque Amber. Amber won twenty-five Bests of Breed and five Group placements, as well as a Group One at the San Fernando Kennel Club show. Amber was the dam of Ch. Blaque's Kitty Mae.

Until 1980 Blanche was content with her breeding program. Then, although she was producing champions and enjoying the shows, breeding seemed to lack the element of surprise and hope. After judging the National Specialty Sweepstakes, however, she experienced an awakening. She saw a high tail set, substance, cobby bodies and lovely fronts and recognized that her dogs might be a bit better in topline, rear drive and underjaw. She bought Ch. Sheffield's Stage Door Johnny from Margery Shriver and bred to Ch. Blaque's Kitty Mae. One of the produce, Ch. Blaque's Streekin Deacon, combined many of the things Blanche had been looking for (and became two-time National Specialty winner). Subsequently, she purchased Ch. Born Free Phire Fox from Walter and Carol Dederick. This dog was very important in her breeding program and with only limited use has produced eighteen champions with many more pointed.

Since she began breeding with a purpose in 1976, Blanche has bred twenty-two champions and has had the pleasure of finishing six more champions not of her breeding. She has been actively involved in the City of Angels Pug Club for years, a member of the board of directors of the Pug Dog Club of America and assistant show chairman for the National Specialty for several years.

She recounts the following memorable moments from her various competitions: "Shahansha's first Best of Breed win as a Special; Amber's Group One; sending Deacon, a thirteen-month-old puppy, to the Pug Dog Club of America American Kennel Club Centennial Specialty Show and having him return with the Best of Breed prize under Judge James Cavallaro; sending Deacon to the Pug Dog Club of America National Specialty Show judged by Edward E. Bivin with a record entry of 255 Pugs and learning that he won the coveted Best of Breed ribbon; watching Ch. Bornfree Phire Fox take the Best of Breed prize at the Pug Dog Club of Greater New York Specialty. Deacon has won seven Specialty shows and Phire Fox has won two."

Goodtime Pugs

Parkville, Missouri, is the home of Ivan and Anita Crowell and their Goodtime Pugs. Their first Pug was a puppy purchased from Marie Donaldson that later became Ch. Donaldson's Goodtime Charlie. During his show career he was consistently in the Top 25 Pugs (Pug Talk Rating System).

The Crowells' foundation bitch was a six-month-old arrival from Ed and Charlotte Patterson, Ch. Ivanwold Desiree of Nice. She produced their first homebred champion, Ch. Goodtime's Centerfold.

In 1980, Donaldson's Tippi Canoe arrived. His breeder was Marie Do-

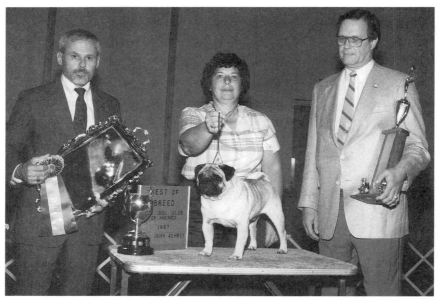

Ch. Blaque's Streekin Deacon winning Best in Specialty Show at the 1987 Pug Dog Club of America show under Edward Bivin. Handled by Ann Storniolo for breeder-owner Blanche Roberts.

Ch. Sheffield's Stage Door Johnny *(left)*, owned by Jacqueline Siegel, and son, Ch. Blaque's Streekin Deacon, owned by Blanche Roberts and shown by Ann Storniolo

h. Donaldson's Tippi Canoe, owned by Ivan and nita Crowell and handled by Mr. Crowell, is a Toy roup winner.

Ch. Goodtime's Centerfold, handled by Anita Crowell

naldson and his sire was owned by Betty Weston. At the age of thirteen months he obtained his championship title, which led to seventy-nine Bests of Breed, forty-four Group placements, twelve Group Ones and an all-breed Best in Show—all within four years. In 1983 "T.C." received the Pug Dog Club of America award for most Best in Show wins–Dog and Most Group One wins–dog.

All the Goodtime Pugs are owner handled—Anita with the bitches and Ivan with the males.

As a sire, T.C. has produced twenty-two champions, which enabled him to receive the following awards: 1982 Second Generation Toy Group Top Producer (Schlintz System); 1984 Register of Merit Award for Top Producing Sire—Pug Dog Club of America; 1985 Register of Merit Award Top Producing Sire—Pug Dog Club of America.

Albelarm Kennels

Mrs. Alan R. Robson of Albelarm Kennels, from Glenmoore, Pennsylvania, has been showing dogs since childhood but has been in Pugs less than ten years. She previously bred and showed Dalmatians, including four all-breed Best in Show winners.

Isabel Robson's first Pug was Ch. Sheffield's Fortune Teller, followed by his daughter, Ch. Gamburg's Wild Oats, who went Best of Winners at the Pug Dog Club of America Specialty Show from the Puppy Class in 1980. Her next Pug champion was the bitch, Ch. Mike Mars Gem of Albelarm (by Ch. Samet Paul of Paramin out of Ch. Sheffield's Careless Love).

After seeing Ch. Charlamar's Ancient Dreamer at a show she fell in love with him and bought him, teaming up with Charlotte and Edward Patterson. Dreamer went on to be the Number One Pug for three years. He won many all-breed Bests plus numerous Specialty Bests and many hearts. His greatest contribution, however, is as a sire. His son, Ch. Ivanwold's Ancient Mariner, has taken over where his sire left off. He was the Number One Pug for 1987 and was leading for 1988 when this was written. He too has won many all-breed and Specialty Bests and is siring winning offspring of considerable merit.

Ch. Manalapan's Carte Blanche finished with three five-point majors. She was bred to Dreamer and earned her Register of Merit by producing Ch. Albelarm American Express, Ch. Albelarm Master Charge and Ch. Albelarm Credit Card. All three finished as puppies, and all were handled by the Pattersons.

Ch. Sheffield's Jersey Bounce was Isabel's third Best in Show and Specialty winner. Other winners include Ch. Chapel Ridges Wonderboy, who finished for the title by going Winners at the 1986 Pug Dog Club of America, and Ch. Albelarm Sound the Alarm, who won the New York Pug Specialty (Fall) 1987. Bounce is shown by Michael Wolf or Margery Shriver. Michael also showed Wonderboy and Sound the Alarm.

Isabel's latest champion is the bitch, Ch. Brittany Teddi Bear (by Ch.

Ch. Charlamar's Ancient Dreamer pictured winning Best in Show at the Columbus KC show under judge Anna K. Nicholas. Owner, Mrs. Alan R. Robson; handler, Charlotte Patterson.

Ch. Sheffield's Jersey Bounce with handler Michael Wolf; owner, Mrs. Alan R. Robson

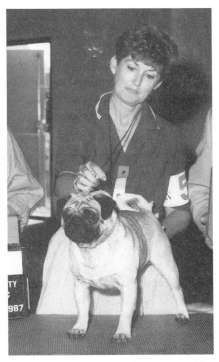

Ch. Ivanwold Ancient Mariner; owner, Mrs. Alan R. Robson; handler, Charlotte Patterson

Cameo's Orange Julius). She too finished from the Puppy Class and is, as Isabel says, truly a heart stealer.

Porter's Pugs

Bert Porter and her Porter's Pugs hail from Pitman, New Jersey. Her family's first Pug was a male puppy, purchased for her daughter in 1979. In November 1981 he became Ch. Wyndshyre's Whipper Snapper.

Ch. Manalapans Ocean Gem was Bert's first Pug. Bred by Bev and Harry DeGraw, she won her first two points at six months of age. She finished her championship at fourteen months. To her credit she has four Bests of Breed and two Group placements.

Bert's next Pug was Manalapans September Song, ROM, who is a full sister to Ch. Manalapans Ocean Gem. In May 1983 Bert got her first black Pug, Manalapans Tootsie Roll. In six years to date, these three bitches have produced ten champions.

Bert cites the Pug's personality as the breed's greatest asset. To her they are a happy, fun-loving dog. She says, "The most serious fault the breed has is a bad topline, as the majority are low in front. This is caused by straight shoulder blades and a short upper arm. With this fault the Pug not only looks bad but also has incorrect movement."

Marvin and Shirley Nelli

Marvin and Shirley Nelli and their daughter Rhonda, from Memphis, Tennessee, are rather new to Pugs. In 1971 they purchased a male Pug puppy as a pet for their two children, their pediatrician having recommended Pugs as being good with children. Rollo was the first dog Shirley had ever owned, and immediately he became an important part of her life. When Rollo died, twelve years later, the Nellis were without a dog for about a year. They investigated several other breeds, but always returned to Pug. From experience they especially liked the Pug's cleanliness, extroverted personality and endearing facial expressions.

In 1984 they purchased their second Pug, but this male was a champion. They had no idea what "champion" meant; they bought him because he looked like Rollo. Later, when they asked a handler to show him at a local show, he went Best of Breed. They were hooked!

In the past few years the Nellis have seen many beautiful Pugs and have tried to learn from them. Marvin and Rhonda like the fawns, Shirley prefers the blacks. In July 1986 they finished their first champion, a black bitch: Ch. Charlamar's Youngford's Bon Ginni of Nelli, bred by Virginia Warner. She was bred to Charlamar's Ancient Dreamer and one female puppy was whelped in March 1988.

In March 1987 a fawn male of their breeding completed his championship, Ch. Nelli's Naughty Elijah. He has since won nine Bests of Breed.

. Manalapans Ocean Gem, owned by Bert Porter

Manalapans September Song, owned by Bert Porter

67

Rhonda shows "Eli" in junior showmanship class and the 1987 Canine Chronicle rated Rhonda and Eli fifth in Toys among juniors.

They are currently showing a black male, Gerrie's Shane of Charlamar (bred by Gerrie Canary, Mary Moxley and Charlotte Corson), who has twelve points, including one major. When he finishes, Shirley plans to learn about obedience with him. A fawn bitch, Ivanwold Patti O'Nelli, is just beginning her show career.

The Nellis especially appreciate straight toplines, good movement and beautiful heads. They treat their five Pugs as family members first and as show dogs second, averaging about one show weekend per month.

Rowell's Pugs

Linda G. and John H. Rowell, Rowell's Pugs, live in Winter Park, Florida. They obtained their first Pug in 1972 and began showing in 1976. Sherman, their first champion, finished in 1979 and was in the top ten for 1980. Several top-ten Pugs followed: Super in 1986 and 1987 and Ch. Rowell's Solo Moon Rising in 1988. This bitch has over 2,000 Group points to date, including four Group Ones from twenty-one Bests of Breed. She was also Best Toy at the 1989 Westminster KC show.

The Rowells have owned and bred twelve Pug champions to date. Linda is currently president of the Tampa Bay Pug Club and treasurer of the Central Florida Kennel Club, as well as a past president of the Central Florida Kennel Club. She also served five years on the Seminole County Animal Control Advisory Board, an appointed position. The Rowells have owned and bred Rottweilers since 1976 and still have two that live with them.

The Rowells would like to see pigmentation, stronger rears and shoulders improved in modern Pugs. The head and expression must attract Linda when looking for a show prospect. Once this happens, she looks to the bone and conformation of the prospect. Attitude, personality and showmanship are also a plus for a good show dog.

In regards to color, the Rowells prefer fawns because of the contrast of the black mask and fawn color. They prefer the silver or beige fawns to the apricots, but color is always secondary to the overall dog.

Bob and Helen Gale

Bob and Helen Gale live in Burlington, Connecticut. Helen has been an active member of the Yankee Pug Dog Club and has held the position of president. The Gales started showing dogs in 1975 with a Doberman Pinscher, and their daughters got interested in junior showmanship. They were told they could have the breed of their choice. Jenny chose a Pug and Sue chose a Soft-Coated Wheaten Terrier, their first champion. Jenny's Pug Ernie (Gale's Hsing Fu of Nazrep) never became a champion but was pointed, including a four-point major from the Puppy Class at the 1977 Springfield Kennel Club show.

. Nelli's Naughty Elijah, owned and handled by
honda Nelli and bred by Marvin Nelli

Ch. Rowell's Solo Moon Rising, owned, bred and
handled by Linda Rowell, is one of the breed's most
successful show dogs of the late eighties. She is
a multiple Best in Show winner and was the Best
Toy Dog at the 1989 Westminster KC show under
judge Harry Smith.

Ch. Cameo's Super Stuff in the ring with owner-handler Linda Rowell

Ch. Rowell's Silver Bullet, owned, bred and handled by Linda Rowell, is shown here in a win under judge James L. Vaughters, Sr., en route to his championship.

Their first Pug champion was Ch. Nazrep Play Me a Melody, ROM, who finished at the Westchester Kennel Club show in September 1981 at the Pug Dog Club of Greater New York Specialty. Melody became their foundation dam. Their first homebred champion was Ch. Gale's Kringle in Time, who went Best of Breed from the Puppy Class at the Eastern Dog Club show. In December 1982, taking back-to-back majors that weekend and finishing in May 1983 with back-to-back majors. The next two champions for Melody's ROM were Ch. Gale's Posey of Warwick (May 1984) and Ch. Gale Be My Valentine of Nazrep (August 1985). The Gales also finished Ch. Simin's Lady Chelsea with all majors. She is a daughter of Gale's Pumpkin Patch, CD.

In summarizing their thoughts on the status of the breed, the Gales noted their belief that the size of Pugs is getting better. For a while, they feel, many were too large, but they now see more breeders trying to breed to the standard. They find color good, but pigment, black nails, the trace, all in the standard need attention. While tail sets are acceptable, many tails need to be tighter and Pugs need straighter toplines. Fronts have improved but rears need improvement. The Gales feel that many breeders are not concerned about white markings when they should be, and competitors are seeing more white in the show ring today than previously. The head, being an important part of the Pug, generally is good but some are too narrow in the underjaw and some nose rolls are too overdone. There is more to a Pug than the head. Movement is very important but too many breeders seem to be ignoring it.

The Gales feel it is all right to breed black to fawn, but note that you must then breed straight fawn or black for at least three generations. Breeding a fawn with poor pigment to a black is not going to improve pigment, they say. Breeding black to fawn has helped to improve the blacks structurally, and they are happy to see more interest in blacks today. However, the Gales do not want to see blacks and fawns separated because this may start an influx of inferior black Pugs in the ring and may compromise the great strides in improvement of blacks.

Warwick Pugs

The Warwick Pugs of John and Joyce Camac hail from Elverson, Pennsylvania. Joyce has been interested in Pugs since childhood, since her family had Melcroft Pugs. After ten years of breeding and showing Labrador Retrievers, John and Joyce went to the Pug Dog Club of America Specialty show in September 1982 and bought a show-quality bitch from Helen Gale (Gale Pugs) out of Silvertown breeding (by Ch. Silvertown Grand Slam out of Ch. Nazrep's Play Me a Melody). Ch. Gale's Posey of Warwick, a nice typy fawn, finished in 1984 at eighteen months of age. She is the Camacs' foundation bitch.

Their first goal in Pugs was to breed a sound Bred by Exhibitor bitch and finish her. They bred Ch. Posey to her half-brother, Ch. Silvertown Sequel, to lock in the points they liked about Silvertown, such as head and movement. The Silvertown son that Posey had was then bred to a Sheffield bitch that the Camacs owned, Somerdane's Pippi of Warwick. From this breeding came

Left: Nazrep Play Me a Melody with owner Helen Gale. *Center:* Ch. Limon's Lady Chelsea, owned by Robert and Helen Gale and shown with Mrs. Gale. *Right:* Ch. Gale's Posey of Warwick, owned and handled by Joyce A. Camac; the perfect diamond which shows on the Pug's forehead is a highly desirable feature.

Somerdane's Pippi of Warwick and Warwick's Grumblethorpe, owned by Joyce A. Camac

Warwick's Pippi's Precious Pup, an outcross of Silvertown and Sheffield. Warwick's Midas touch resulted from a breeding of Posey and Ch. Gas Hollow's Mickey (a Sheffield-Wiselore mix).

The Camacs ultimately came up with a third generation outcross of mostly Sheffield and Silvertown to produce Pugs that are sound, with heavy bone, dark pigment, black nails and trace. They are cobby, have good movement and great temperaments. The Camacs are concerned about the size of some dogs that they have seen in the show ring. They heartily believe that Pugs weighing twenty-five to twenty-seven pounds are too large and that breeders should work on down-sizing dogs of this size.

Alabee's Pugs

Abby and Al Fox, of Alabee's Pugs, live in West Caldwell, New Jersey. Abby and Al have been active members of the Pug Dog Club of Greater New York since 1982 and members of the Pug Dog Club of America since 1983. They purchased their first Pug in 1981 from Dan and Anne Fischetti, Vandonna Pugs. Ch. Vandonna's Excellent Choice, handled by Dan Fischetti, finished her championship with four majors at sixteen months of age and went on to many Best of Opposite wins handled by Abby Fox. Eve was grand sweepstakes winner at the February 1982 Pug Dog Club of Greater New York Specialty Show and Sweepstakes under judge Marilyn Brantley.

Their second Pug, also purchased from Dan and Ann Fischetti, was Vandonna's Flicka of Alabee. Flicka attained her championship handled by Al Fox, taking, along the way, Best Puppy at the September 12, 1982 Pug Dog Club of Greater New York Specialty Show and Sweepstakes. Flicka was bred to Ch. Shirrayne's Victorious Vance and produced Ch. Alabee's Asta Risk, ROM.

Asta had a five-point major at the Pug Dog Club of Greater New York Specialty Show and Sweepstakes, finishing with a Best of Breed on August 31, 1985. Bred to Ch. Bornfree Jac Daniel of Tori, she had a litter from which all became champions. They are Ch. Alabee's Billie Jean (owned by Dan and Anne Fischetti), who finished with four majors, three of them five-point majors; Ch. Alabee's Brazen Marge; and Ch. Broadway Danny Rose, who finished with four majors and was Best of Winners for a four-point major at the Progressive Dog Club show. Asta was tied for the Number Two, Top Producing Pug Bitches for 1987 and achieved her Register of Merit status for producing three champions—all from her first litter.

Barbara Braley and Anitra Hutchinson

Barbara A. Braley of Plant City, Florida, is one of the founders of the Tampa Bay Pug Club and is active in quite a few all-breed dog clubs. Barbara Braley purchased her first Pug, Pug-Haven's Tag-A-Long Jim, in 1960 from the Hornbecks of Pug-Haven Kennels in Clearwater, Florida. One of their best known is the black Pug Eng. & Am. Ch. Mirandus Invader of Harloo, who

Ch. Alabee's Broadway Danny Rose, shown with owner-handler Abby Fox after he was awarded Best of Winners at the 1987 Progressive Dog Clubs' all-Toy show for four points under judge Shirley Limoges.

Ch. Chauncelear's Dhandy Andy, a multiple Group and Specialty winner, owned by Patricia L. Park and Barbara A. Braley. *Paulette*

went Best in Show from the classes at Palm Beach Kennel Club in the 1960s under James Trullinger.

Tag-A-Long Jim was sired by Ch. Pug-Haven's Cactus Jim. In 1961 Barbara purchased Pug-Haven's Cactus Pandy, who was also sired by Cactus Jim. Pandy was finished by Barbara in 1962.

Meanwhile, Anitra Hutchinson got her first show Pug, Pug-Haven's Sho Hotel, in 1958 and put a CDX obedience degree on him. She obtained Ch. Velvet Tracey from Pug-Haven Kennels and bred her to her grandson, Ch. Pug-Haven's Cactus Pandy in 1963. The two boys, Ch. Ah-Ya Gung Ho Murphy, owned by Anitra Hutchinson, and Ch. Dhandy's Marco Velvet, owned by Barbara Braley, were the strong foundation of the Dhandy line. Marco was a top-ten Pug with very limited owner handling, a Group winner and producer of champions.

In 1965 Barbara obtained Crowell's Pandora, of the Fahey line. Pandora was bred to Ch. Dandy's Marco Velvet and produced champions from that litter. Then she was bred to Ch. Ah-Ya Gung Ho Murphy. That breeding produced two bitches and one male. One bitch was not shown; one bitch became Ch. Dhandy's Doryble Kippi. She was a Best of Breed winner and obtained a CD with Peggy Kaspar after retiring from breed competition. The male was Ch. Dhandy's Doryson Buccaneer, Group winner and the winner of the Mary Pickhardt award for 1973–1977 as top sire for a five-year period. He obtained his Register of Merit in 1979.

Buccaneer was bred to Merle "Bunny" Osborn's Bleuridge line and produced Dhandy's Bleuridge Robin and Ch. Bleuridge's Link. Link was co-owned by Barbara Braley and E. G. Willard and was the Pug Dog Club of America Best of Breed winner in 1974. Robin was co-owned by Barbara Braley and Peggy Kaspar and, when bred to Ch. Sheffield's Dancing Tiger (owned and campaigned by Barbara Minella), produced Ch. Dhandy's Skylark, a Best of Breed and Register of Merit winner with three males in one litter sired by Ch. Chen's a Favorite of the Gods. They were Dhandy's Sky High, ROM, who went to Texas and produced many outstanding progeny in that area; Ch. Dhandy's Sky Rocket, campaigned by Ralph Adair to top Pug in 1980; and Ch. Dhandy's Sky Rider, co-owned by Barbara Braley and Betty Page. Sky Rider, known as Jello to his friends, produced Specialty and Group winners. Ch. Heritage Wicket Witch, who was also sired by Dancing Tiger, was finished by Barbara Braley and Anitra Hutchinson and then bred in 1977 (as was her half-sister Ch. Dhandy's Skylark) to Ch. Chen's a Favorite of the Gods. This litter produced Ch. Dhandy's Favorite Chipmunk and Ch. Dhandy's Favorite Woodchuck. Woodchuck was the Sweepstakes winner at the Tampa Bay Pug Dog Club under Gordon Winders. At ten months of age he was also Best of Winners at this show while his sister, Chipmunk, came from the Puppy Class at her first show to be Winner's Bitch.

Woodchuck started out as a special in the Fall of 1978 and won eight Groups. In January 1979, on the Florida circuit, he won Group One under Dr. Harry Smith. During this Group he was spotted by Bobby Barlow, who later started negotiations for Woodchuck to go to Robert A. Hauslohner of Phila-

Ch. Dhandy's Coopertown Classic, with breeder-owner Barbara A. Braley *Alverson*

Ch. Dhandy's Favorite Woodchuck, owned by Robert A. Hauslohner, achieved a first for the breed when he was selected Best in Show at the 1982 Westminster KC dog show. The judge was Langdon L. Skarda. *Booth*

delphia in September 1979. Mr. Hauslohner has had numerous top-winning dogs under his guidance, but Woodchuck was his first Pug.

Woodchuck became the top-winning Pug of all time, with a record as yet unequaled. He was handled through his show career by Bobby Barlow. His record includes 56 all-breed Bests in Show, 6 Specialty Bests in Show, 145 Group Ones, 30 Group Twos, 21 Group Threes, 9 Group Fours, and 231 Bests of Breed, including the coveted Best in Show win at the Westminster Kennel Club in February 1981. Woodchuck will always be remembered for his great record and for being the first Pug in the history of the breed to win Best in Show at the prestigious Westminster Kennel Club.

Woodchuck was bred to Ch. Goodwin's Misty Dawn, a half-sister, and produced Ch. Dhandy's Woodstock, CD, owned by Peggy Kaspar. Woodstock is one of the few Pugs in America with a Pet Therapy degree and has worked thousands of hours with Peggy over the years in nursing homes, schools, educational exhibits, etc., as well as having started tracking. He is known to hundreds of children for his obedience demonstrations at schools in Tampa, Florida.

Youngsters in the Dhandy household include Ch. Coopertown Classic, the 1988 Sweepstakes winner at the Tampa Bay Pug Club who finished in January with three majors while still a puppy. Several hopefuls are waiting their turn to enter the ring under the Dhandy name.

Barbara Braley and Anitra Hutchison commented on the current state of the Pug breed:

> Since we have seen Best in Show Pugs from fawn to black breedings, we know it can be successful. As all our breedings have been fawn to fawn, we have not personally studied the genetics involved in such a program.
>
> Through the years, sometimes the competition has had the quality in dogs; some years the bitches have the overall better quality. We believe that generally where a Pug club is in the area to foster and promote the breed, the entry is of overall good quality. We believe one of the big problems the breed has is a top winner being of questionable quality, but because he is heavily campaigned, he is a "top" Pug. Therefore, as a stud, the next generation will probably have the same problems—widespread—as he does. So let us hope wise breeders consider the quality of the dog (and bitch) rather than their show record to continually strive to have each generation improve as nature tries to pull the quality toward average.

Ivanwold Pugs

Destin, Florida, is the home of Charlotte and Edward Patterson and their Ivanwold Pugs. The Ivanwold kennel was established in Virginia in 1960 when Edward was married to Janet Patterson and in the ensuing years produced the multiple Specialty and Toy Group winner, Ch. Ivanwold High Tor, as well as Ch. Johnny Appleseed and Ch. Ivanwold High Barbary, both of whom won Group placements.

The kennel was reorganized and relocated to Florida when Edward remarried in 1974. Since that time Charlotte and Edward Patterson have bred and exhibited some of America's top Pugs. Among the sixty champions bearing the Ivanwold name, three are multiple Best in Show winners: Ch. Ivanwold Senator Sam, owned by Mrs. R. V. Clark; Ch. Ivanwold Pistol Pete of Rontu, owned by Charlotte and Edward; and Ch. Ivanwold Ancient Mariner, owned by Mrs. Alan R. Robson. Senator Sam had fourteen Best in Show wins. Pistol Pete boasted a career record of five Best in Show wins, while Ancient Mariner also had five such wins. All were also multiple Specialty winners, and Senator Sam was the Toy Group winner at Westminster in 1980.

While both Charlotte and Edward have been active as agents for the past eight years, they consider themselves primarily as breeders. During his career Pistol Pete sired thirty-six champion get and was twice winner of the prestigious Mary Shipman Pickhardt Award (1981 and 1983). Two Ivanwold bitches have also won this award: Ch. Ivanwold Gayberry Carolina, CD (1979), and Ch. Ivanwold Tip Top (1984).

The Ivanwold Pugs have also competed successfully in obedience trials. Handled by Charlotte and Edward, Ch. Ivanwold Apple Jack and Ch. Ivanwold Gayberry Carolina both won their Companion Dog titles, while Ch. Ivanwold Lord Cecil was handled to his title by owner Patricia Scully. More recently, Ivanwold Peter Gunn won his CDX with owner Michelle Bjorke-Barnes and is currently working on his Utility degree.

All in all, Edward and Charlotte have attained the championships of over one hundred Pugs for their clients.

Trafalgar Pugs

Jeff and Mariette Keefe, who live in Cornish Flat, New Hampshire, are known for their Trafalgar Pugs. Jeff's "love affair" with the Pug began in 1968 when he saw a Pug in a pet shop window in Queens, New York. It was not until four years later that he was able to get his first Pug, Bowzer, and he bought him at a pet shop.

He entered Bowzer in a half-dozen shows and they were defeated soundly, but through Bowzer, Jeff learned ring procedure, sportsmanship and a respect for the breed.

Jeff then joined the Pug Dog Club of Greater New York and through Shirley Thomas, then secretary, acquired Ch. Shirrayne's Hot Shot, bred by Shirley's brother, Al Meshirer.

Hot Shot finished his championship in nine months and was specialed for three years, gaining many Bests of Breed and Group placements.

From that point, Jeff acquired another Pug, Shirrayne's Wonder Woman, and started occasional breeding. Ch. Shirrayne's Hot Shot and Shirrayne's Wonder Woman produced a quality bitch named Ch. Trafalgar's Naughty Marietta. She also finished her title at nine months but, unfortunately, she never produced a litter.

Jeff and Mariette became involved with starting the Yankee Pug Dog

Club, a Springfield, Massachusetts breed club that is now one of the most successful Pug clubs in the country.

The Keefes moved from Massachusetts to New Hampshire to purchase a commercial kennel, which they established as Trafalgar Kennels. They are still active in Pugs and along with the Yankee Pug Dog Club, Pug Dog Club of Greater New York and the Pug Dog Club of America, they are also members of the Wachusett Kennel Club and the Woodstock Dog Club in Vermont.

When discussing the overall advancement of the Pug breed, Jeff writes:

> Blessed are the true Pug breeders for they shall receive honors. The Pug breeders in this country are making a genuine effort to improve the Pug breed, although they might disagree in the direction that the Pug should be improved. Let's face it, we all breed Pugs differently: pigment, topline, tail set, bone, temperament, fronts, head. But we all agree on a few points: type, soundness and balance. Perfection in any breed has not yet been achieved and I doubt it ever will. But with the constant persistence of any breeder, this perfection may be achieved at least in the mind of the individual.

Shep's Pugs

In East Point, Georgia, you can find Larry and Pat Shepherd and a few of the Shep's Pugs. They began their association with Pugs in August 1968 after seeing them in the movie *The Great Race.* Their first Pug, purchased in 1972, was Shep's Li'l Tamu of Dunroamin, ROM. She became their foundation bitch, producing nine champions with many more pointed. She received the first Mary Shipman Pickhardt award for top-producing dam during a five-year period. She also received a silver certificate from *Kennel Review* for top producer. Shep's Miss Georgia Peach, ROM, was also nominated by *Kennel Review* as a top producer. The following is a list of other Shep's Pugs who have earned a Register of Merit award: Ch. Shep's Major Top Cat, Ch. Shep's Peach Puddin, Shep's Glowing Yo Yo, Ch. Shep's Li'l Golden Rooster and Ch. Shep's Cassia of Holly Springs.

The Shepherds' first champion finished in 1974 and since then they have produced thirty-one home-bred champions, finished five champions from other breeders and have had a total of forty-one champions in all.

The Shepherds note that the Pug of today compared to twenty years ago is a much improved dog. The earlier Pug was a larger dog, had a longer back and longer legs. Today it is a cobbier and better balanced dog. They think a Pug should be small, square and well balanced, with a nice head that is in proportion to the body.

What concerns them most is the Bulldog look—wide chest, incorrect shoulders, narrow rears and poor toplines. They have also seen some viciousness, which they say should not be tolerated: "Pugs are gentle and playful by nature, and as breeders we must do everything possible to keep this characteristic in our breeding programs."

Ch. Ivanwold Princess Jasmine, owned by Edward and Charlotte Patterson

Ch. Shirrayne's Hot Shot, owned by Jeff and Mariette Keefe

Trafalgar's Wise Guy was Best of Sweepstakes at the 1985 Pug Dog Club of Greater New York Specialty show under judge Cecilia Geary; handled by breeder-owner Jeff Keefe.

Ch. Shep's Sassafras Coco with breeder-owner Larry Shepherd

Ch. Shep's Rising Son winning Best Puppy at the 1985 PDCA National Specialty under judge Joan Gordon Alexander; breeder-owner, Larry Shepherd.

Wisselwood Pugs

One of our new breeder-judges, Lorene M. Vickers-Smith, lives in Grand Ledge, Michigan, with her Wisselwood Pugs. Lorene has been interested in breeding black Pugs. Her childhood dream was to breed and show fine dogs when she grew up, and she had several Boston Terriers around throughout her early days.

While waiting for a light in Alexandria, Louisiana, at around eleven one night, Lorene saw a whole yard of Pugs! She had been without a dog for three months. She got her hands through the chain link and was being covered with Pug sneezes and delight when a spotlight came on. Her hands were "hand-cuffed" fast in the fence. Fortunately, instead of being shot, she was invited in to tea by a gentle elderly lady and she went home with her first Pug. Teto was a spayed granddaughter of Int. Ch. Pugville's Mighty Jim. Why she ever wanted more Pugs after Teto she will never understand. While her Bostons were intelligent ladies who worried every moment they weren't pleasing her fast enough, this self-centered little lout turned her life upside down. No waste basket or paper roll was safe and she practiced every trick ever written on stubborn antics.

Lorene feels she was either born with, or was helped by her father to acquire when very young, an eye for structure and balance. Teto had type. These things helped her decide what to start with when she wanted to breed. She purchased many show puppies only to sell them later as pets rather than breed them. Helen Camp, of Pugacre in Phoenix, warned her that light eyes or too much underbite could hide and pop up in later generations to haunt a breeder. Lorene wanted bone, perfect structure—perfect type—everything perfect, please!

When she finally kept a bitch puppy to breed, it was Morfa Madcap from Diana Woolstencroft. Diana brought Doms and Cedarwood dogs into Canada with her from England. Due to an incident with an incompetent veterinarian, Madcap had only one live puppy by Dick Paisley's Eng. & Am. Ch. Phidgity Phircone, then was spayed. This puppy was Ch. Heathers Honey of Wisselwood, Register of Merit.

Lorene feels that the key to an overall strong breed in a country must be the breeders working together:

> If we breeders cover up problems, it is the dogs that suffer the most. They are the ones that end up with health problems. Inherited faults should be weighed with regard to the severity of the effect on the long-term health and functioning of the dog. If you breed for any length of time you find yourself dealing with something. Certainly it is most important for the health of the dog to have a sound structure. The unique part of breeding and developing our own line is that we make all these decisions for ourselves. By hiding things we take the right away from those using our stock. They aren't going to find a stud free of everything!

Lorene adds that some known inherited defects cannot be tolerated by any standards once a dog is proven to pass them on. What about entropion? Entropion used to be found in black lines. From what she sees all over the country, Lorene is now convinced we have it in a staggering number of fawn lines as well. We need to be aware that this is in our breed and be honest with ourselves and each other, she says; the alternative is to end up with automatic surgery on our puppies, like Chow Chow or Shar-Pei breeders.

As a breeder, Lorene states that she wants perfect color, but first she wants a super structure and lots of Pug type. Color is important but not to an unreasonable degree. Unfortunately, she feels, some breeders and judges are lacking in knowledge of type and structure; color is the easiest of the three to see and judge. Ideally, it is best not to mix the colors, she says, but she has found it necessary to throw a fawn in from time to time (when what she was really looking for was a black to use instead).

When she first started to breed blacks it was next to impossible to find breeding stock that was both sound and typy. She notes:

> The greatest overall fault was lack of bone and substance. If you found one in proportion, too often it had a bad mouth or light eyes. A lot were high stationed and really big. When you were lucky enough to find a black that was close to what you wanted, who could you breed to it? Most of the early black imports were many generations black bred but had the same problems. I knew some Pugs bred only black for at least six generations that were very rusty and threw a lot of white on the chest of their get with different bitches. This white, then, does not only come through our fawn lines. You need to stay away from it behind your blacks as well as carefully screening any fawn line at birth that you want to mix with black.
>
> The choices were fairly limited in black. Some of us tried to improve by selecting an extremely typy fawn to use with our black. I really don't feel the fawns have hurt me—again, I can only speak for my own experience.

In twelve generations of mixed colors, Lorene doesn't feel that poor color in either color has resulted from black/fawn matings. She has gotten what she bred from. If poor-colored fawns or blacks were used, poor-colored fawns or blacks were the product, at least by the second generation. If clear fawns and black blacks were used, clear fawns and black blacks were the products. Lorene's goal was black, and she has been lucky enough to work with two typy studs that were dominant black, Dick Paisley's Ch. Tick Tock of LeTasyll and his grandson, Ch. Wisselwood Velvet Tubby, ROM.

Lorene believes that breeders are dealing with a lot of different and complex genes and no established rule of thumb. She cites such incidents as seeing a good solid black Pug with pink toenails and white hair on the bottoms of her feet! About seven years ago in her blacks she got what she believes was a blue and a year later a liver. The culprits were neutered and spayed, and using basically the same stock, neither color has surfaced again. Lorene says of the liver, "Her eyes were light brown instead of black, but her type was gorgeous. We called her Agent Orange."

Some people have found their blacks have coarser, longer coats than fawns, but this has not been true for Lorene. She notes having bred generations of solid blacks without loosing density, texture or increasing coat length. Some breeders associate the blue-black coat only with the coarser texture. She says she is lucky enough to have gotten some blue-black coats (which, by the way, can lie in the sun all day and never fade) that were soft, short, thick and shiny.

Lorene Vickers-Smith sums up her hopes for the breed this way: "Do we want to win or do we want to be unified in breeding the best Pugs in the world? The competitive spirit won't die as a result of helping each other or being honest about our stock to serious breeders. Being helpful and honest will not only improve the breed but will also help you minimize damaging faults in your Pugs that love you."

Vandonna Pugs

Staten Island, New York, is where Donald and Ann Fischetti and some of their Vandonna Pugs live. Dan and Ann are active members of the Pug Dog Club of Greater New York, and Dan has been recording secretary for many years.

Vandonna Pugs originated in 1976 when the Fischettis purchased two foundation bitches from Rayne and Shirley Thomas of Shirrayne Kennels.

Dan had been interested in the dog show game since the late 1940s. At that time he was primarily interested in Boxers and Bulldogs and he bred and exhibited them with moderate success for some ten years.

By this time it became quite apparent that the limited space of their Staten Island home was not ideal for breeding and raising dogs the size of Boxers and Bulldogs. A decision to go to a smaller breed was made, and the choice was the Pug.

After considerable research, a visit was made to the Thomases' Shirrayne Kennels. The Fischettis were told that to obtain a bitch of the quality desired they would have to be patient until the right one came along. The patience paid off in the form of Ch. Shirrayne's Pert Prima Donna. She not only completed her championship in short order but went on to produce five champions. A short time after acquiring Prima Donna—and after much arm twisting—Ann and Dan were able to purchase Ch. Shirrayne's Vivid Vanessa, who also finished her championship quickly and produced four champions. The kennel name of Vandonna is comprised of part of the names of these two foundation bitches.

Vanessa was most unusual in that she had four litters, each litter consisting of one female puppy. Each of these puppies completed its championship and became a producer of note.

Some of the better known Vandonna Pugs were:

Ch. K.O. Katie, who was most successful in Sweepstakes, having been
Grand Prize winner at the Pug Dog Club of America, Yankee Pug
Dog Club and Pug Dog Club of Greater New York Specialty shows.
She was also a multiple Breed winner, Group placer and was invited
to participate in the first Showcase of Pugs held in 1987.
Ch. Vandonna's Diggy of Shirrayne won many breeds and was a Group
winner when shown under the Shirrayne banner.

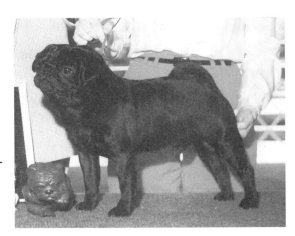

Ch. Wisselwood Velvet Tubby; breeder-owner, Lorene M. Vickers-Smith

Ch. Shirrayne's Vivid Vanessa, owned by Dan and Ann Fischetti

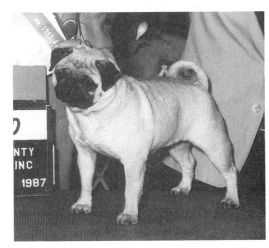

Ch. Vandonna's K. O. Katie, bred and owned by Dan Fischetti

Ch. Alabee's Billie Jean completed her championship with three five-point majors. She was bred by Al and Abbey Fox. Billy Jean was also a Grand Prize Sweepstakes winner, having obtained that award at the Yankee Pug Dog Club.

Vandonna's Matchmaker was lost tragically before his first birthday. He did, however, manage to be Grand Prize Sweepstakes winner at the Pug Dog Club of Greater New York Specialty and earn seven points toward his championship under the ownership of Lloyd Alton and Bill Gorodner of Ging's Kennels.

Ch. Vandonna's Excellent Choice was also a Grand Prize Sweepstakes winner. She was owned and campaigned by Al and Abbey Fox of Alabee Kennels.

Among others were Ch. Vandonna's Adam; Ch. Vandonna's Baby Snooks; Ch. Vandonna's Bubbles, owned by the Shirrayne Kennels; Ch. Vandonna's Bojangles, owned by Mr. and Mrs. Sam Castleman; Ch. Vandonna's Adorable Aimee, owned by Andy and Bobby Mraz; Ch. Vandonna's Cherrio; Ch. Vandonna's Extra Special; Ch. Gings Flapjack Fever, a multiple Breed winner who was bred by Lloyd Alton and Bill Gorodner and was a son of the illustrious Ch. Dhandy's Favorite Woodchuck; Ch. Vandonna's Golly Gee, another outstanding producer; Vandonna's Hot Rod Henry, a Grand Prize Sweepstakes winner; and Ch. Vandonna's Latin Lover.

The Fischettis wish to acknowledge that whatever success they have obtained as Pug breeders is owed in no small part to the teaching, guidance and assistance of two couples in particular: Bill and Marjorie Rankin of the well-known Huck Hill Boxer and Pug Kennels and Rayne and Shirley Thomas of Shirrayne Kennels.

It is the feeling at Vandonna that the bitch is the backbone of the Pug breed. The Fischettis also feel, therefore, that something should be done to enhance the position of the bitch in the breed; it is sad to so often see a superior bitch fall to defeat at the hands of an inferior dog simply because the dog is larger and more massive. The bitch is meant to be feminine, they say, and judges should take this into account when comparing a dog to a bitch. Several Pug bitches have established good show records but there never has been one to earn a show career of true greatness. The Fischettis feel it is difficult to believe that there never has been a bitch capable of consistently beating the boys and earning a comparable record.

Upon first turning attention to the Pug it seems that there were many overdone, coarse, "Bulldoggy" Pugs exhibited. To the breeders' credit, that no longer seems to be the case. However, the breeders may have overcompensated. We now see too many light-boned, straight-in-shoulder, Terrier-type Pugs. This is just as objectionable as the coarse Pug. Breeders should try breeding for Pug type: a square, well-balanced dog with a good straight hard topline and high set of tail; good layback of shoulder with enough angulation both in front and rear; having the ability to double-track freely and fluently; having good reach in front and rear. A Pug should have a large, heavily wrinkled head, but not so large as to be out of balance with the rest of the body.

Let us try for a tight curl in the tail, good pigment, including black nails, muzzle and ears with clear color, be it fawn or black. Let us try to produce a head in which the muzzle is in balance with the rest of the skull and in which the ears are properly set. This is true Pug type.

Corinne Black

Corinne Black, who lives in Lake Worth, Florida, was a former member of the Pug Dog Club of Greater New York. She fell in love with Pugs twenty years ago. Not knowing what kind of dog she wanted, she went to a local department store. Back then they had pet departments, with a great variety of breeds. She spotted a Pug and promptly feel in love.

Going to her first dog show awakened a latent competitive spirit within her, and she was hooked. She purchased a Sabbaday bitch from Mary Pickhardt that had a bad front foot and couldn't be shown, but she was otherwise lovely, with an excellent pedigree. She turned out to be a good brood bitch.

In 1969 Ch. Barney of Martlesham, an English import, took Best of Breed at Westminster; a local breeder, Ann Gries, had bred her champion bitch, Wheatland's Little Sue, to him. She had two bitch puppies for sale and Corinne bought one—Auburndale Robin. She had eight points, including one major on her when Corinne, for personal reasons, had to give showing up. But the dream persisted. Over the years she bred just enough to keep going, and five years ago was able to start over again.

In the last five years Corinne has finished seven Pugs, five of whom were "flyers"—finishing in anywhere from four to ten shows.

In discussing the show ring today, Corinne notes a greater and greater disparity between the dogs and bitches:

> The bitch entries, especially down here in Florida, are always quite a bit larger than the dog entries. The quality of the bitches is superlative: We're seeing shorter and shorter bodies, lovely to gorgeous heads and, for the most part, pretty good movement.

In her opinion the quality of the average males shown needs much improvement. She writes of seeing dogs going up with lovely bone and body, but hardly a wrinkle. They have small bitch-like heads, and light eyes. Worst of all, many have terrible rears that go in every direction but forward. She questions:

> What's happening to males? Are breeders only using their own studs to breed to, and then selling all but their outstanding bitches? Is it that campaigning a male to the top, where he'll get recognition and stud services, is getting so expensive that the average breeder can't afford it? Or is it that the bitches, by producing puppies, generate more income than the males do via stud fees, and therefore are expendable?

All in all, Corinne thinks the breed is in good shape, with more and more Pugs placing in Groups. Much emphasis lately is being placed on movement,

Head study of Ch. Morningstar's Cookie Bear, foundation sire of Stabradav's Pugs; owner, Corinne Black. He has lovely wrinkles and a nice, wide underjaw and widely spaced eyes.

Melissa Monterossa with Stabradav's Rebecca.

Which of these babies is the most curious? Puppies bred by Corinne Black.

more than ever before. She believes breeders have done an excellent job in improving fronts, but still have a way to go with rears.

Spacknkil's Pugs

In Poughkeepsie, New York, live Bill and Jean Richards and son Chris, who own the Spacknkil's Pugs. Bill has served as treasurer of the Pug Dog Club of Greater New York, and Jean and Chris are also active members.

After noticing a pair of Pugs while strolling in Washington, D.C., in the fall of 1977, the Richardses became enamored of the breed. They happened upon a pet shop in a local mall and soon ended up with Winston, a light fawn with a black mask. His papers indicated that he had been whelped on a Kansas puppy farm.

In April 1978 they were permanently transferred to Poughkeepsie, New York. Their new residence included a swimming pool, and three months later, Winston succumbed by drowning in the pool. Heartsick, the Richardses set out to find an immediate replacement. A phone call to the American Kennel Club for names of reputable Pug breeders in the New York area put them in contact with Shirrayne's Kennels. Shirrayne's Ambitious Berton replaced Winston, and in December 1978 they also acquired Shirrayne's Fabulous Gal.

In early 1979, Christopher started entering and handling the two Pugs at a few selected dog shows. In October 1980 the Richardses co-owned a second male from Shirrayne's Kennels, Ch. Shirrayne's Jolly Kid. In September 1981, at fourteen months of age, Jolly became a champion. Because of Jolly's exceptional qualities, he was continued as a special, and had great success, ending up as the Number One Pug in the country for 1982. In 1983, he finished fourth on the top-ten list.

In the spring of 1983 the Richardses acquired a second bitch, Ch. Shirrayne's Serene Tammie, whom Christopher showed and championed. In February and October of 1984, Tammie had two litters, each sired by Jolly. Two Champions resulted from these litters: Ch. Spacknkil's Amazing Cerric and Ch. Spacknkil's Charming Sir Echo. Outside their kennel, Jolly sired many champions. In 1986 they chose Alabee's Atta Boy Angus to sire Tammie's third litter. This produced Ch. Spacknkil's Eminent Guy, Spacknkil's Elegant Gal and Spacknkil's Empress Grace.

The Richards family has come a long way and has gained immeasurable experience over the last ten years. As cute as their little pet-shop Pug was, they have learned that there are vast differences in quality between a Pug that is properly and selectively bred and one that is produced by a puppy farm and sold over the counter. Having such an outstanding specimen as Ch. Shirrayne's Jolly Kid, finished by their son Christopher and campaigned so successfully by Shirley Thomas as a special, has given them valuable knowledge concerning confirmation to the Pug standard, overall correct skeletal structure, form and movement. In the show ring Jolly demonstrated an excellent topline with correct tracking while being moved. His size, structure and weight are in close agreement with the Pug standard.

Ch. Shirrayne's Jolly Kid, owned by Bill, Jean and Chris Richards

Ch. Kesanders Miss NoBody, owned by Jean and Bob Anderson

In reviewing all the aspects of their involvement with the Pug, the Richards agree that the part that still excites and challenges them the most is the planning, creating and maintaining of a realistic breeding program that will not only produce quality now, but also reasonably assure this level and/or something significantly better many years down the road. It takes considerable patience to carefully linebreed for quality, and it is hoped that Pug fanciers who try their hand at breeding will keep it paramount in their minds that a great deal of patience and a good understanding of what is involved in correct linebreeding are essential for maintaining and bettering the Pug long range.

Kesander's Pugs

Naperville, Illinois, is where Jean and Robert Anderson live with their Kesander's Pugs. Their first Pug, Bridget, was eight weeks old when she joined their family on St. Patrick's Day in 1964. A very ordinary pet Pug in appearance, she could not have endeared herself more had she been the most magnificent show dog. She would sit, dressed in doll clothes, in the wagon as the Anderson children pulled her up and down the street.

The Andersons bred Bridget once in 1968, to a beautiful champion, but managed to save only one puppy out of five, Sheba. Then both mother and daughter were spayed.

Early in 1969 a breeder friend gave the Andersons a beautiful male pup that had been returned to her. His sire was Quad. Ch. Hedlund's Jimijon, CD. The friend suggested that they take the puppy to Vera Hedlund, Jimijon's breeder, so that she could evaluate him. "Show him, show him," she said, so they entered their first dog show and have been going ever since.

The Andersons feel that Pugs as a breed have improved steadily over the years:

> Today we are seeing cobbier bodies, heavier bone, more substance generally and better fronts. It is often said, "heads are the easiest things to get," but it is not always that simple to produce a correct head. Pug gait is improving because more and more breeders are aware that a good specimen of any breed must be able to move well.

They also note that toplines are often sloppy lately, the dogs being down at the shoulder, high in the rear, roached or slightly swaybacked.

The Andersons believe that breeders must become more aware of and alert for the problems that can be found in the Pug today such as patella luxation, entropion and related disorders and even hip dysplasia. If breeders can be open and above board with each other, they say, we will see a vastly improved breed and much less heartache for all involved.

When commenting on the quality of black Pugs the Andersons point out that those who have not raised any black Pugs do not realize how difficult it is to produce an excellent specimen of that variety. He must be superior to his counterpart, partially because of the optical illusion his color presents. A black will appear longer in body, finer boned, weedier in general, although this may not be the case at all. The breeder of blacks is also faced at times with rusty coats and puppies born with white on their chest and feet, both unacceptable in the show ring.

Jean and Robert have interbred the black with the fawn extensively with excellent results. Dramatic improvement in the substance of the blacks has been achieved by this method, and a much sounder, cobbier black Pug is the result.

The Andersons point out that while Pug people feel that it is necessary to breed their fawns to a black periodically in order to keep the masks and ears darkly pigmented and distinct, the gene for the masks and ears is separate and distinct, carried by each fawn Pug and having nothing to do with the blacks. Similarly, the smutty fawn coat is not a result of a fawn-to-black breeding but is instead caused by a gene for that characteristic. They add:

> A surprisingly common misconception among a few less-experienced breeders is the belief that if you mate two fawns, each of whom has some black ancestors, you may have a few black puppies in the litter. This is totally impossible; nothing but fawn pups can result from a fawn-to-fawn mating. Fawn-to-fawn is pure recessive, therefore one parent must be black in order for a mating to produce any black offspring. Every serious breeder must be a student of genetics.

The Andersons mention one final guideline for all who are trying to improve the Pug dog, both fawn and black: *breed to the Pug standard!* A lot of the Pugs being shown today greatly lack neck. Many of these pups have massive heads that rest squarely on their shoulders, and the total look is coarse, especially as the dog grows older. Another weakness is the lack of underjaw in some dogs.

The Andersons currently have only two "old men" at stud, Speaker and P.R. They have not used Speaker for some time, although a breeding to a black bitch is planned. He produces a lovely, square offspring with super bone and a lovely head. He will now and then throw a pup with white on the chest and toes. He is heterozygous and will produce both fawn and black, depending upon who he is bred with.

P.R. Man is their "size-reducer." Almost always he will produce smaller Pugs, no matter to whom he is bred. He often throws his beautiful, clear apricot coat, and nearly always a beautiful, well-wrinkled head. He produces better when bred to a bitch with ample bone and good topline, although he himself possesses these characteristics.

Jean has two Dreamer males ready for use, and she still officially owns Ch. Kesander's Siwasher, who lives nearby and can be used any time. He is a Register of Merit, P.R.'s sire.

Cheryl Neese

Cheryl Neese, of Spartanburg, South Carolina, has been in Pugs for only several years, but is extremely proud of her first show Pug, which she owner-handled to his championship.

After several interviews, Joe Campisi decided Cheryl was serious about showing and sold her "Bubbie." It was love at first sight. Joe's associate, Rodney Merry, taught her the basics of handling and grooming. Being that both Cheryl and Bubbie were novices, it took them a while to reach stride. Bubbie won seven reserves, one of them at the Bluebonnet Pug Club Specialty.

Then Cheryl and her husband moved from Texas to Florida. At the first show in Florida Bubbie got his first points. It snowballed from then on, and he finished within the year.

Bubbie—or Ch. Campisi's Aldonova to Cheryl—died not long after that, on his third birthday of a blood clot in his heart. Cheryl writes, "His background was Shaw and Purifoy on his sire's side and Sheffield and Paragon on his dam side, and all this came together to make a nice little package."

Since then the Neeses have moved again, this time to South Carolina. Cheryl hopes to begin showing in the near future, and writes that she particularly admires the looks of the Shirrayne Pugs.

Jesswin Pugs

Jesswin Pugs was started in New Rochelle, New York, by Winifred M. Mullen, who had a lot of determination and faith in her Pug.

Winifred's family had owned a pet Pug for twenty-five years. She bought her first, Dinty M, from a pet shop in 1973. The local breeders had no pups at the time, and she wouldn't wait. He was healthy and sound, and grew so beautifully that she decided to show him.

Unfortunately, he was untrained and Winifred could not control him on the lead or in the ring. Winifred admits that even despite her "mishandling," he won his first points when he was a year and four months. He was Best of Winners at the Progressive Kennel Club under Judge Ruth Turner from the Novice Class.

From then on they struggled stubbornly. Dinty loved going to shows, and Winifred finally, with great help from her teachers and friends, Ruth Kayser and Tom Okun, learned to handle. Dinty's second major came at the age of six years under "all-rounder" Judge Vincent Perry, who raved about his beautiful movement. Dinty M finally became a champion—probably with one of the shortest names on record—when he was six and one-half years old and still in condition.

Meanwhile, his too-long showing and no championship meant no suitors coming to be bred to him. Winifred's good friend and partner, Tom Okun, advised her to buy a bitch with a similar background. Both the new bitch and Dinty M went back four generations to Ch. Pugholm's Peter Punkin Eater, a famous Pug of the 1950s.

The bitch, Dinty's Sweet Birdie, became a champion, and between them they produced two litters. There have now been five generations of the "Jesswin Tomlor" line.

Tom Okun heads up the breeding program, as he has great knowledge of pedigrees and a long memory for good and bad characteristics. Winifred's

Ch. Campisi's Aldonova to Cheryl;
owner, Cheryl Neese

Ch. Dinty M; owner-handler, Winifred M.
Mullen

Jesswin Tomlor's Blk Adonis; breeders-
owners, Winifred M. Mullen and Thomas
H. Okun

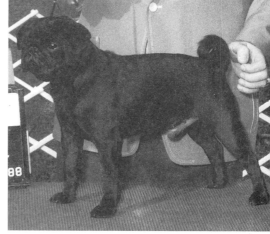

and Tom's object is to produce sound and healthy dogs with legs that are capable of jumping and moving without fear of injury.

Maggie and Rosie from the first litter were first mated to Tomlor's Vulcan, a lovely black. Annie and Tommy, of Dinty's and Bridie's second litter, were mated to their nephew and niece respectively. Altogether the champions number fifteen, both black and fawn.

Jesswin Pugs have won at the specialties of the Pug Dog Club of Greater New York, of America, of Maryland and the Yankee Pug Club. They have won at Westminster and other all-breed shows in New York and the neighboring states in the East.

Sheffield's Pugs

Margery A. Shriver lives in Baltimore, Maryland, with her Sheffield's Pugs. Showing dogs began when Margery was eleven or twelve years old and attending local American Kennel Club dog shows. At that time a youngster could participate in a children's handling class by borrowing anyone's dog and appearing at ringside at the proper time. Everyone received a box of candy and the four placements won a gift. During those years there was a Whippet breeder and exhibitor living across the street who kindly allowed Margery and others to borrow his champion dogs to run in nearby fields and woods. All her friends were given Whippets to show and breed, but unfortunately Margery's mother had a prejudice against thin, smooth-coated dogs and denied her the pleasure. Instead, she was given a Kerry Blue Terrier puppy but, despite her skill and dedication with the scissors, he never grew a show coat. Instead, she spent these years as a junior member of the newly formed Dog Owners Training Club of Maryland, one of the first obedience clubs, and trained her own crossbred hound as well as Whippets and Afghans.

Soon college and marriage intervened, but then, in 1950, Margery acquired two Toy Manchester Terrier bitches, believing at long last that she could begin showing and breeding dogs. Alas, they were too small for either.

More years passed while she raised her three children.

A visit to the Maryland Kennel Club benched show acquainted Margery with the enthusiastic group of Pug exhibitors in the newly formed Pug Dog Club of Maryland. This led to the acquisition of her first Pug, Honey, on breeder's terms. Her rationale was that since the breeder kept this bitch until it was a year old she must feel that it had breeding potential. Instead of trying to show, Margery raised some puppies, satisfied her obligation, and became owner of her Pug. She bred her first litter, from which she kept the first Sheffield Pug, Sheffield's Sunny Peach. Although never quite "enough" for a show dog, "Peachy" gave Margery three champions and a lifetime of devotion.

About the time Peachy had her first litter, Margery bought a puppy bitch from Louise Fyffe Baker. Sired by import Ch. Paramin Farmford Flarepath, she was a real doll, known as Sarah: Ch. Serenade of Sheffield. Flarepath's son

Scottish import Ch. Ardglass Tansy pictured going Winners Bitch and Best of Opposite Sex at the Berks County KC under judge Joan Alexander en route to her championship. Owner: Margery Shriver.

Ch. Sheffield's Kitten on the Keys pictured winning Best of Breed at the 1983 Westminster KC under Mrs. George Wanner. Breeder-handler-owner: Margery Shriver.

in England, Eng. Ch. Paramin Dillypin Pantaloon, became a dominant influence on the breed there. Sunny Peach was bred to Flarepath, and from one of her champion daughters, Ch. Sheffield's Lucy Locket of Shogo, got Am. & Can. Ch. Sheffield's Sure Fire, who holds the current record for top-producing dam (eleven) at this writing. Both Serenade and Lucy Locket were bred to another Paramin dog linebred from Flarepath, Ch. Wall's Warrior of Paramin, imported by Sue and Bill Wall and later owned by Louise Baker, who also owned Flarepath. The litter brother of Wall's Warrior in England was Eng. Ch. Patrick of Paramin, a dominant sire in the breed and foundation stud dog of the Nanchyl Pugs. From this mating Serenade produced Ch. Sunday Punch and Ch. Sally Sunshine.

Both Sure Fire and Sally Sunshine were then bred to Best-in-Show winner Am. & Can. Ch. Wolf's Li'l Joe, with successful results. The two lines intercrossed until Margery was able to import another Paramin-bred dog, Am. Ch. Samet Paul of Paramin. Sally Sunshine and Sure Fire between them had twenty champion offspring, all but two sired by Li'l Joe. One of these from Sure Fire was Ch. Sheffield's Dancing Tiger, owned by Mrs. Walter Jeffords, Michael Wolf and Barbara Minella. He went Best in Show the day after the national specialty.

Margery Shriver has bred sixty-six champions and owned and finished eight champions bred by others. Ch. Sheffield's Stuff 'N' Nonsense is the sire of sixty-four champions (two Best-in-Show dogs) and Ch. Little Red Wagon is the sire of thirty-six champions so far. Four of her other champion stud dogs have accounted for more than seventy champions among them.

The Pug that Margery is most proud of is Ch. Sheffield's Country Cousin, a bitch who did a lot of winning in her day. She achieved fifty Bests of Breed, forty-eight Bests of Opposite Sex, four Group Ones, twenty-eight other Group placements and a Best in Specialty win, all owner-handled. Her one litter produced three champions: Ch. Sheffield's Little Red Wagon, Ch. Sheffield's Kitten on the Keys and Ch. Wild Clover, who was the first bitch in nearly twenty years to win the breed at the Pug Dog Club of America National Specialty and Westminster Kennel Club.

In 1983 Margery was able to acquire a lovely little bitch puppy from the Ardglass Kennels in Scotland, Ch. Ardglass Tansy. She has made her own contribution by producing five champions.

Ch. Sheffield's Spitfire is now beginning her career and has won Best Puppy in Sweepstakes over eighty-six puppies from the four- to six-month class.

A recent addition to Sheffield Pugs is Nanchyl Girasol, who was bred by Nancy Tarbitt in England. His pedigree traces back to English Pugs previously mentioned. It is hoped that through Girasol the breeding program will be able to produce correct smaller Pugs with proper pigment. Time will tell, as every generation brings another challenge.

In Margery's opinion the biggest problem in the Pug breed is the same now as it was twenty years ago—incorrect shoulder structure and the accompanying faults of low shoulders and often straight stifles:

An astonishing number of Pugs currently being shown (and bred from) have steep shoulders and very short upper arms. This often makes them loose in the elbows and too wide in front, as well as causing a topline low in shoulders and high in rear. The length of the shoulder blade and the length of the upper arm should be approximately equal, with the shoulder laid back so that the neck blends smoothly into the back. A quick check is to feel the width between the shoulder blades at the withers—good shoulders are about two fingers apart, while steep shoulders can be as much as four fingers apart. A straight front is more than two straight legs. Those legs must be attached to correct shoulder assembly in order to move freely. Correspondingly, the rear legs must have adequate bend of stifle to balance out movement. It should be noted that a Pug with wide, muscular thighs (as desired) might appear to have a slight bend of stifle, but if you identify the points of the knee and the hock, you will see that the angulation is there.

Margery lists her next biggest frustration with Pugs today as the incorrect movement that is so prevalent in the ring. Needless to say, she says, it is the result of the above-mentioned structural flaws. When a Pug moves toward you, his hind feet should not be visible on the outside of the hind leg. No judge of working or sporting dogs would tolerate in those breeds the movement that is so commonly accepted in Pugs. Pug structure and movement belong in the same category as normal dogs, a majority of breeds, not in the same category as exceptions for normally structured dogs.

She notes an unexplained phenomenon whereby a Pug moving away from you in wet grass often moves in a sloppy fashion even though it may move perfectly true on a hard surface. A matter of controversy is the "Pug roll," which Margery describes as just a springy or jaunty rear action that should not prevent the Pug from double-tracking.

Regarding breeding blacks and fawns together, Margery feels it should be avoided if it is at all possible. The time is past when the quality of blacks was so rare that it was necessary to introduce fawns to improve blacks. She feels that interbreeding will complicate things, perhaps not in the first generation, but in the later ones:

It is a fallacy that one can or should breed a poorly pigmented fawn to a black to get black toe nails and better pigment. Ironically, a fawn puppy from black parents is often lacking pigment. There are ample fawn stud dogs with excellent pigment for those who seek it and nowadays quite a few excellent black stud dogs to choose from. The one quality that might excuse a cross between the colors is improved structure, which is often in short supply in both colors. Once accomplished, however, one should stick to one color for many generations—it is said at least five generations of black breeding before bringing in a fawn.

Certainly, she adds, color is a problem currently in blacks, no doubt because of crossing so often with the fawns.

What follows is some background information on Margery's stud force to help everyone to improve the Pug breed.

Ch. Sheffield's Little Red Wagon: A fawn dog, 23 pounds, light golden fawn and good shoulders, moderate length of back, high tail set, soft expression, very dark eyes, black nails, very wide muzzle and deep underjaw, good strong rear with good angulation, and extremely good rear movement. His detriments are a somewhat muscled-up front, legs that aren't always conducted well, and some of his pups do not have much pigment around their eyes and/or nose-roll, while some have light nails.

"Reddy" 's pups just about always are a clear light fawn, no matter the color of the mother, and they usually have a sweet, soft expression. Margery would not recommend him for a bitch who is washed out and needs pigment. However, ears always get black. The size of the pups usually is dominated by the bitch.

Ch. Sheffield's Jersey Bounce: A fawn dog, 23½ pounds, orange apricot color, well pigmented, with a short back, very high tail set, very straight front and good shoulders. He has a lovely arch of neck, angulated rear, clear coat color, lots of pigment, dark eyes and black nails. Margery would not breed a smutty bitch to Bounce, as his mother is very smutty. Some pups have turned out quite small, although he is rather large. Puppies are quite a bit like Stuff 'N' Nonsense (his grandfather) and might have rather furry coats.

Ch. Stuff 'N 'Nonsense: A fawn dog, 22 pounds, with an orange-apricot color, very heavy bone, short back, good shoulder assembly and straight front. He has a thick-set neck, very dark eyes and pigment, black nails, moderate rear angulation and a large round head. He is predominant for good bone, short bodies and good fronts, while bitches dominate wrinkles and usually size, color and coat type. *Note:* Little, short, cloddy Pugs often turn up for several generations.

If other breeders were as knowledgeable and forthcoming enough to contribute this kind of data, we might be able to control or improve some of the shortcomings in the Pug breed. I thank Margery for her contribution.

Paulmar's Pugs

Paulmar's Pugs, owned by Martha J. and Paul Pratt, are located in Toledo, Ohio. The Pratts bought their first Pug in 1969, having never seen one. They loved the dog so much that eight months after getting the first Pug, they couldn't resist getting another. Not being familiar with the breed or ever being at a dog show, they only wanted pets.

In 1970 they had a litter of three. The puppies were so nice that the Pratts decided to go to their first puppy match. They came home with a Group One, and they were hooked.

They bought a show dog, and for several years purchased different lines and showed them to no avail. Then they bought a male, Ritter's Benji of Monaco, whom Paul showed to championship.

In 1976 the Pratts purchased Rosened's Lovin Abby, who later became their third champion and foundation bitch. Abby was bred to Benji and produced their first homebred champion, Ch. Paulmar's Serene Serena. Her second breeding was to Ch. Gore's Up'N Adam, ROM, from which there were four champions: Ch. Paulmar's Trace of Excellence, Ch. Paulmar's Trace of

English import Nanchyl Girasol, owned by Margery Shriver

Ch. Paulmar's Little Luke, owned by Martha J. Pratt

A head study of Ch. Paulmar's Trace of Fascination, CD, owned by Martha J. Pratt

Virtue, Ch. Paulmar's Trace of Antiquity and Ch. Paulmar's Wagga De Ann. The breeding was repeated and produced Ch. Paulmar's Trace of Fascination, CD ("Flash").

In 1983, at one year of age, Flash became the Pratt's first obedience champion with a high score of 192. Shortly afterwards he became a champion.

After owning, breeding and finishing many Pugs, the Pratts decided to special Ch. Paulmar's Trace of Antiquity. Andy placed in many Groups, then along came his son Luke—taking Best of Breed from the classes over his papa and top specials. Ch. Paulmar's Little Luke finished with a five-point major at the Great Lakes Pug Club Specialty, April 12, 1985.

In 1986, at two years of age, Luke won two all-breed Bests in Show and the national specialty, making him Number One Pug. He's been in the top five for 1985, 1986, 1987 and 1988.

The Pratts note that when they started in Pugs, breeders were few and far between, so they had to learn by trial and error. It took them many years of studying to establish a line they could be proud of.

Harper Kennels

Alan L. Harper, a breeder/judge, lives in Alexandria, Virginia. He has been associated with Pugs since he was ten years old. He acquired his first Pug, which was bred in Ashville, North Carolina, from a pet shop and named him Pugsy. They started on the match circuit and that was the extent of their show career. Not one to be discouraged, he purchased another Pug, a bitch named Hoshi, and commenced showing her also. A very kind Canadian judge told him it was obvious Hoshi was very unhappy at being a "show girl"; he felt, however, that properly bred, it was likely she could produce well for Alan. Alan took that advice and bred her to a dog named Buccaneer. She produced a litter of three bitches, one being Fawn-C-Pants.

In the meantime, Alan took handling lessons from Lee Sleeper and made his debut at age eleven in the junior handling classes. His confidence soared and he entered in regular competition with Fawn-C-Pants. Ed Bivin was judging dogs on that occasion, and Alan won his first points—a four-point major, Best of Winners, and Best of Opposite Sex. He was fourteen when Ch. Harper's Fawn-C-Pants attained her title. Subsequently, she received Breed and Group placements.

Alan recalls how the odds were stacked against him because of his age, but he was able to hold his own, and overcame many obstacles that inhibit some judges' decisions when young aspiring exhibitors are only asking to be judged on the merits of their dogs. He was helped by further tutoring with other professionals in the sport, and this added to his background and handling expertise, not to mention self-confidence and discipline.

Alan got a job with a local veterinarian after school hours and during summer vacations. This continued for five years, but it wasn't enough to satisfy his incessant appetite for dog shows. He and his mother attended approxi-

Ch. Harper's Tommy Tune, an all-breed BIS winner, pictured winning Best of Breed at the 1984 Gloucester County KC under judge W. C. McGough, Jr. Owner-handler: Alan Harper.

mately sixty-five shows each year for the next three years, and Alan writes that "my generous and compassionate father helped subsidize this venture."

To date, the Harper Kennels have produced over fifty champions, both fawns and blacks. This is in addition to Maltese, Yorkshire Terriers, Pekingese, Pomeranians, Brussels Griffons, Shih-Tzu and a specialty-winning Boston Terrier.

At age twenty-three Alan applied for and received his judge's license, and his love of dog shows has taken on yet another dimension. With the help of knowledgeable and patient judges, and the efforts and encouragement of two supportive parents, Alan has been able to get the opportunity to give something back to the sport and to encourage and promote others to find their niche in the sport of dogs.

John Marsh

John Marsh has had a long career in Pugs. He recently moved from Long Island, New York, to his new home in Forest, Virginia. His parents, James and Mae Marsh, raised Boston Terriers and Boxers and John helped to show them. After World War II he bought a Pug bitch from Grace Heerwagon and Janet Kosvik, who bred to Mighty Jim. She produced many champions and was a top show Canadian and American winner.

John became a professional handler a few years after I did. He finished over one hundred Pugs and many other breeds. I remember when the Shih Tzu breed was recognized. John and I stayed up all night grooming John's dog because his coat had been stained by wet grass. It paid off! It was the first time Shih Tzus were shown in this country, and John went Winners Dog, Best of Breed, Group One and on to win Best in Show, under James Trullinger.

But John's first love will always be the Pug. He has worked hard over the years to try to breed quality dogs. John is always there if some one needs a hand.

The Author and Shirrayne Kennels

In bringing this chapter to a close, I will relate to you how I, Shirley Thomas, became involved in dogs. I was born in Flushing, New York, and I have an early memory of having a dog with me in my crib. It might have been a Chow Chow—my family had them—I was too young to tell.

Being a mischievous child I used to bite the Chows, and consequently they would bite me back. My father, not knowing who was at fault, was in a dilemma. Left with no alternative, he got rid of the Chows.

A few years later he bought me a Bulldog, Mitzi. My constant companion, Mitzi helped get me temporarily expelled from school for a week. My teacher did not appreciate her attendance in the classroom. Mitzi provided me with my first show ring experiences and became my first champion.

I was busy with school, training in all phases of dancing, dramatics, singing and skating for the next few years. I appeared on the "Children's

Ch. Albelarm's American Express, pictured with owner-handler
John Marsh

Hour" radio show, and in my spare time became the best kennel help Dad ever had.

My father and my brother Al became involved in Boxers in 1937, under the prefix of Dahlia Crest. At the time I was performing after school at some of New York's top nightclubs, such as Leon and Eddie's and the Latin Quarter. In 1938 my brother took me to the greatest dog show I have ever seen, the Morris & Essex show. A wonderful lady named Mrs. Dodge took me under her wing. I was totally enchanted and fell in love with the dog show scene.

While on tour with the Skating Vanities, I traveled with a Maltese, who was from Dr. Vincenzo Calvaresi's stock and appeared in the show. Dad also bought Ch. Dapper of Kesthal for me, who was campaigned by my brother Al and me. Dapper became the top Boxer in the country in 1944 and 1945. When the revue was back in New York for rehearsals I would travel to all the shows with my brother Al and exhibit Dapper.

In October 1944, in Milwaukee, Wisconsin, I was seriously injured while on tour with the Skating Vanities. I shattered most of the bones in my face. In between the many operations on my face I attended all the dog shows I could, as the doctors would not allow me back on skates. I couldn't bear not skating any longer, so one evening I took off for a skating rink in New York City. My brothers must have known what I was up to because the three of them followed me. While there, my brother Al introduced me to Rayne Thomas, who later became my husband.

My father and my brother Al decided to buy me any dog I wanted to keep me happy and away from skating. Dad imported the third Weimaraner into the country for me. I bred and showed a few of those for a while and then worked with a smooth Dachshund bitch named Candy. She finished her championship, and we bred her once. My brother brought me home an angelic Keeshond, whose record has only recently been bested. We bred Keeshonds for a time and also continued to breed Boxers.

After I was married, my husband and I moved to Old Westbury, Long Island. I then decided I wanted my own kennel name and started off with the prefix Raynebeau. Under the Raynebeau prefix I bred and showed Toy and Miniature Poodles, Labrador Retrievers and a colored Bull Terrier bitch. I also endeavored once more to return to my first love, skating. Unfortunately, trouble arose. I had blackouts and still needed several operations on my face. I finally realized I had to give up skating completely, I settled down and had three children. Raising the children slowed me down for a few years. In 1952 I acquired my professional handler's all-breed license, and knew this was the way I wanted to go. I had two Pugs at my home at the time for training and fell in love with the breed.

We decided to register our Raynebeau kennel prefix with the American Kennel Club, but due to a name too close to ours they would not permit it. We changed our prefix to Shirrayne.

In 1959 Dapper passed away at eighteen years of age. There will never be another Boxer to take his place in my heart.

My mother was indisposed, and I wanted to be closer so I could take care of her. We were able to purchase a house that bordered my parents' property in Flushing, New York. We continued to breed and show the Labs and Poodles, and I finally located the right Pug for me. I imported Am. & Can. Ch. Bitterwell Broth of a Boy from England. The next year I went to England and purchased my black male, Ch. Rouleyn Shere Khan and also brought back an eight-week-old Pug bitch and a white Toy Poodle. I also purchased Anchorage Killer Joe and Ch. Candy's Almond Joy. A few years later I purchased another English import, Ch. Greentubs Busy Bee, and Barbarella of Gore, who was co-owned by John Marsh. The combination of these lines created the Shirrayne Pugs.

I have owned a few other breeds that have touched my heart. Included are Ch. Mignon's Cotton Candy, a Chihuahua; several Bichon Frises; a Siberian Husky and my daughter's blue Great Dane, Cleo, who still raids the refrigerator.

I have also been active in dog clubs. Currently I am president of the Dog Judges Association of America, president of the Bronx County Kennel Club, president of the Progressive Dog Club, president of the Pug Dog Club of Greater New York, which I had founded with my brother Al Meshirer and John Marsh. I am also an active member of the Pug Dog Club of America. I have finished well over 150 dogs, which is probably a short count.

I presently own a Toy Poodle, a Scottish Deerhound, one cat, two birds, and many Pugs. I have been honored to have a Pug place in the top ten every year until 1984. At that time Ch. Shirrayne's Jolly Kid, co-owned by the Richardses, was retired at the peak of his career because someone poured acid on his front toes and pads. He was the number one contender when this terrible incident occurred.

Shirrayne Pugs have won the honors of Most Bests of Breed, Breeder of the Year, and Register of Merit awards at the Pug Dog Club of America.

For the last three years it has been quiet at Shirrayne Kennels because of my brother Al's illness and subsequent death. I had helped him by managing his business. We shall soon be back out at all the shows, however.

It is important that breeders know some of the dominant and recessive genes in the Shirrayne lines. I will start off with Am. & Can. Ch. Bitterwell Broth of a Boy, affectionately known as Tiger. He reproduced cobby-type Pugs. He was dominant in producing beautiful correct heads with a perfect diamond. He was strong in rears, straight toplines, short backs and magnificent coat texture, markings and color. You had to breed a potent front line to Tiger because in his ancestry there were some short upper arms and bowed fronts. Tiger weighed 18½ pounds.

Ch. Rouleyn Shere Khan, my black male, was dominant in reproducing type, heavy bone, short backs, excellent toplines and good fronts. Khan was also dominant in throwing blue-black puppies. Khan's head was lovely but was a result of a recessive gene. He was also a little straight in rear and weighed 18¾ pounds.

Ch. Shirrayne's Victorious Vance was dominant in producing outstanding correct heads and, most of all, an impeccable layback of shoulder and

English import, Am./Can. Ch. Bitterwell Broth of a Boy at eight months. Owner: Shirrayne Kennels.

English import Ch. Rouleyn Shere Khan. Owner: Shirrayne Kennels.

upper arm. Vance also produced type, coat color and short backs. Eye color was a matter of concern with Vance because he went back to Stormie of Martlesham, who had light eyes. He could also throw roached backs. Out of twenty-six litters he had four puppies with this blemish. He had to be bred into a strong line of good toplines. His son, Ch. Scampish Tattoo, who was his sire's double, carried the same dominant and recessive traits. Vance and Tattoo both weighed 18½ pounds.

If I wanted spectacular strong rears, movement, toplines, massive bone and head it was Am. & Bda. Ch. Shirrayne's Earthquake Earl. Earl had a nice front but was not dominant in passing it along. His great-grandfather, Ch. Auburndale Aquarius, carried this as a recessive trait that Earl acquired. Aquarius's front could also have been better. Earl was dominant in passing on his strong rear, bone and correct head. Earl was bigger than I liked, weighing 21½ pounds. Size was a matter of concern with Earl, as there was an abundance of sizeable dogs behind him. Occasionally he would produce an open overnose wrinkle, which is behind his line.

Ch. Shirrayne's Music Man, who is co-owned by Carol Schmidt, is dominant in producing extraordinarily correct heads, excellent bone, straight toplines, color, strong rears and movement. Music Man is 20½ pounds. His recessive genes are his fronts, and he was a little long in body. His son, Pinewoods Elegance, also carried the same traits except he was better balanced and would also pass on his lovely jet black markings.

Ch. Shirrayne's Jolly Kid is exceptionally dominant in producing type, straight toplines, short backs, good bone, high tail sets, color and lovely correct heads. His recessive genes are his fronts and rears. Jolly is 19 pounds.

My Int., Braz. & Am. Ch. Shirrayne's Golddigger, who is owned by Tracy Williams, produced Pugs of correct size. "Diggy" is 26 pounds. His dominant genes are his lovely correct head, straight toplines, high tail set, short backs, strong rears, lovely color and movement. He has a correct front but carried this as a recessive gene. Golddigger has won four Bests in Show and six Group Ones in four months of showing in Brazil and holds the honor of being the top dog in Brazil, all breeds, for two years. His American record stands at thirty-four Bests of Breed with many Group placements. He was in Number Five Pug in the nation in 1975 before leaving for Brazil.

It is difficult to tell you what Tara's Jeb Stuart of Dixie is dominant in, as this young dog has only been used three times at stud. His puppies are too young to evaluate, but what I have seen thus far in the three litters is good bone and correct heads.

A few of Shirrayne's top producing bitches are Ch. Shirrayne's Brash Buffi, 16 pounds; Ch. Candy's Almond Joy, 17½ pounds; Ch. Greentubs Busy Bee, 18 pounds; and Ch. Shirrayne's Lotsa Lovin, 15½ pounds. All the females were dominant in producing excellent type, fronts, heads, bone, short backs and toplines, with the exception of Candy's Almond Joy. She had to be bred to a proper short-back dog with an appropriate rear and correct topline. Busy Bee, Lotsa Lovin and Buffi were also dominant in producing strong rears and high tail sets. Pugtowne's Barbarella of Gore was dominant in producing good

Am./Bda. Ch. Shirrayne Earthquake Earl. Owner: Shirrayne Kennels.

fronts. Although Barbarella had a good rear, she carried this as a recessive gene. She was 18 pounds.

My goal for our future Shirrayne Pugs is to maintain all the dominant genes within my lines, which are breed type, correct heads, square balanced bodies, soundness, level toplines, movement, color and coat. Many years of trial, error and sweat went into achieving these features in my Pugs. One of my most difficult tasks was achieving the perfect forty-five-degree angle layback of shoulders and upper arms that is now dominant in my line. This project of linebreeding, which took me fifteen years to develop, was reproduced and made dominant in Vance. In doing so I also accomplished reproducing a perfect duplicate of Vance, his son Tattoo, who also carries this dominant gene.

Shirrayne is also working on a project to produce a dominant line of correct legs and rears. This we all know might be impossible to achieve due to the fact that the Pug was cross-bred. There are so many hidden genes that trace all the way back to Pugs in China and England. We may never be able to eradicate them. Never forget that when you breed you can throw back twenty and thirty generations. This is because Pugs were cross-bred in China to the Lion Dog, Pekingese, and a few unknown breeds. Also, in England, they were cross-bred to the Bulldog and many other breeds. Inbreeding then took over for many generations. As the result of these many factors you can see what we are up against, but I am looking forward to this challenge.

I would like to say thank-you for the interesting autobiographies I have received. Your opinions will be a great help to the future of the Pug breed, especially for beginners, judges and the many of us who have been trying to control genetic faults while maintaining the positive virtues of the breed. I hope they serve as a useful depiction of what we would like to accomplish in the breed. The general consensus of the above autobiographies is a desire to correct toplines, fronts, rears, size, tails and movement, to learn where these problems originate and to try and delete them from your breeding program even though you know they may resurface again.

It astounded me to find out how many breeders and breeder-judges look for soundness before type. They might as well pull a mutt off the street and judge it. Most of them are sound. Without proper breed type, however, you do not have a Pug. Upon reading all these autobiographies I have found that everyone suggests that there is no perfect Pug. All our goals are geared to achieving type and soundness.

In the 1940s through the early 1960s we had some lovely cobby, sound black Pugs with heavy bone and dark eyes. We also had some nice cobby fawns. Our fawn colors were much better then. They weren't being destroyed by the fawn and black crosses. The blacks owned then by Dr. Nancy Riser, Florence Bartel, Fred Greenly, Margery May, Russel Hicks, Dick Paisley and others, including my Khan, were all far better in quality when compared to a few bitches that we are seeing today.

Many are of the opinion that our Pugs are better today. I personally don't think so, because the Pug breed runs in cycles. You will see excellent quality for a few years and then it disappears and returns with the help of a few dedicated breeders, striving, as they have for centuries, to unlock the many secrets of the Pug. There will always be new theories added to the many extraordinary ones already found. I look forward with great expectation to our future Pugs and the advances that will be made through modern technology, improved veterinary medicine and an era where information will be available from more reliable sources. I also look forward to our breeders working together for the betterment of our wonderful breed, the Pug.

Michael Sim's daughter, Maria, pictured with (*from left*) Mo Mo, Jumbo and Ginger

The Pugs' afternoon swim at the home of Michael Sim

An Australian imported bitch out at sea off the coast of Hong Kong. Owned by Otto Lau Kin Fung and Michael Sim.

4

The Modern Pug
Around the World

I GREATLY ENJOYED the experience—and challenge—of contacting and speaking to all the exceptional Pug people around the world. Try calling Hong Kong sometime! I finally got through after locating a few interpreters. It was an interesting encounter that I will recount through the biographies. Pug type, soundness and the pursuit of excellence is also their goal.

Pugs in Hong Kong

We shall begin in Kowloon, Hong Kong, with Michael W. Y. Sim and his charming Pugs. Together with his partner and good friend Otto Lau Kin Fung, he breeds Pugs in his spare time.

There are two major kennel clubs in Hong Kong: the Hong Kong Kennel Club (HKKC) and the Hong Kong and Kowloon Kennel Association (HKKKA). They hold only four all-breed shows each year, so it takes a while to finish a dog there. A dog needs three challenge certificates (CCs) to become a champion.

The top-winning Pug in Hong Kong is currently Dido of Arrow Kennel, owned and handled by Otto, Michael's partner. Bred by Mr. Liang Yang of the Arrow Kennel in Taiwan, the dog is also known as Jumbo. He is a beautiful two-year-old fawn male. He started his showing career in 1987 when he was ten months old at the HKKKA twenty-fifth all-breed show, held in the spring.

The show was judged by American Kennel Club all-round judge Bill Harvey. Although Jumbo was still a puppy, he was already showing perfection of the breed and was moving beautifully. That day Jumbo took Best of Breed and Best Toy Dog, then went on to win Best Puppy in Show and finally Best in Show out of nearly 400 entries. It was really a great moment. Never before had a Pug placed Best in Show there in dog show history.

Jumbo showed his ability once again in the Spring of 1988 when he took Best in Show again at the twenty-seventh HKKKA all-breed show, judged by American Kennel Club all-round Judge Dorothy Welsh. This was his second Best in Show in a short career of only three shows. Michael and Otto have great confidence in his future and hope that one day he will become one of the top-winning dogs in the show ring.

The dog's breeder, Liang Yang, is the owner of the top Pug breeding kennel in Taiwan and has donated many years of his time carefully planning breeding programs of the stocks he so treasures. Many people believe that Mr. Yang has the most outstanding bloodline in Asia, and Michael and Otto are very proud to be able to own some of his best stocks.

Competition in Hong Kong

In Hong Kong the Pug entries at the dog shows usually number around ten to fifteen, and at the larger shows may go as high as twenty Pugs. The cost of a lifetime membership is $1,000 for the Hong Kong and Kowloon Kennel Association. Entry fees are $70 for the first entry of lifetime members and $20 for each additional entry. Nonmembers of the HKKKA are charged double. A lifetime membership in the Hong Kong Kennel Club is $4,000. Entry fees are $50 for the first entry and $20 for each additional entry, with the exception of those who enter an Open class only, for which the fee will be $60. Nonmembers are charged double. All prices above are stated in Hong Kong dollars.

In both clubs, in cooperation with the Agriculture and Fisheries Department, all exhibits must be examined by the honorary veterinary surgeon in attendance by 8:00 A.M. Each dog entered in the show must have its dog license with it. In HKKKA shows, bitches in season cannot be shown, and their entry fee will be refunded with a certificate from the veterinarian. On the other hand, bitches in season *may* be shown at Hong Kong Kennel Club shows, with a certificate from a veterinary surgeon recognized by the club proving that prevention treatment has been given or she will be treated by the club's honorary veterinary surgeon at the gate of the show at the owner's expense. It is interesting that males with one testicle can be shown at HKKC shows, but at the Hong Kong and Kowloon Kennel Association shows males with none or one testicle cannot be shown.

The Elimination Classes that a dog can be entered under at HKKKA are: (AA) Young Puppy—dogs and bitches over three months of age; (A) Puppy—dogs and bitches over six months to twelve months; (B) Novice—dogs and bitches over twelve months that have never won a first prize at a championship show; (C) Local Bred—dogs and bitches over twelve months of age bred in Hong Kong; (D) Open Dog—dogs over twelve months; (E) Open Bitch—bitches over 12 months; and (H) Handler's Classes—exhibitors can handle any dog entered in the show (judging based on handler's skill, entry fee $100 for members and $200 for nonmembers). Winners of Class AA and A will compete for a special Best Puppy in Show Class.

At the Hong Kong Kennel Club you can enter your Pug in the following Elimination Classes: (A) Puppy; (B) Novice; (C) Local Bred; (D) Open Dog; (E) Open Bitch; and also in the following classes, which are called Variety Classes: (F) Litters—at least two puppies aged six weeks to three months; (G) Locally bred and still owned by breeder at the time of show—dogs and bitches over six months old whose parents were mated and the puppies born in Hong Kong and still owned by the breeder at the time of show; (H) Brace—two of the same breed, same sex or opposite sex, over six months old and both being the property of the same owner; (I) Veteran—dogs and bitches over eight years old; (J) Junior Handler Class A—children of members under thirteen years old, no charge; Class B—children of members thirteen to eighteen years old, no charge; (K) Adult Handling Class—members only, no charge; and Exhibition Only—any dog or bitch over three months old entered for exhibition only, not for competition in any class, fee $100, handler's badge charge for nonmembers, $100.

The classification of groups is Terriers, Hounds, Utility, Gundogs, Toys, Working, Any Other Variety Classes and Handlers Classes. After elimination they move to Best of Groups, Best Puppy in Show, Best in Show and Reserve Best in Show.

Dogs entered in the Hong Kong Kennel Club show will not be excused until the dog show has closed. Litters are permitted to be removed from 4:00 P.M. onward. Exhibitors may state on their entry forms the price at which they are prepared to sell their dogs. The sale must take place through the office of the club's secretary to the first acceptance at the stipulated price. A commission of 10 percent will be charged to the seller on all sales. Exhibitors may reduce the price of their dogs on giving notice to the club's secretary. The HKKC's new by-laws on dog shows state that dogs under six months of age will not be accepted for dog shows. The qualifying date is the first day of the show. Another change is that the winner of any Breed class or any Group class of either sex may, if the judge deems it worthy, be awarded a Hong Kong Kennel Club Challenge Certificate.

The HKKC is affiliated with the Kennel Club of London and is a member of Federation Cynologique International. Pugs are judged by the English standard and need three Challenge Certificates to become a champion.

Cavalier King Charles Spaniels, Chihuahuas (long-coated and smooth-coated), English Toy Terriers (Black and Tan), Brussels Griffons, Italian Greyhounds, Japanese Chins, King Charles Spaniels, Lowchen, Maltese, Miniature Pinschers, Papillons, Pekingese, Pomeranians, Pugs and Yorkshire Terriers are shown in Hong Kong in the Toy Group.

The Hong Kong Kennel Club Limited held their first championship dog

A class of Pug puppies at the Hong Kong Kennel Club show

Best in Show at the Hong Kong and Kowloon KA under American judge Dorothy Welsh was Jumbo. His handler and co-owner is Otto Lau Kin Fung.

show in 1948. They have now held fifty-five championship shows and thirty-seven obedience trials. They did not hold any show in 1950 and 1956.

Pugs in Denmark

As we leave the Far East, let's travel to Dianalund, Denmark, and visit with a lovely and interesting lady, Britta Husted, whom I had the pleasure of talking to a few months ago.

Denmark has a tradition of Pugs that dates back to at least the sixteenth century. Denmark is the oldest kingdom in the world, and they are currently celebrating their most famous king, King Christian IV. He was only eleven years old when, in 1588, he succeeded his father King Frederick II on the throne. In the National Museum there is a beautiful tapestry showing Frederik II and his young son, standing with their dogs at their sides. The king has a big hunting-type dog and the young Christian is shown with a playful little Pug.

King Christian was a real Renaissance king, for good and for bad. When his first queen, Anna Catherine, died in 1612, he remarried, but since this time it was a "left hand" marriage, Kirsten Munk, his new wife, never became Queen of Denmark. The king was the father of at least twenty-three children. His favorite daughter, Princess Leonora Christina, was portrayed by Karel van Mander with her tame wolf and her Pug. This Pug is typical of the time with its long ears. It is very light in color with no mask. Others were golden or brownish with big white markings on head, chest and legs. The black Pug was very common as well, but it too had white markings.

There is an exhibition at Frederiksborg Castle dealing with King Christian, his family and the era of the sixteenth and seventeenth centuries. In many of the paintings showing the royal family there were Pugs as well, and always in a position showing that they were beloved pets.

In the following centuries in Denmark, the breed experienced many ups and downs. In 1899, in an article in a Danish dog magazine about Pugs, the author states that the Pug could be seen on all the streets of Copenhagen. Pugs were almost never seen in dog shows because they were in such low esteem that nobody wanted to pay even the small amount of money that was the charged fee.

Britta Husted first met the Pug in the late 1970s. At the time the breed was very rare in Denmark. There were only one or two breeders with an occasional litter, and one was lucky if one saw one or two Pugs at the shows.

She remembers very clearly her first meeting with a Pug. She was visiting her mother-in-law, who at that time bred French Bulldogs and Great Danes. They were all gathered in the sitting room, with Bulldogs and Great Danes in every corner, when suddenly they had visitors, a young couple with an extraordinary little dog. They all stood in the doorway, and the little dog looked around. It crossed the floor and jumped on Britta's lap, as if they had been friends forever. He stole her heart on the spot, and it became a "must" for her to own a Pug.

Danpug Little Lion, at six weeks, owned by Bettina Kyed of Denmark

Danish Ch. Diamond, bred by Baron and Baroness Raben- Levetzau and owned by Britta Husted

Four litter brothers from Britta Husted's Danpug Kennels show a remarkable evenness of type.

Though this was more easily said than done, finally, through the Danish Kennel Club, she contacted the representative of Pugs, the late Rita Bonde, of Kennel Ribo. Mrs. Bonde told Britta about a litter, the first litter born at Aalholm Castle with Baron and Baroness Raben-Levetzau, of three black bitches—and Britta became the owner of little Diamond. She was later to become Dan. Ch. Diamond and foundation bitch of Kennel Danpug. Diamond, who was shown six times, three times with Best of Breed, gained her title in March 1982. Diamond is the mother of two Danish champions and a German junior champion.

In 1981 Britta bought a black puppy dog from Renee Sporre-Willes of Sweden. The dog, Sidney, is of British origin on both sides and has had a beautiful career in the show ring.

How would you like to place Best of Breed Number One, Number Two, Number Three and Number Four? Well, that's how it's done in Denmark. They have four Best of Breed placings (and the sex of the Pug doesn't matter!). Shown fifteen times at championship shows, Sidney has taken fifteen First Prizes, eight Bests of Breed and a number of other awards. He became a Danish champion at only fifteen months of age. Sidney was Pug of the Year in 1982 and Number Two in 1983. He was not shown in 1984, but made a comeback in 1985, when he again was Number Two. In 1985 the first Pug specialty show in Denmark was held, with forty-seven entries, and Sidney ended his show career by winning Best in Show. Sidney and Diamond had a litter in 1982. Two bitches from that litter became Danish champions, and a litter sister became a German junior champion. Sidney is also sire of Dan. Ch. Nicolaj, out of Danpug Beige Bonnie. Nicolaj's breeder and owner is Lise Garde.

To continue the black line, Britta kept a black bitch from the first litter after Dan. Ch. Cobby's African Drakensberger and Dan. Ch. Diamond. Her name was Danpug Diamond's Daughter and she became of great importance for Britta's breeding program. She was shown at championship shows twenty times, always with a first prize and ten Best of Breed placings. She became a Danish champion in 1984 and the same year she was Copenhagen winner. She was Pug of the Year Number Three in 1983 and Number Four in 1984. Two of her litter sisters also did very well. Danpug Debsie, owned by Mrs. Ludvigsen, Kennel Tidselbakken, gained her title in 1987. Another sister was bought from Barbel Wohlers of Kennel Ut Heid in Germany, and became German junior champion and Europajugendsieger.

Daisy had three litters. The first one, by Int. Ch. Cyrene Black Jack Ut Heid, produced three black males and a silver. One of them was Danpug Giant Panda, who was sold to Mrs. Ludvigsen. Panda became a Danish champion in 1986. He was the best black Pug of the Year Number Four in 1985, Number Two in 1986, and best black Pug again in 1987.

In 1985 Britta imported a fawn dog from England, Cyrene Dandy Dick, bred by Renee Meadows. He became the sire of Daisy's next litter, consisting of two black and two fawn bitches. Britta kept one of the fawn bitches, Danpug Isabella, as a foundation bitch of fawns. She became a Danish champion at

Danish Ch. Cobby's African Drakensberger, owned by Britta Husted. *Drawing by Jane Bank Rasmussen*

In 1986 the Danish Kennel Club celebrated 100-year jubilee. Danish Ch. Danpug Diamon Daughter and Britta Husted were invited to repres the Toy Group in 1886 period costume.

Part of Britta Husted's collection of Pug figures

Danish Ch. Danpug Isabella, at six months. Owner: Britta Husted.

Danish Ch. Danpug Giant Panda. Sire: Danish Ch., VDH Ch., Int. Ch. Cyrene Black Jack Ut Heid. Dam: Danish Ch. Danpug Diamond's Daughter.

Ch. Cyrene Dandy Dick, bred in England by Renee Meadows and owned by Britta Husted

sixteen months of age, has many Best of Breed awards and was best bitch Pug of the Year Number Three in 1987.

Isabella's litter sister, Danpug Ivory and Ebony, was Best of Opposite Sex at the 1987 Pug specialty show with fifty-five entries under judge Mrs. Meadows of England. She gained her title in 1988, and the final ticket was awarded by Bob Flawell of England. Ivory and Ebony is owned by Mr. Steen Hansen.

From Daisy's third and last litter Britta kept a black bitch, Danpug Double Diamond. Britta hopes she will have success in the show ring and continue her black line.

Dan. Ch. Danpug Isabella had her first litter by Dan. & Ger. Champion Peter Pan Ut Heid, who is bred and owned by Barbel and Klaus Wohlers of Germany. (Peter Pan has done very well in the show ring and is the sire of many super Pugs. His background is mostly British, with such well-known names as Cedarwood Willapop Isawonderboy, Paglesham Sage and Sneezwort Tufry Tufnut in the pedigree.) It was a litter with males only.

In Britta's opinion, the Pug is the best companion you can have—always in a good mood, following you everywhere, trustworthy and friendly, even with small children.

Britta is concerned that the appearance of the Pug has changed a great deal during this century. The noses have almost disappeared, causing a lot of trouble for a great number of Pugs. It is Britta's hope that future breeders will take care of this problem and not go to further extremes. She notes that we also have a problem with correct size and weight according to the standard. It is difficult to breed a Pug that is both small and cobby; most of the small Pugs are lacking in bone and body substance. She admits that she prefers the bigger but correctly built Pug. Still, it is her aim to obtain the correct size and confirmation.

Competition in Denmark

It is difficult to finish a Pug with only twelve championship shows and one Pug specialty a year. They have six all-breed shows and six club shows. The club show is when a few of the smaller breeds who do not have their own specialty shows join together and put on a championship show. They also have a few open shows, which are equivalent to our match shows. Entry fees are $10 to $12, which is said to be expensive.

To finish a Pug in Denmark the dog must receive three challenge certificates, the third coming after eighteen months of age. Approximately twenty to twenty-five Pugs are entered at today's shows in Denmark. They are judged in Denmark according to the standard of the Kennel Club of England.

Pugs in Australia

Our travels now bring us to Tullamarine, Victoria, Australia, the home of Sandra and Jeff Chivell. Sandra informed me that they have a cut-off date of 1950 on dog books written in Australia and present-day breeders are left out.

The Chivells are relatively new to breeding Pugs. They purchased their first Pug (a dog, Don Diego) from Esme Stringer of Gilgai Kennels. Mrs. Stringer has been a well-known and very successful breeder of Pugs in Australia for more than thirty years. Don Diego is from Gilgai Hollyanna and Aus. Ch. Gilgai Tarsun.

Don Diego was very slow to mature, not winning a challenge certificate under an Australian judge until he was fifteen months of age. An American judge, Mrs. M. Kay, awarded a CC and Best of Opposite Sex in Toy Group to him at twenty-three months of age. The Chivells always felt he had the potential to become a good show dog so they persevered with him, given a lot of encouragement from Mrs. Stringer.

In 1984 he started to live up to his potential. He was always a brilliant moving dog, and he filled out into a well-balanced Pug. Early in 1984 he was beaten by his brother, Aus. Ch. Gilgai Peter, for Best Exhibit at the Pug Club of Victoria Championship show. With the improvement Don Diego demonstrated as the show season progressed that he was able to become Victorian Pug of the Year. The Pug Club of Victoria conducted the Pug of the Year in conjunction with ten all-breed shows, points being awarded for placing in classes and bonus points for challenge winners. Don Diego's sister, Aus. Ch. Gilgai Dolly, was the previous Pug of the Year winner. To finish off a great year, Don Diego was Best of Breed at the Royal Melbourne Show. The Melbourne Royal is the biggest dog show in the southern hemisphere, with approximately 8,000 dogs exhibited.

Two of Don's offspring are being exhibited in South Africa and are producing good results for their owner, Julia Van Rogen.

Mrs. Stringer presented the Chivells with a little bitch from Gilgai Hollyanna but sired by Aus. Ch. Anoky. Aus. Ch. Gilgai Hollylee is a lovely little bitch, full of herself and a pleasure to show. While campaigned, she gained her title and along the way several Toy Group awards. Hollylee now lives in Tasmania, having retired from the show ring.

In 1985 Sandra heard that Don's brother, Aus. Ch. Gilga Peter, was for sale. Peter had a great career, gaining his title in very quick time and winning Best Exhibit at the Pug Club Victoria show and the Ladies Kennel Club show in Tasmania. Peter was a little out of condition when he came to the Chivells. He adopted their daughter, Kirsty, and under her training and handling he won Runner Up Best Exhibit in Show at Belconnon in Canbessa out of 1,300 dogs and in 105-degree heat. The judge was a Canadian, Mr. M. Dixon.

Peter won the challenge at the 1986 Royal Melbourne Show and with Don won the Brace class at two successive Victorian Pug Club Championship shows. He passed away in Brisbane after competing in the Royal Brisbane Show.

All of the Chivells' Pugs participate in obedience training. They enjoy the work, and the training also helps with showing. The Chivells have five Pugs at the moment. Two are Don's offspring out of a black bitch and they will be the first Pugs that they will have exhibited with their own kennel name.

Sandra and Jeff like the Pugs to have a moderate length of leg, so as to

Australian Ch. Gilgai Don Diego, owned by Sandra and Jeff Chivell. *Robin Twigg*

Australian Ch. Gilgai Peter, owned by Sandra and Jeff Chivell. *Robin Twigg*

present a balanced dog. They also like dogs that cover the ground well with good muscle tone, so the dogs are exercised every day.

Breeders in Australia are following the breed standard and are constantly on the lookout for defects and are trying to eliminate the faults from the breed. Although a long way from America and Europe, the Pug is alive and well down under. The Chivells have had Pugs in their family for many years, at least as far back as Jeff's great-grandfather, who brought his Pugs out of England late last century when he immigrated to Australia. None until the present has been shown, but only kept as pets, and many of the descendants still have Pugs as pets. The Chivells believe they have had Pugs in the family for at least one hundred years.

Pugs in England

Bournle Pugs

Les and Elizabeth Elbourn are breeders from Lee-on-the-Solent, Hants, England. They became interested in Pugs through, of all things, their daughter's rabbits! She required an Ermine Rex, and after purchasing one they were returning to the house from the breeder's rabbit hutches when they heard a peculiar snuffling noise. Peeking into what turned out to be a kennel they spotted two little fawn dogs. It was a case of love at first sight, and six months later they purchased one from the same breeder to replace their much adored Boxer.

Mandy of Purland was the foundation bitch of Bournle Pugs and now, more than thirty years later, all their Pugs have descended in an unbroken bitch line. Mandy was pet quality and she had many faults, as they found later, but with careful linebreeding most of these were eliminated. Within three generations they bred what they now consider their best litter ever.

Showing has been the main attraction for the Elbourns, and breeding litters has not been of paramount importance, usually being undertaken when they decided another addition was required. The sires their bitches have been bred to have been very carefully chosen. Behind their present ones are what they consider the greatest influences in English dominant sires: Ch. Justatwerp of Cedarwood, Ch. Stormie of Martlesham and Ch. Isawonderboy of Cedarwood.

The Elbourns believed it was the combination of Stormie on Twerp's daughter Olive Beaute that culminated in that one-in-a-hundred litter. Galahad was sold to Nancy Gifford, who added Martelsham to his name. "Laddie," as he was known, was later sold to Dick Paisley, so through Laddie came their introduction to the American Pug scene.

Since few champions are made in Britain, the Elbourns' number of champions are few, but all their bitches had some of those elusive Challenge Certificates, three of which are required to become a champion.

In 1971 Les and Elizabeth flew to New York for the Westminster show. At this show they had one of their greatest thrills when they saw Dick Paisley go Best of Breed with their Laddie, Ch. Martlesham Galahad of Bournle.

Since that time they have made many trips to the United States. In 1975 Elizabeth received the honor of judging the American Pug Club Specialty at Allentown. Following have been several judging engagements, including Great Lakes Pug Club and the Bluebonnet Pug Dog Club Specialties.

Les arrived on the judging scene much later than Elizabeth because of his work. With Elizabeth one of the top breed specialist judges, Les was eventually induced to enter the judges list. Since then he has officiated at both the Pug Club Open show and the Pug Club Championship show. Elizabeth had the honor of judging Pugs at the Cruft's show in 1985.

At the present time the Elbourns are showing Ch. Bournle Leon Le Seul and his daughter Leonora, out of Ruby of Bournle (two CCs). Leon is the first male they have kept for many years. He was the only one in the litter, hence his name.

Les and Elizabeth believe that the breed is at as high a level of quality at the present time as any during their experience. They implore all breeders to keep the wonderful temperament the Pug has and to remember that the Pug is a Toy dog and breed to keep the size down—*multum in parvo* (much in little).

It is now one hundred years since Pugs entered England with William of Orange and Queen Mary. The Pug Club commemorated this historic landmark at the Paignton Championship show. Les was given the honor to judge the Pugs at this great event. The Pug Club colors have been orange and black in recognition of William and Mary's contribution.

Nanchyl Pugs

Nancy Tarbit and her Nanchyl Pugs live in Sunderland, England. Nancy started to breed Pugs in 1962 and has owned or bred thirteen champions who have accumulated more than 150 CCs.

The first contact she ever had with a Pug was when she spotted a Pug dog waiting patiently outside a shop while his owner did some shopping. The wrinkled face and curly tail fascinated her, and she vowed that when she got another dog it would be a Pug. At that time she had a smooth Standard Dachshund and had previously had Scottish Terriers, a Bullmastiff and an Elkhound.

Sometime later, after the death of her Dachshund, she contacted Miss Thompson of the Tyerfield Pugs, who had a litter due in three weeks. Nancy purchased the only bitch in the six puppies and she turned out very well, winning at all types of shows. She was eventually mated at about eighteen months of age to Ch. Paramin Dillypin Pantaloon and produced six puppies, one of which died. A bitch puppy, Nanchyl Amber, was retained, and her brother Ajax became a Finnish champion. Amber also won a goodly amount and was mated to Ch. Tempest of Martlesham. This litter of eight, unfortunately, was a disaster and five of the puppies died. None of the survivors was kept.

Nancy then bought a Dillypin bitch both of whose parents were cham-

Bournie Leon Le Seul, sire of Leonora,
owned by Les and Elizabeth Elbourn
Diane Pearce

Bournie Leonora at eighteen months,
owned by Les and Elizabeth Elbourn

Bournie Josephine, dam of Leon,
owned by Les and Elizabeth Elbourn

pions. She was shown a little but did not turn out as well as hoped. She had several litters and several of her puppies won CCs, but none became champions.

After some time Nancy brought in a dog puppy, Patrick of Paramin, and made him into a champion. He won his first CC at ten months, and it was from him and Amber that the Nanchyl line was established. They produced Ch. Nanchyl Gossamer, who was sold as a show puppy and ten days later became a champion. Nanchyl Imp also gained her title. She won nine CCs and was also a Group winner.

Nancy also acquired a bitch named Plenipotentiary of Pyebeta, who had eight puppies by Patrick, one of which became Am. Ch. Nanchyl Hobgoblin. She was never bred again, as she hated the puppies and had to be held down to feed them.

Nancy then retained another bitch, Nanchyl Elf, from a mating of her Dillypin Allegra to Pantaloon. She won one CC and one reserve CC but after an illness was not shown any more. She was mated to Nanchyl Igor (they were half-sister, half-brother). Igor is the litter brother to Imp, who had gained his junior warrant at eight months. From this litter came Ch. Nanchyl Jasper, who won ten CCs and several reserve in Groups.

Elf was not bred from again, as she had difficult whelping and partial inertia, so Imp was mated to Ch. Adoram Faro, who had done a lot of winning, and from this litter came Ch. Nanchyl Kelpie, who was born in August 1972. She was a beautiful bright-apricot color and became a champion in 1974 and won seven CCs. She unfortunately died after only one litter in January 1975, and was thought to have eaten poison of some sort. Four puppies from this litter survived and two became champions. They were by Patrick. The dog Obetan was sold for showing and Ophelia became a champion before eighteen months of age. She won eleven CCs and was top-winning Pug in 1977.

Imp was then mated to Gallant Knight, a Pantaloon son, and had six puppies—two dogs and four bitches. She raised five of these and the bitch Nancy kept was Ch. Nanchyl Roxanna, who won thirty-two CCs and is the record holder in the breed. She was top-winning Pug in 1978, 1979 and Best of Breed at Cruft's in 1979. She won many Groups and Best in Show at the United Kingdom Toy Dog Society Championship show.

Ophelia was mated to Paramin Paul, another Pantaloon son. Ophelia had followed her mother in being a beautiful apricot color with velvety black ears and muzzle. This, Nancy believes, was due to Faro having been sired by a black dog. Ophelia produced two champions in this litter, Tabitha, who was sold for showing, and Troglodite, who was kept. He went on to be the top-winning Pug in 1980 and 1981 and won thirteen CCs and several Groups.

Ophelia was then mated to Ch. Stepe Kerrygold, a son of Patrick. This half-brother, half-sister mating yielded six puppies, all dogs except for one. The bitch became Ch. Nanchyl Venus.

Roxanna was mated to Nanchyl Ninbul (one CC—an Amber and Patrick son) and from this litter of five came Ch. Nanchyl Xerxes. He is joint top winning dog with Ch. Rexden Rubstic and finished with twenty-seven

Eng. Ch. Patrick of Paramin, owned by Nancy Tarbit

Eng. Ch. Nanchyl Roxanna, owned by Nancy Tarbit

Eng. Ch. Nanchyl Ophelia at ten months, owned by Nancy Tarbit

CCs—and twenty-six of these wins were Best of Breed. He won several Groups and was Best of Breed at Cruft's in 1983, 1984 and 1985, and in 1984 was Reserve in the Toy Group.

Nancy had great difficulty in getting Venus into whelp. At last in 1983 she proved to be in whelp to Xerxes. She had to have a Caesarean operation for one puppy, and through this it was found that she had a very long vagina, making it difficult for her to get into whelp. The lone puppy became Ch. Nanchyl Zechim, who at the moment has twenty-three CCs and was top-winning dog in 1986 and 1987.

Xerxes was top sire in 1986 and Zechim in 1987. Zechim was mated to Nanchyl Yamadou, a daughter of Troglodite and Roxanna, and the bitch Nancy kept became Ch. Nanchyl Cachucha. She won her first CC at seven and one-half months and her title at thirteen and one-half months old.

Over the years Patrick sired six English champions, as did Xerxes. Zechim has so far sired three champions in England, and Trog, who was never used at stud very much, sired one.

Nancy writes that over the years it has been very interesting and enjoyable working out breeding programs. She is a great believer in linebreeding, but only if you have really good sound stock in the first instance. She will occasionally do an outcross, but stresses that this will not work out well if mediocre stock is used.

Before closing our discussion of English Pugs, it is worth noting that in the early 1980s Mrs. E. L. Bowden's Ch. Rexden Rubstic was the only Pug to win Best in Show twice at an all-breed championship show in England. The first Pug ever to win a Toy Group at Cruft's was Pauline Thorp's Ch. Cedarwood Blunshills Nimrod.

Pugs in Germany

Barbel and Klaus Wohlers and their Ut Heid Pugs hail from Germany. They became fascinated in 1974 by a Pug in a pet shop window. The dog in question, Kibbo Kift Black Bijou, had a noble pedigree and was in whelp at the time. About three months later they purchased one of her puppies, Hindemith, who became the playmate of the Wohlerses' two-year-old Afghan.

The following year they bought a bitch, Jette von Pehrengrund (by Rosecoppice Oliver, out of Kibbo Kift Fawn Sirikit).

In 1976 they decided to breed dogs under the kennel name of Ut Heid, but their male dog Hindemith was not willing to serve. Other Pug breeders didn't want to make a male dog available, but at last they found a privately owned dog to breed to, Alichang Ceravir von Mops. The mating yielded three puppies, two males and one female. They kept the bitch, Annelie.

The Wohlerses visited several dog shows and decided to continue to breed a Pug (called *Mops* in Germany) like the type of Oliver. This was contrary to the more common heavy Pugs popular at that time in the Federal Republic of Germany. Since then many other breeders have followed this

Eng. Ch. Nanchyl Xerxes winning at the 1983 Pug Centenary. Owner: Nancy Tarbit. *Diane Pearce*

Eng. Ch. Nanchyl Xerxes, owned by Nancy Tarbit

decision. After careful consideration the Wohlerses purchased Gershwin vom Rosencavalier from a kennel with only English bloodlines. He became the progenitor of their kennel and was frequently used by other breeders, especially in Denmark, and has in many ways impressed his mark on the breed.

Because he lacked ring discipline, Gershwin wasn't used as a show dog. He is, however, the sire of eighty-six puppies, and many of them have been used for further breeding.

In 1981 the Wohlerses purchased two dogs from Mrs. Purbrick of the English kennel Sneezwort. By means of these two dogs from England, the Ut Heid kennel reached its first success on the dog show scene. The brother and sister Sneezwort Solara and Jenny Wren (after Sneezwort Tufry Tufnut and Sneezwort Chamari) both became German champion, VdH champion, Federal Youth champion, Areal champion and Best of Breed.

Solara died at the age of two from acute heart failure on the way home from a show in Berlin. He had just been mated to a bitch in Denmark, and two bitches out of this litter attained their Danish championships.

Jenny Wren gave birth to her first puppies in 1983: one male and three females. The male, Napoleon, lives in Vienna, Austria, at the kennel Baby Grand of Mrs. Brach and has already produced a litter of champion puppies. From Jenny's second litter of puppies the Wohlers kept two dogs, Penny Lane and Peter Pan. At the same time they bought another British dog, Cyrene Black Jack Ut Heid (by Sneezwort Zulu Warrior, out of Cyrene Black Rhapsody) from Renee Meadows. Jackie was their first black male Pug. While he has been an absolutely beautiful dog with an excellent character, the Wohlers nevertheless feel that he is a little too big.

That same year they purchased another female black Pug from Denmark, Danpug Danish Delight, from Britta Husted. From this they finally accomplished their expectations of four champions in 1984: Olita Ut Heid (by Gershwin; out of Annelie); Youth Ch. and Federal Youth Ch. Danpug Danish Delight (by Cobbys African Dracensberger, out of Ch. Danpug Diamond); Youth Ch. and Europe Youth Ch. Cyrene Black Jack Ut Heid and Youth Ch. Peter Pan Ut Heid. They also won several Bests of Breed.

In the following years Peter Pan and Jackie fulfilled the expectations for the German and VdH championships, and two sons of Jackie by Danpug Danish Delight—Royal Black Lover and Royal Black Diamond—acquired the Youth championship. Another son of Jackie's by Upside Down Ut Heid, Xenium Black Ut Heid, gained his Youth championship, German and VdH championships, as did Royal Black Diamond.

In 1986 Barbel Wohlers became ill and was forced to sell most of the dogs. With the help of Miss Veldhuis in the Netherlands, the Pugs went to fitting homes there, private homes as well as those of other breeders. Miss Veldhuis loved Sophisticated Lady and kept her herself. Another black female went to Denmark to Britta Husted.

In 1987 Ut Heid presented the first kennel group with black Pugs in the Federal Republic of Germany, and became the winners of kennel group competition in Berlin.

Peter Pan Ut Heid (*left*), Cyrene Black Jack Ut Heid (*rear*) and Gershwin Von Rosencavalier. Owners: Klaus and Barbel Wohlers.

Royal Black Lover Ut Heid, owned by Klaus and Barbel Wohlers

Because of Barbel's illness, the Wohlerses were not very active showing, but the kennel Ut Heid continues to exist in order to promote further breeding of healthy and typical Pugs. Their ideal Pug is a dog of a good size; this means a bitch weight of about 7 kg. (15.43 pounds), the male a bit more. A clear color is also essential—for bright colors as well as for the blacks. Eyes and nails should be dark, the best being black. They note that this point of the standard is more and more neglected. The ears and tail should show a good posture and great attention should be put on a wide and strong lower jaw.

Their male dog Peter Pan approaches more or less their ideal concept of the proper Pug. They also feel that with their acquisition of Britta Husted's six-month-old Danpug Luck Luke Ut Heid (by Ch. Peter Pan Ut Heid out of Ch. Danpug Isabella) they have accomplished another step toward a maintenance of their kennel ideal.

Pugs in Canada

Shirley Limoges, Bernalee Pugs, resides in Ottawa, Ontario, Canada. Shirley, a breeder-judge, is approved by the Canadian Kennel Club to judge Hounds and Toys. Shirley began showing dogs when she was fourteen, when her great uncle, a former president of the Canadian Kennel Club, started taking her to dog shows with him. She did not acquire her first Pug until 1962, and she cites the breed's "wonderful, outgoing, cheerful temperament" as what most attracts her.

Over the past twenty-six years she has bred approximately twenty litters and has never campaigned a Pug. Despite the small scale of her program she has bred and showed four generations of Winners Bitches at American specialties, and two of these bitches were also Best of Winners.

In Shirley Limoges's opinion the Pug has improved steadily over the years, with minor problems becoming apparent periodically. She is pleased to see that most breeders are attempting to breed Pugs of correct size and most thankful that breed temperament has been maintained, as this has not been the case in many breeds.

She feels that in some cases color could be improved and that clear fawn or apricot (which is not often seen any more) with black points and dark eyes gives a most pleasing effect.

Pugs in Taiwan

Liang Yang of Taiwan has worked hard over the years to promote dog shows and breed quality Pugs. Liang has imported quite a few Pugs from the United States and is the foremost breeder of Pugs in Taiwan. Many of his Pugs are Best in Show winners under the banner of Arrow Kennels.

Taiwan is just a hundred miles off the Chinese mainland. When the army and government of Nationalist leader Chiang Kai-shek retreated to Taiwan in 1949, most of the world believed Taiwan would be overrun by the communist forces from mainland China. This little island state, 240 miles long and from

Australian Ch. Gilgai Mai Tai with breeder-owner Felicity Way

Judging at the 1984 Sydney Royal Easter show in Australia

Competition at the Pug Club of New South Wales Championship show 1984

Australian Ch. Gilgai Boiwata Newsance owned by Felicity Way

Enno of Arrow Kennel with his Best in Show trophy, won at the Taiwan Kennel Association dog show. Owner: Liang Yang.

Taiwan Ch. Arrow of Liang Yang is photographed with a famous Taiwanese actress, Ton-Chie.

137

60 to 90 miles wide, survived and is flourishing. Today the population is about 18 million.

The Chinese are undergoing many changes and their enthusiasm and interest in the development of pure-bred dogs have grown. In Taiwan there are three major kennel clubs. The Taiwan Kennel Association (TKA), Taipei Kennel Club (TKC) and the Taiwan Police Dog Association (TPDA). Each club holds one major show a year. At each of these shows one of the judges must belong to the show-giving club. He will be assigned to judge the Adult Class, Group and Best in Show. If a foreign judge is invited to officiate at one of the three major shows, the honor of selecting the top winners will be given to their guest. The local judges who are not members of the show-giving club can only judge the three- to six-month and six- to twelve-month classes. They only have the three breed classifications at their shows.

It is very difficult to finish a dog in Taiwan. To become a champion in Taiwan the Pug most go Best of Breed, Group One and Best in Show. Thus there can only be one champion made up in a given show. Their dog shows are not scheduled on a regular basis. The Taiwan Kennel Club has eleven branches throughout the island and no shows are held in July and August. The two other clubs also have branch clubs around the island; these branch clubs can hold a show every month. The dogs are judged on our American Kennel Club point system. It is interesting, however, that no points are awarded to the dogs. Entry fees are $25 (American) per dog. The Taiwan Kennel Club is currently contemplating a change whereby it would adopt the rules and regulations of the American Kennel Club.

5

Official Standards for the Pug

The American Standard

> **Symmetry**—Symmetry and general appearance, decidedly square and cobby. A lean, leggy Pug and a dog with short legs and a long body are equally objectionable.
>
> **Size and Condition**—The Pug should be *multum in parvo,* but this condensation (if the word may be used) should be shown by compactness of form, well-knit proportions, and hardness of developed muscle. Weight from 14 to 18 pounds (dog or bitch) desirable.
>
> **Body**—Short and cobby, wide in chest and well ribbed up.
>
> **Legs**—Very strong, straight, of moderate length and well under.
>
> **Feet**—Neither so long as the foot of the hare, nor so round as that of the cat; well-split-up toes, and the nails black.
>
> **Muzzle**—Short, blunt, square, but not up-faced.
>
> **Head**—Large, massive, round—not apple-headed, with no indentation of the skull.
>
> **Eyes**—Dark in color, very large, bold and prominent, globular in shape, soft and solicitous in expression, very lustrous, and, when excited, full of fire.
>
> **Ears**—Thin, small, soft, like black velvet. There are two kinds—the "rose" and "button." Preference is given to the latter.
>
> **Markings**—Clearly defined. The muzzle or mask, ears, moles on cheeks,

thumb mark or diamond on forehead, black-trace should be as black as possible.

Mask—The mask should be black. The more intense and well defined it is the better.

Trace—A black line extending from the occiput to the tail.

Wrinkles—Large and deep.

Tail—Curled tightly as possible over the hip. The double curl is perfection.

Coat—Fine, smooth, soft, short and glossy, neither hard nor woolly.

Color—Silver or apricot-fawn. Each should be decided, to make the contrast complete between the color and trace and the mask. Black.

Scale of Points

	Fawn	Black
Symmetry	10	10
Size	5	10
Condition	5	5
Body	10	10
Legs and Feet	5	5
Head	5	5
Muzzle	10	10
Ears	5	5
Eyes	10	10
Mask	5	—
Wrinkles	5	5
Tail	10	10
Trace	5	—
Coat	5	5
Color	5	10
TOTAL	100	100

The Dalziel Standard—England

The following is taken from Hugh Dalziel's *British Dogs* (1881):

The Pug Dog Club was formed in 1883, and in a copy of its rules, dated 1887, I find the following statement:

"Standard Points of Pugs. On the 26th January, a meeting was held at 86, Hatton Garden, when the points of the Pug were defined, and set down in minutes."

Now, I venture to say that the vast majority of readers—all, in fact, who are blest with fair minds and a modicum of intelligence—will agree with me that it would have been honester, and altogether more creditable to the Pug Dog Club, to have modestly and truthfully stated that the points of the Pug, and the language in which they were defined, had been mainly adopted from "British Dogs," a work published years before the Pug Dog Club existed. In that work I gave the following as my own opinions on the points of the Pug:

The **General Appearance** and **Symmetry** of the Pug are decidedly square and cobby; a lean, leggy dog and a long-backed, short-legged one are equally out of harmony with the ideal Pug, which, although not so graceful in contour as the Greyhound and some of the Terriers, should yet be so well proportioned that each part is, as to size, in harmony and conformity with every other, and in combination forming a symmetrical whole. Condition, which materially affects a dog's chance in the judging-ring, alters the general appearance, and destroys the symmetry when it represents extreme poverty or excessive obesity. The Pug is a *multum in parvo* but this condensation, if I may use the word, should be shown by compactness of form, in well-knit proportions, and hardness of developed muscle.

The **Head** should be round and short, the skull well-domed and large, to correspond with the general size—bigness is the better word—of this delightful ladies pet. The *Muzzle* must be short and square (a pointed muzzle is a serious drawback). The *nose* is short, but the Pug is not up-faced like the Bulldog. His nose should be decidedly of the snub variety, but not *retrousse*. The protrusion of the tongue is a deformity often arising from partial paralysis of that useful organ, and apt to appear in all short-faced dogs; but it should always be looked on as a fault.

The *Ears* should be small, thin, soft and velvety, and black in colour. Some are carried flat, and close to the face, corresponding to the "button ear" of the Bulldog; others have the ears part partially thrown back, the edge again slightly folding forward, and a portion of the interior shown. This also corresponds with a variety of ear of the Bulldog called the "rose" ear. I prefer the rose to the button in both breeds, the latter giving a dull, heavy almost sulky look to the countenance.

The *Eyes* are very dark in colour, very large, bold, and prominent, globular in shape, soft and solicitous in expression and very lustrous, and when excited full of fire. There should be no tendency to water, or weep, as it is called.

It has been insisted that there should be a black mole, with three hairs growing out of it, on each cheek. "Stonehenge," in his valuation of points, gives five for this. "Idstone" lays down that it is important, and hundreds re-echo the opinion. I think, however, that these two eminent writers have themselves merely echoed the extremely foolish cant of dog-fanciers. A mole on each cheek is not peculiar to Pugs, but will, on examination, be found in every breed, and is easily enough seen on all smooth-faced dogs; and I cannot, therefore, see why these marks should be claimed as a special point in the Pug. I would not allow a single point for them.

The *Mask* is the black colour of the face. The more intense it is, the better, and it should include the eyes, running in a straight line across the forehead; the more sharply defined this mask is, the better, as the contrast between it and the body colour is thereby more strongly marked. Separate from the mask is a black patch, or thumb mark, rarely met with, but much to be desired, and no Pug can be considered absolutely perfect without it. The loose skin of the head forms into wrinkles, which alter in depth with the varying emotions of the dog; when seen at their greatness, they give a frowning look to the face. The lines of these wrinkles can be traced when the skin is stretched, or smooth, by deeper shades of colour.

The *Trace* is a dark line—the blacker the better—running along the back, right to the end of the tail. It should be clearly defined, and narrow, ½ inch to one inch at broadest.

The *Colour* of the pure Morrison is yellow fawn, the pure Willoughby a cool stone or light drab; but two strains are much interbred, and good Pugs of many shades are met with. What is called the *apricot fawn* is now in vogue with many, but the great consideration is to get the colour—whatever its shade—decided enough, and with a very pronounced contrast between it and the black of the mask, trace and vent. The most common fault in colour is smuttiness, the mask spreading over the whole head, the trace extending down each side, and the fawn hairs of the body being more or less shaded with black. A correspondent informs me that Mr. Beswicke Royd's family, who for many generations owned a very fine breed of Pugs, now lost, had one pair—the last—that invariably threw one pure white pup in each litter. The eminent veterinarian, Blaine, records a similar instance in a Pug bitch of his own, which in three consecutive litters had one pure white pup. A white Pug with good points would be a curiosity, and the production of a strain of them does not seem impossible, and is well worth the attention of speculative breeders.

A great fault with many Pugs shown now is coarseness of coat. The coat should be fine, smooth, soft, and glossy. The skin is extremely loose, and when a handful is taken, the coat, although thus handled, must on one side be felt against the grain, should be neither hard nor woolly.

The *Neck* is short, thick, and fleshy, and with the skin loose and free; although there is seldom a decided dewlap, still there must be an abundance of skin, or the head will be void of wrinkles.

The Pug is wide across the chest, wide through the barrel, and square in the quarters; the back is fairly broad, and the whole body stout and thick-set.

The *Legs* must be straight, and well under him, of moderate length. The dog should stand about 12 inches high, and at that height should weigh about 15 pounds. The legs should be strong, and the feet rather long, or hare-shaped; the toes well split up, and the toenails black.

The *Tail* is of great importance. The more tightly and closely it is curled over the hip, the more is thought of it; and in a winner nowadays the double curl is almost indispensable. Many fanciers insist that the dog should curl the tail over the right hip, and the bitch curl her tail over the left hip, and this is very often the case; but I have seen these positions reversed, and many good specimens curl the tail straight between the hips.

Stonehenge Standard of the Pug (England)

Points of the Modern Pug (1867)

	Value		*Value*		*Value*
Head	10	Trace	5	Legs and feet	10
Ears	5	Colour	10	Tail	10
Eyes	5	Coat	10	Symmetry and	
				size	5
Moles	5	Neck	5		25
Mask, vent,		Body	10	Grand Total: 100	
wrinkles	10		—		
	35		40		

142

1. The *Head* (value 10) should have a round, monkey-like skull, and should be of considerable girth, but in proportion not so great as that of the Bulldog. The face short but again, not "bully" or retreating, the end being cut off square; and the teeth must be level—if undershot, a cross of the bull is almost always to be relied upon. Tongue large and often hanging out of the mouth; but this point is not to be accepted for or against the individual. The cheek is very full and muscular.
2. The *Ears* (value 5) are small, vine-shaped and thin and should lie moderately flat on the face (formerly they were invariably closely cropped, but this practice is now quite out of fashion), they are black, with a slight mixture of fawn hair.
3. The *Eyes* (value 5) are dark brown and full with soft expression. There should be no tendency to weep, as in the toy spaniel.
4. A *Black Mole* (value 5) is always demanded on each cheek, with two or three hairs springing from it; the regular number of these is three, but of course it is easy to reduce them to that number.
5. *Mask, Vent, Wrinkles* (value 10). These markings must be taken together, as they all depend mainly on colour. The wrinkles, it is true, are partly in the skin, but over and above these there should be lines of black; corresponding with them, on the face and forehead. The mask should extend over the whole face as a jet black, reaching a little above the eyes, and the vent also should be of the same colour. In the Willoughby strain the black generally extends higher up the skull, and has not the same definite edge as in the Morrison Pug, in which this point is well shown, and greatly insisted upon by its admirers.
6. A *Trace* (value 5) or black line is exhibited along the top of the back by all perfect Pugs; and the clearer this is, the better. As with the mask, so with this—the definition is more clear in the Morrison than in the Willoughby Pug. When it extends widely over the back it is called a "saddle mark," and this is often displayed in the Willoughby, though seldom met with in the Morrison strain; of course, it is admired in the one, and deprecated in the other, by their several supporters.
7. The *Colour* (value 10) of the Morrison is a rich yellow fawn, while that of the Willoughby is cold-stone. The salmon fawn is never met with in good specimens of either, and is objected to. In the Willoughby the fawn coloured hairs are apt to be tipped with black, but its rival the fawn colour is pure, and unmixed with any darker shade. Of course, in interbred specimens the colour is often intermediate.
8. The *Coat* (value 10) is short, soft, glossy over the whole body, but on the tail it is longer and rougher. A fine tail indicates a bull cross.
9. The *Neck* (value 5) is full, stout and muscular, but without any tendency to dewlap; which again indicates when present, that the bulldog cross has been restored to.
10. The *Body* (value 10) is very thick and strong, with a wide chest and round ribs; the loin should be very muscular, as well as the quarters, giving a general punchy look, almost peculiar to this dog.
11. *Legs and Feet* (value 10). The legs should be straight but fine in bone, and should be well clothed with muscle. As to the feet, they must be small, and in any case narrow. In both strains the toes are well-split-up; but in the Willoughby the shape of the foot is cat-like, while the Morrison strain has

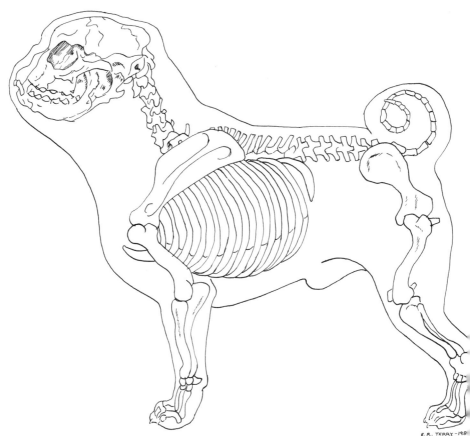

Skeletal anatomy of a Pug—correct bone structure and angulation, front and rear. *Drawing by E. Ruth Terry*

a hare-foot. There should be no white on the toes, and the nails should be black.

12. The *Tail* (value 5). The tail must curve so that it lies flat on the side, not rising above the back to such an extent as to show daylight through it. The curl should extend to a little more than a circle.

13. *Size and Symmetry* (value 5). In size the Pug should be from 10 inches to 12 inches high—the smaller the better. A good specimen should be very symmetrical.

The Pug Standard in England has just been revised. A few of the changes are as follows:

Ears: The "rose" (a small drop ear folding over and backward), "button" (the ear flaps folds forward, with the tips lying close to the skull and pointing toward the eyes).

Forequarters: Shoulders should be well laid back.

Hindquarters: Legs very strong, moderate length, good turn of stifle, appear parallel and straight when viewed from behind.

Tail: Tail is referred to as the "twist."

Gait: In front the forelegs should rise and fall with the legs well under the shoulders, feet moving directly forward, not turning in nor out, behind the action should be the same. The Pug should move strongly, putting forelegs well forward and driving freely with his hindquarters. Slight roll of the hindquarters is quite typical.

When Mrs. Graham Weall was judging, she introduced the idea that the Pug roll was from the rear. In my opinion, the slight roll in the hindquarters is not correct movement for a Pug. A swaying gait that is interrupted as a roll is an unsteady gait which places more weight on the forelimbs. This is a sign of an abnormal hip joint.

In judging, the first thing to consider is the entire Pug. *All drawings by Pauline Thomas*

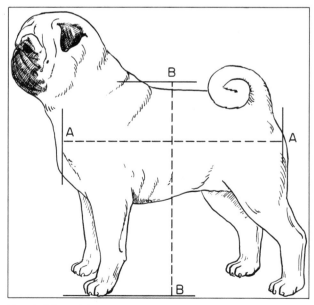

How height and length are measured: Length is measured from point of shoulder to the point of buttock (line A). Height is measured from a point horizontal with the withers straight down to the ground (line B).

146

6

Blueprint of the Pug Standard

Amplification and Clarification of the Pug Standard

Symmetry—Symmetry and general appearance, decidedly square and cobby. A lean, leggy Pug and a dog with short legs and long body are equally objectionable.

The description of the Pug, in its official standard, is excellent up to a point but does not sufficiently clarify the true picture of the Pug.

In judging, the first thing to consider is the entire Pug. Does the individual Pug mirror good breed type? Do all of the parts belong together? Is some feature too big or too small for the other parts of the dog?

The Pug is square in appearance, and the height at the highest point of the withers equals the length from the breastbone to the point of rump.

Size and Condition—The Pug should be *multum in parvo,* but this condensation (if the word may be used) should be shown by compactness of form, well-knit proportions, and hardness of developed muscle. Weight from 14 to 18 pounds (dog or bitch) desirable.

We should remember that the Pug is a Toy dog, but built like a cob horse (short and thickset). The correct Pug should be neither too big nor too small. The Pug should be a solid, stocky little dog, square in outline and *sound,* which is the proper functioning of the various parts of the Pug, *well balanced* to achieve the whole and well confined within the bounds of symmetry.

Temperament (which the standard omits)—The Pug is a small dog with charm and appeal and the perfect companion. They are accommodating, faithful, mischievous, stubborn and strive to be the center of attention. They are a bit temperamental and quite jealous at times, but would rarely attack anyone. They are a good watchdog, playful, spirited and very fond of children. There is a difference in temperament between the blacks and fawns: the fawns are rather placid and loving, whereas the blacks are often more alert and energetic. Serious faults: dogs that are shy or appear to be nervous should be penalized.

Hardness of Developed Muscle—This trait is important and must not be overlooked because a structurally correct Pug's movement can be hampered if he is out of condition. We do not want a fatty Pug or one that is weedy.

Weight—From 14 to 18 pounds (dog or bitch) is desirable. In my opinion weight alone is a most unsatisfactory method of determining size. The standard also implies that a dog and bitch should be the same size. I like my bitches to be approximately 16 pounds, and my dogs to be approximately 18 to 22 pounds. We are seeing too many Pugs ranging from 22 to 38 pounds and a few under 14 pounds.

I would like to see a desired height of 10 to 12 inches at the withers for bitches and 12 to 13 inches at the withers for dogs. A dog or bitch measuring under 10 inches or over 13 inches at the withers is not desirable, and this should be added to the standard.

The weight of the Pug has always been a topic for debate. As judges and breeders we must accept the standard, which states 14 to 18 pounds for dogs or bitches desirable. Ribbons should not be awarded to Pugs under 14 pounds. If ribbons are given to ones over 18 pounds, their breed type, soundness and balance must be superior to everything else in the ring. Excess weight should not be held against them unless their weight exceeds 22 pounds. Any Pug that is far in excess of the standard should not be considered for ribbons or points.

I have completed a survey of fifty Pugs using an official American Kennel Club wicket for height, and each dog or bitch was also weighed.

Neck (which the standard omits)—The head and body should be joined by a strong neck, well muscled, with enough length to be carried proudly. The neck should have a slight rise, or crest, just behind the skull. The length of the neck is an important factor to achieve a well-balanced look and blend smoothly into the shoulders. Faults: too short—governed by the layback of shoulder—therefore the neck cannot blend into the shoulders; too long—gives the Pug a weedy or "Terrier-type" look; ewe neck—faulty front movement.

Body—Short and cobby, wide in chest and well ribbed up. Legs—Very strong, straight, of moderate length and well under. Feet—Neither so long as the foot of the hare, nor so round as that of the cat, well-split-up toes, and the nails black.

The body is square in appearance, cobby with a short back. Topline is level, extending from the withers to the croup with a high tail set. The level topline is important. We are seeing too many Pugs with their topline running down—hill to the shoulders (lower in front). A few roached-backed or sway-backed. Serious faults: lower in front, short shoulder blade or upper arm or

148

	Dogs				Bitches	
	Height	*Weight*			*Height*	*Weight*
1.	12½"	19½ lbs.		26.	13"	19 lbs.
2.	13"	18¼ "		27.	12"	16½ "
3.	13"	19 "		28.	10"	14¼ "
4.	14"	22 "		29.	13"	14½ "
5.	11"	19 "		30.	12"	15 "
6.	12"	17 "		31.	11"	17 "
7.	13"	21 "		32.	11½"	17 "
8.	13"	19 "		33.	10"	15 "
9.	12½"	20 "		34.	12"	14 "
10.	12½"	18 "		35.	12"	16 "
11.	12½"	19 "		36.	12"	18 "
12.	14"	25 "		37.	13"	18 "
13.	12"	18¼ "		38.	12"	16 "
14.	15"	26 "		39.	12"	16⅛ "
15.	14"	23¼ "		40.	11"	19 "
16.	13½"	20½ "		41.	12"	14 "
17.	13"	17 "		42.	10½"	15½ "
18.	12"	18 "		43.	11½"	17 "
19.	12"	25 "		44.	12½"	16 "
20.	14"	26 "		45.	14 "	32 "
21.	10"	14 "		46.	11¾"	17 "
22.	11"	14 "		47.	12⅛"	18 "
23.	11 1/16 "	17 "		48.	13"	22 "
23.	12"	28¾ "		49.	11¼"	16¾ "
24.	12"	14 "		49.	11¼"	17 "
25.	10½"	15 "		50.	12¼"	21 "

both; straight rear, shelly; sway backed, roached, or arched back; coarse, narrow chest; excessive tuck-up.

Brisket—Reaching deep to the elbow with the front legs well under the dog. The brisket should ascend gradually to the rear with the belly slightly tucked up.

Chest—Broad, wide, *but not as wide as the Bulldog. This is a fault.* Chicken-breasted is an abnormal projection of the breastbone sternal region and such a Pug *must* be penalized.

Ribs—Well sprung, pear shaped and short coupled.

Shoulders—Well laid back. In the ideal shoulder blade, the scapula should slant at a forty-five-degree angle to the ground, forming a right angle with the upper arm, humerus at the shoulder joint, putting the front legs well under the Pug. Length of the shoulder blade and the upper arm must be equal.

In Pugs, where a *short back and cobby outline is sought,* we find many with moderately sloping shoulder blades and too short an upper arm, or both, which gives a pleasing but faulty profile. A major fault commonly seen in today's Pug is a slightly sloping shoulder with an upper arm that is too short, causing a "Terrier-type" front. If the shoulders are well laid back, and they have a short upper arm, they cannot cover ground. Steeply set shoulders tend to give the Pug an undesirable length to the back and a neckline that joins the

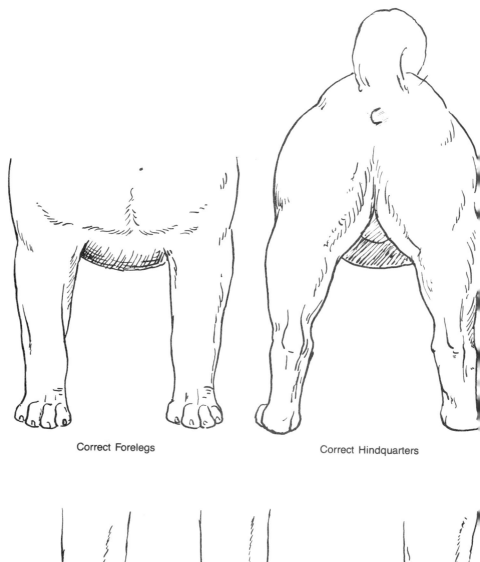

Correct Forelegs   Correct Hindquarters

Pasterns: A. Correct, B. Straight, C. Broken-Down

withers abruptly and unattractively. Overloaded shoulders are also a fault. Straight shoulders are a serious fault.

Elbows—They should lie close to the body facing the rear of the dog. Faults: out at the elbows—the elbows must stay close to the body and not turn in or out while the Pug is standing or moving.

Legs—Very strong, straight of moderate length and well under.

The forelegs are straight with heavy bone, muscle and strong pasterns. But the standard omits that a mature Pug will have a hard muscle buildup on the outside of the legs, forming a slight curve and giving the mistaken impression of a bowed or curving bone. This buildup of muscle is not a fault. If you check the inside of the front legs the bones are straight. A small fold of loose skin in the region of the pastern joint, running across the forelegs will form tiny wrinkles. The forelegs are well under the dog, and form a straight line from the point of the withers to behind the elbow to the ground, when viewed from the side. We do not want Terrier-type fronts.

Pastern (which the standard omits)—In my opinion the pastern should have a slight bend and not be straight, so it can absorb the shock as the Pug's foot strikes the ground on his heel pad. A straight pastern will cause a Pug to knuckle over while standing still or in motion. A sloping pastern should not be confused with a broken-down pastern. The broken-down pastern will not properly support the weight of the heavy front of the Pug, and puts a burden on the muscles. Faults: fiddle front, bowed front, down in the pasterns, poor bone, leggy or too short in the leg.

Hindquarters (which the standard omits)—The Pug's hindquarters have big, full, muscular hams and buttocks, with a good bend of stifle and a short hock. This must be in balance with the heavy head and front, never appearing higher than the shoulder. The croup is full and slightly rounded. The standard means that the hind legs should be squarely set and parallel to each other when the Pug is standing. Many interpret the wording to imply the stifles are straight—this is totally wrong. The pelvis should have a thirty-degree slant, forming a right angle with the femur at the hip socket. If the Pug has a good front that is well laid back and a straight rear, his stride will be broken and you will see him hopping or slashing from side to side. *This is not how a Pug rolls.* If a Pug lacks angulation in both the front and rear he can appear to be moving correctly, but watch him from the side. Remember the Pug's hindquarters are responsible for how he moves. With a straight rear you will also see his topline running down hill to his shoulders. Faults: straight stifles, cow-hocked, patella luxation, bowed, light bone.

Feet—Neither so long as the foot of the hare, nor so round as that of the cat; well-split-up toes and the nails black.

The feet should be round, the pads thick and black, the toes well arched and also well split up, being neat in appearance. The two middle toes should be slightly longer than the others and the nails black. Dewclaws on the forelegs may be removed. The natural tendency of the Pug's toes is to turn slightly outward to balance the heavy front. Faults: splayed, or spread out, down on the pastern, white toe nails.

Correct Balanced Head

Muzzle—Short, blunt, square, but not upfaced.

The standard does not clearly define the muzzle. The muzzle on the black and fawn Pug is another important feature and must be as short or flat as possible. The Pug's muzzle is well padded, large, wide and set squarely on the front of the skull. It must be in balance with the rest of the head. If the muzzle is not well padded you will get a falling away below the eyes. It will also make the muzzle look long and you will lose the flat, wide typical Pug look. The muzzle must not have a backward slant toward the nostrils; this is called a *layback,* or *upfaced,* which is correct for a Brussels Griffon and the Bulldog. The upper lip must be neat and clean, with no suggestion of being pendulous or heavy. The whiskers should be cut off for the show ring.

Head—Large, massive, round—not appleheaded, with no indentation of the skull.

The head of the Pug is also important, but do not get carried away by a massive head. It can be overdone and out of balance with the rest of the Pug. Remember, there is more to the Pug than just a head. The Pug's head is round and massive but must be in proportion with the whole dog (well balanced). Looking at the head from the front, the top of the wide skull should be as flat as possible between the ears. The skull must not be domed or appleheaded. The underjaw should be as wide as the skull and slightly show the chin. A Pug with a weak or pinched underjaw will also have a falling away under the eyes and you will lose the typical Pug expression. This is a major fault.

Teeth and Mouth (which the standard omits)—In my opinion it is essential to check the Pug's bite and mouth, which the standard fails to mention. A Pug should be slightly undershot, but not more than ⅛ inch. The teeth should be sound and white. In the Pug's underjaw the six teeth between the eye teeth should be in a straight line. Crowding and displacement of the teeth are caused by the underjaw being too narrow and is a fault. Serious faults: extremely undershot or a layback like the Brussels Griffon or the Bulldog. Teeth showing. A wry mouth should be penalized to the point of withholding ribbons and the same applies to one that is overshot (where the top teeth are over the lower teeth). Sometimes with a bite that is even or scissor, you will also find a weak underjaw and lose the typical Pug expression. The presence of missing, crooked, or misaligned teeth should be penalized. Usually when you have a wry mouth the tongue will protrude from either side of the mouth. A Pug with a protruding tongue or wry mouth must be penalized and ribbons withheld.

Eyes—Dark in color, very large, bold and prominent, globular in shape, soft and solicitous in expression, very lustrous and, when excited, full of fire.

The eye is of great importance, and the standard neglects to state that the large dark eyes are set wide apart. The center of the eye should be in line with the top of the nose. The eyes are also placed in front of the brow. If the Pug has a pinched or a weak underjaw, you will find small eyes that are set too close together. The typical Pug expression, of keen alertness and mischief, is lost. There are far too many light eyes and small eyes seen today; judges should penalize a Pug for these faults. The eye rims are black and encompassed

The Pug Skull

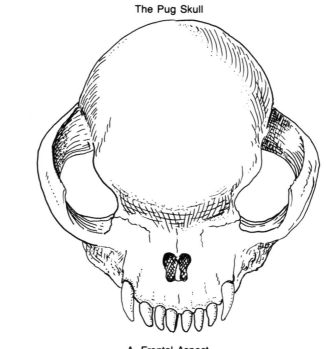

A. Frontal Aspect

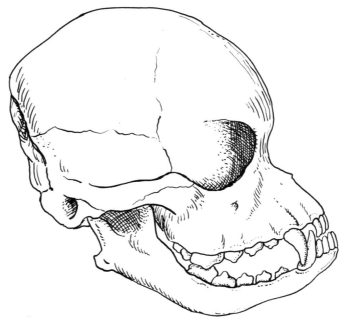

B. Lateral Aspect

154

Teeth and Mouth

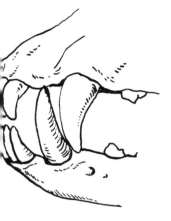

A. Level Bite

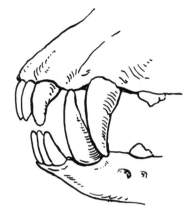

B. Scissors Bite

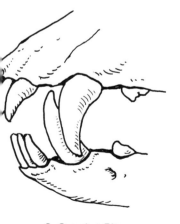

C. Overshot Bite

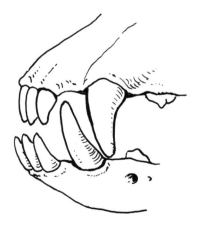

D. Correct Undershot Bite
or Reverse Scissors Bite

by the mask. The whites of the eyes must not show. They must not be wall eyed. Serious faults: light eyes, wall eyes, East-West eyes, white showing around the eyes, eyes that bulge or protrude like they are popping out of their sockets, eyes too small.

Nose (which the standard omits)—The black nose of the Pug should lie as flat as possible against the face, set high, and even with the inside corner of the middle of the eye. Nostrils are large and the nose is set straight from the stop to the end and in balance with the whole head. The nose should not show any sign of layback or sloping down. A little length of nose is permissible. The overnose wrinkle, which is unbroken across the bridge of the nose, is preferred. It is not a fault if a Pug has a broken wrinkle over the nose, but the nose must be short and set properly. Faults: butterfly, Dudley.

Ears—Thin, small, soft like black velvet. There are two kinds—the "rose" and "button." Preference is given to the latter.

All reference to the placement of the ears is omitted in the standard. In my opinion the visual effect of the ears is governed by the width of the skull. However, the inner edges of the top of the ear should be placed perpendicular to the outside corner of the eye and even with the top of the flat skull. The top of the "V"-shaped button or rose ear should not extend past the eye and must be in balance with the whole head. Pugs' ears are mobile when they wrinkle up their face and look alert. The ears are brought forward on the face and are set moderately high on the skull. The button ear gives a wider appearance to the skull, and the rose ear tends to make the skull appear smaller. A true rose ear is seldom seen in Pugs. Many interpret a flying ear to be a rose, which is often seen in puppies while they are teething. Light ears are often seen on puppies and usually darken when they mature. A button ear turns over and the lobe falls down in a triangle to the front of the face. The rose ear folds with the inner edge against the side of the skull, rather than showing the inner burr as in the Bulldog. The texture of the ears should feel and look like black velvet. Faults: flying ears, light ears, ears that are too thick and too long, ears that are set too high on the skull, or too low.

Markings—Clearly defined. The muzzle or mask, ears, moles on cheeks, thumb mark or diamond on forehead, back-trace should be as black as possible.

The mask should be as dark as possible, black. A diamond or thumb mark in the center of the head is preferred, but do not fault a Pug without one. The loose skin on the head or wrinkles must be deeply embedded and can be highlighted with dark hash marks that break up the face. We do not want a *black smutty skull or one without wrinkles.* The size of the forehead limits how deep the wrinkles can be. We do not want a head that appears plain, nor one that is overdone. By this I mean masses of small surface wrinkles. The cheek spots or moles are not mentioned in the standard; they should be large, must be black, and will give a finished look to the Pug's head. The nose must be black. A two-toned, butterfly, or Dudley nose should be penalized. The eye rims are black. Too many Pugs have white toenails, and this is a fault. The trace is a fine black line, as the standard states, but I feel it is just a highlight.

Mask—The mask should be black. The more intense and well defined it is the better.

The black mask on the fawns should be well defined. The depth and width of the mask may vary in each individual Pug. This can also affect the whole expression of the Pug. The mask should be as dark as possible, framing the eyes and brow, and it should cover the upper and lower jaw. There must be a definite break in color between the black mask and the fawn's forehead.

Wrinkles—Large and deep.

Another very important characteristic of the Pug is his wrinkles and looseness of the skin. The wrinkles on the face are essential. His surplus skin under the throat should be present in large folds or wrinkles. *Wrinkles are across the neck and the looseness of the skin must be there, forming deep rolls behind the neck in the adult dog.* Tiny wrinkles, or small folds of loose skin, are seen across the pastern joints. The unbroken over-nose wrinkle that crosses the bridge of the nose is preferred. Serious fault: *the pug must not have wrinkles or deep rolls running down its back.*

Trace—A black line extending from the occiput to the tail.

The original Stonehenge standard states: "A *Trace* (value 5) or black line is exhibited along the top of the back by all perfect Pugs. . . . the definition is clearer in the Morrison than the Willoughby Pug. When it extends widely over the back it is called a "saddle mark," and this is often displayed in the Willoughby, though seldom met with in the Morrison strain; of course, it is admired in one, and deprecated in the other, by several supporters."

Webster's Dictionary defines "trace" as: "A barely observable amount; a visible mark, a very small quantity, a drawn or traced mark."

In 1905, the first book on Pugs was written by L.J.E. Pughe. I would like to quote from the book: "In fact, good black Pugs are now more numerous in shows than fawn—so many of the latter being faulty, either wanting the traces or black toe nails."

Since 1900 a trace—a black, thin line—was seldom found except for the highlight that I consider the trace. The research that I have done over the years in regard to the trace has proven that the trace is just a highlight, except on newborn puppies. My puppies are born with approximately $\frac{1}{16}$-inch-wide black trace that fades and turns into a highlight approximately ¼ inch wide. *We do not want a big, black, broad, smutty saddle mark, 1 or 2 inches wide or wider,* which blends into the fawn coat. This leaves the dog's body color smutty and dirty looking.

Why all this on the trace? It is upsetting when I hear judges say, "Give me a black trace down the back of the Pug or a double twist tail and it will win." In judging Pugs today, I feel the highlight is the trace and always has been. A Pug's trace should only be credited if two dogs are equal in everything else. You may still occasionally find a thin black line down the back of a Pug, but remember it should not be a smutty saddle mark—this is a major fault. Black Pugs do not have a trace.

Tail—Curled tightly as possible over the hip. The double curl is perfection.

The Pug's tightly curled tail is his prized possession. It is closely curled and set high, and carried over the hip on either side. The tail carried in the middle of the back is technically a fault, but it is overlooked by judges in today's Pugs and no one seems to penalize them for it. The tail is nice and full, the soft hair on the tail is a little longer than the body coat. A double twist is perfection, but do not fault a Pug with just one curl. Serious Faults: too short—so you do not have a complete curl, too thin, set too low, too loose a curl, or carried straight down, no curl. *A straight tail must be penalized to the point of withholding ribbons.*

Coat—Fine, smooth, soft, short and glossy, neither hard nor woolly.

The standard has just about said everything, but the Pug has a double coat. A soft, thick undercoat, and a fine, smooth, short, glossy, outer coat are desirable. The black Pug's coat is a little coarser than the fawn's coat and some do not have any undercoat. The black has fewer hair follicles to the inch than the fawn and their skin is also blue. We are seeing too many Pugs with coats that are too long and coarse. Faults: too long, too coarse.

Color—Silver or apricot-fawn. Each should be decided, to make the contrast complete between the color and the trace and the mask. Black.

Silver fawn is a clear, cold fawn, or a grayish silver color and must not be sooty or smutty or darker than apricot. Apricot-fawn is any of the light yellowish shades, from a cream to a deep apricot, which is almost golden. The black should be a solid jet black, like a deep solid raven black, without any intermixing of fawn, rust, or white hairs or spots throughout the coat. Dull coats, rusty, or fawn hairs showing through the coat is a serious fault. Beware of the hair particles that are even in color from the roots out to the end. It should be a shaded black color. Too many of our Pugs today have bad color. This is due to the intercrossing of both colors and it is a serious fault. The fawn's color may be any shade, but the black mask, ears, diamond mark, nails and trace must stand out in a definite contrast. The fawn areas must be free of soot and smuttiness. This usually will show on the forehead, legs, chest or across the back, or appears as a wide saddle mark, leaving the coat looking dirty. This is seen more often in the silver fawn color and is a very serious fault. Judges must penalize the Pug for bad color.

Movement (which the standard omits)—I was appalled to have read that the gait of the Pug is impossible to define. The overall breed type tells us how a Pug should move regardless of size. If the Pug is correct breed type he can only move one way. The Pug double tracks, moving slightly into the line of gravity. He starts away with hocks parallel one to the other, neither cow-hocked nor bowed. He comes toward you without paddling or weaving, turning his feet neither in nor out. The Pug's gait should be normal, springy and stylish.

The Pug stands naturally with his weight evenly distributed at all four corners of his body. Viewed from the front the column of support is reasonably straight. The natural tendency of the Pug's toes is to turn slightly outward for balance. If he has a Terrier-type front he will not turn his toes outward. Seen from the rear his legs are parallel to each other. When he trots, his body is supported by two legs at a time, which move alternately in diagonal pairs. He

Correct Ears

A. Button Ear

B. Rose Ear

Correct Movement

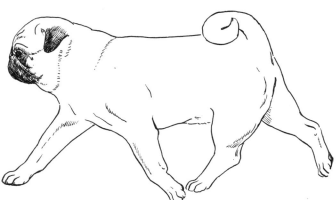

A. Correct Side Movement

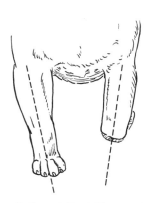

B. Correct Front Movement

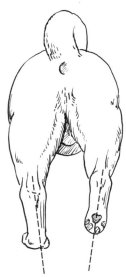

C. Correct Rear Movement

Incorrect Movement

A. Too Wide

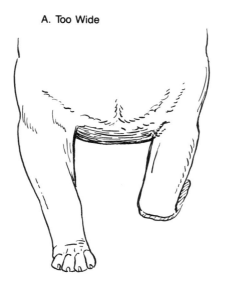

B. Bulldog Front

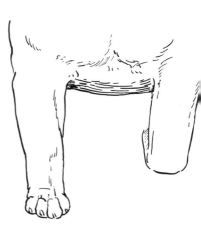

C. Rope Walking

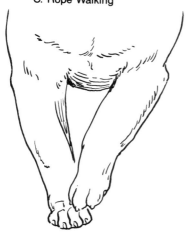

D. Paddling

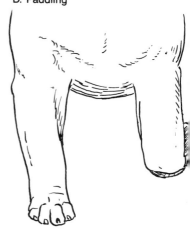

Pekingese: Bowed front, wide in front, narrow rear, short neck, short legs

Bulldog: Wide front, narrow and higher rear, short neck

161

must balance himself over the center column of support, otherwise he will wobble from side to side. To achieve balance the Pug's legs angle inward toward the center line of gravity.

The Bulldog, and the Pekingese, whose front quarters are wider than their rear quarters, tend to roll in the rear because their hind feet track inside of their front feet. This is not how a Pug moves.

How does the Pug roll? The Pug's roll comes from the reach of the forelegs. As the Pug reaches his front leg forward his shoulder drops and you will get a slight roll.

Summary

I have herein expressed some of my own opinions clarifying the Pug standard. What counts is the overall appearance of the Pug, which encompasses his type, balance, soundness, character and presentation.

The Pug standard allows forty points for the fawn's head and thirty-five points for the black's head. Obviously the Pug is a "head breed". But just as importantly it is also a "body breed". The level topline, square body and the hardness of developed muscle tell the whole story. Without these, the necessary attachments of his body, feet, neck and tail set will be out of balance.

Do not get carried away with one particular feature of the Pug. Although the standard does not mention movement, the Pug must be sound, and if he is sound he will move correctly. Please do not overlook movement. The Pug should move on a loose lead, and slowly. Do not let the handler run the dog around the ring or string him up on a tight lead.

Color and coat are another very important aspect of the Pug. Remember, we do not want smutty dogs or Pugs with long coats. This is difficult to breed out, and judges must discourage this.

Your consideration of weight is also not to be overlooked. Although weight should be more closely examined, the weight is relative to the size of the Pug and the amount of bone and muscle he has. We do not want a weedy dog that lacks proper substance, but the Pug is a Toy, and the smaller dog that is square, balanced and has substance should be rewarded and not the Terrier-type Pug.

I must point out that a Pug must not be "chicken breasted." It is appalling to me when I see judges placing and awarding ribbons to Pugs with this abnormality.

In judging Best of Breed or Best of Winners competition, judges should take enough time to evaluate both the dog or bitch equally as representing the better of the breed. Too many judges place the dog over the bitch because of the massiveness of the dog's head and bone, or to divide a major. It is important to evaluate each part of the animal whether dog or bitch. Many inferior dogs are placed over outstanding bitches. Let's not overlook a good bitch, as bitches are the foundation of any breed.

The Pug is not an easy dog to judge or breed. In closing I would like you to remember: The Pug is a lot in a little.

7

Judging the Pug

As A BREEDER-JUDGE, I strongly feel I must lock in breed type. I want a well-balanced, sound, square, cobby Pug with a level topline, short back and high-set curled tail. The Pug's head must also be correct breed type and in balance with the rest of the dog.

There is a great deal of controversy concerning size in the Pug breed. A typy, well-structured and balanced Pug will not be penalized by me because he is slightly over the ideal size. However, as a breeder-judge, I will not tolerate a Pug over twenty-two pounds or one under fourteen pounds because we will be losing breed type.

Soundness is also important, but I will give a little on soundness to maintain breed type. A Pug must be correctly gaited on a loose lead and not run around in the ring. He should double-track and cover ground.

Color and markings are also part of breed type. I will excuse or withhold ribbons on a Pug whose color and markings are erroneous and cannot be clearly defined. If the Pug is not properly marked it does not represent breed type. I will also withhold ribbons on a Pug with a wry mouth, a straight tail or a lolling tongue, and one that is not structurally sound.

The Pug is not a Chinese Shar-Pei and must not have rolls down his back. I will penalize a Pug who does because this is not breed type. I will penalize a Pug who is straight in shoulder and whose upper arm is too short or is out of condition. I will penalize an obese or flabby Pug. I will penalize a Pug who is too long in body, slab sided or whose topline runs downhill to his shoulders because this, too, is not breed type.

To be considered, bring me a Pug who is alert, covers ground, is balanced and most of all conveys true Pug breed type. A quality Pug will always be a winner.

Ch. Shirrayne's Darling Eve winning Best in Sweepstakes under judge Betty Dullinger at the 1979 Pug Dog Club of Greater New York Specialty. She also won Best Puppy in Show at the Pug Dog Club of America Specialty the following week. Bred, owner and handled by the author. President of the PDCGNY, A. J. Meshirer, presents the trophy.

Ch. Cameo's Super Stuff (*left*) and Ch. Rowell's Solo Moon getting ready for a little holiday fun. Both dogs are owned by John and Linda Rowell.

8

Choosing and Caring for a Pug Puppy

IF YOU DECIDE that you want a puppy, always give it a great deal of thought. This is an important step in your life. The puppy will become part of your family, and once you purchase the puppy you are committing yourself for ten to sixteen years. You must carefully consider the need for proper housing, grooming, feeding, exercise, training and health care. It is a responsible job that demands a lot of attention.

Ask yourself the following questions:

1. Is the puppy going to interfere with my job or household duties?
2. What about vacation time? Do you have someone to leave the puppy with?
3. Will the puppy get along with my children and friends?
4. Who is going to walk the dog?
5. Is the puppy a house dog or do you intend to kennel him outside?
6. The most important question of all: What breed of dog will best fit into our lifestyle?
7. Is anyone in the household allergic to dogs?
8. How do I find the correct puppy for my family?

The first step that you should take after deciding that a puppy will fit into your lifestyle is to attend some dog shows in your area. Look at all the different breeds. Talk with the breeders and exhibitors about the temperament,

Two litters of Pug puppies, born three weeks apart, pictured with owners Carolyn and Albert Bradshaw

grooming, exercise and care of the breeds that interest you. Know the history of the breed and what purpose the breed serves.

Once you decide to purchase a puppy, call the American Kennel Club. They will send you information on the breeders and dog clubs in your area. Read all the dog books you can find on the breed you have chosen; contact the breeders.

If you have decided on a Pug, now you are ready to look at Pug puppies. I have to warn you, there is nothing cuter than a Pug puppy. He wriggles himself into your heart.

Visit a few reputable Pug breeders who show dogs. Do not buy the first Pug puppy you see. Please go home and sleep on it. Visit one or two more kennels. Remember, you can go back and purchase the other puppy you saw the day before. A reputable breeder will suggest that you think it over for a few days. Have your mind made up whether you prefer a male or female.

A reputable well-known breeder will cross-examine you on the reason you want a Pug puppy. Do you live in a house with a fenced-in yard? Does the apartment building allow dogs? How old are your children? Do you know if they have an allergy to dogs? Is your puppy going to have the run of the house? Is there a good veterinarian in your area? Are you looking for a puppy to breed, show or just a lovely pet?

After all the important information is out of the way you should be told a few facts about the Pug. Pugs shed and you will always have Pug hairs on your clothing. Pugs are not barkers, but will notify you if someone rings your doorbell. The Pug is a house dog and cannot adjust to outdoor living. You must be careful with the Pug in hot or humid weather and also in extreme cold weather.

It is advisable to ask the price of the puppies before making your final selection or expressing your preference. The average Pug puppy costs between $500 and $800 dollars, depending on the quality of their bloodlines.

Make sure the breeder's premises are neat and clean. Ask to see the mother and the sire of the puppies. Sometimes the sire is not available, as the breeder went to an outside stud dog. Have the breeder show you the American Kennel Club registration papers or the litter registration papers. Do not purchase a puppy without papers. Also ask to see the pedigree of the puppies.

Pug puppies are usually kept in a whelping box or exercise pen. Just watch them bouncing around and playing with each other! Germs can be carried in on hands and clothing and most breeders will not allow you to handle the puppies. Please don't be offended by the restrictions placed on you. A lot of long hours, no sleep and hard work went into rearing the puppies.

Most of the time the breeder will bring only one puppy out for you to see. There is a good reason for this. For example, the American Kennel Club registered 462 Pug litters in one typical month. There were 951 puppies born out of those litters. So you can figure about two puppies per litter. Once in a while a bitch will give birth to a larger litter, but you must realize that most breeders breed only when they wish to keep a Pug puppy for themselves. That is about once or twice a year. They are looking for a top-quality show specimen or one to carry on their lines.

Beware of the kennel that has four or more litters of Pugs at one time, or the breeder who tries to talk you into breeder's terms or any type of deal. They are only out to make a fast buck.

Every puppy born is not a show dog. The pet Pug puppy should not be an inferior dog. You are paying the same price for the pet as you would a promising show puppy at three months of age. Do not buy a Pug puppy under three months of age or let anyone talk you into it. Make sure the puppy has been wormed and had all its protective inoculations. A reputable breeder would not sell anyone a Pug puppy until they are twelve weeks old.

When you are buying a pet you want it to look like a Pug, which is what we call breed type. The puppy must be clean, playful, have clear eyes, be alert and move well on all four legs. The puppy you want is outgoing and friendly not reluctant, cringing or sitting off in a corner disconsolate.

If he is fawn, the Pug puppy should not have any black on his chest, inside his legs or under his belly. White markings on the puppy's chest or feet are a no-no. The combination of the clear fawn color with the black mask and ears is an important characteristic of the breed. A black Pug puppy has no white markings. White markings on a black Pug puppy is attributable to a breeder crossing the black Pug with a fawn indiscriminately.

Make sure the Pug puppy is chubby, solid, sound and well fed. You do not want a puppy whose ribs are showing, is bony or has a weedy body. Your main concern in choosing a Pug puppy is a healthy, sound puppy with a wonderful temperament. Also, if you want a show dog or a stud dog, check the male puppy to make sure the testicles have descended.

If you wish to pick the puppy up, let the breeder show you how to hold the puppy. The Pug puppy may jump out of your arms and hands, which could result in an injury. Never pick up a Pug puppy by his front legs or the nape of its neck.

Pug puppies are adorable creatures and spirited, and it is difficult for the inexperienced person to make a selection. Do not rush into buying that puppy. If this is the puppy for you, an ethical breeder will insist that you have the puppy checked by your veterinarian within forty-eight hours of purchase. If your veterinarian finds any congenital defects, return the puppy to the breeder instantly, even though the attachment formed between you and the puppy will make it difficult for you to return him to the breeder. Be sure you ask the breeder for the puppy's diet and get all the necessary information about worming and inoculations.

Let's say you are interested in a promising show puppy. Many Pug breeders will tell you they pick their puppies when they are born. This is hogwash. A Pug puppy goes through many changes in its development. At birth you can see if the puppy is going to have a proper layback of shoulder. You can tell if his hams are going to be full enough and if he is going to have sufficient angulation. From day one until he is three months old his coat color will lighten.

Pug puppies playing with a show lead. Owner: Blanche C. Roberts.

There are also many changes going on in the development of the Pug puppy's head and body. Between four and six months the underjaw can narrow. The puppy can start to fall away under the eyes, *lack of fullness under the eye*. His nose can protrude too far out. This is a critical time in his development. The puppy's front legs can start to bow out between four and seven months. His rear legs can start to hock. His topline can *fall apart*. That is, instead of retaining the desirable straight line it can develop a sway back, a roached back or a higher-in-rear-than-shoulder condition.

At eight months we know how the puppy's head is going to develop. We know if he is going to have a good front, rear and topline. At this point we still hope that his ribs spring enough and his chest drops and that he is not going to overload in the shoulder (a muscle beneath the top of the shoulder blade can overdevelop and push the shoulder blade outward from the body). At this age we know whether we have a promising show puppy. At eighteen months, if he is correctly constructed and everything properly falls into place, you have a show dog.

So if your interest is in a top-quality show bitch or dog you should not consider one until it is over eighteen months old. Remember, it is still a big gamble between the eighth and eighteenth month of age.

The cost of a Pug puppy at eight months runs between $1,000 to about $1,500. At eighteen months of age a top show dog can cost $1,800 and up, depending on bloodlines and if the Pug is a finished champion.

Spend a long time looking around the dog shows. Check your catalog to see who the breeders are. Look for the type you like, who breeds it and check to see what dogs win. Watch the novice with the top breeders' dogs; see if they are winning. If you find a line you like, prepare yourself to wait one to two years for a top-quality dog or bitch to come along. Don't let a dozen shows sway you. Spend a year, if you can, looking around for that ideal type and a sound dog. It will save you a lot of money in the end. In the meantime you are developing an eye for a dog and gaining knowledge about the Pug breed.

If you buy a promising puppy, a breeder cannot guarantee you a show winner or a champion. This is up to you. It is in the way you condition and feed the puppy and the way he continues to develop. A breeder should know his lines, so listen to his or her advice when you are considering a top show dog. The final and most important bit of advice I can give you is to memorize and learn how to interpret the Pug breed standard.

Bringing Your Puppy Home

You have just received in writing the following information from the breeder:

1. The puppy's normal diet.
2. Dates of past worming and the medication used.
3. Dates of inoculations and who manufactured the product.
4. A vial of the serum used if the shots were given by the breeder.

5. The American Kennel Club registration papers.
6. A copy of the puppy's pedigree and a bill of sale.
7. A written guarantee against hereditary diseases, if the breeder supplies one.

Make sure you bring cash with you for the puppy. Many breeders will not accept checks. This is quite reasonable because a few years back there was a ring of dog thieves going around buying puppies with bad checks. At that time legal authorities suggested that sellers should never accept checks for livestock.

You must bring someone with you when you pick up the puppy so he can travel in their lap. Being placed in a box for travel can be a terrifying experience for the puppy from which he may never recover. It is advisable to bring two turkish towels and paper towels with you in the event the puppy becomes car sick. This occasionally happens with puppies on their first few car rides. Comforting him through this experience is one way of reassuring the Pug puppy so he will learn that car rides are fun. It also helps the puppy to form that special emotional attachment to his new owner.

Pug puppies adjust very well. The first night should be uneventful if you purchase a wire dog crate. You can purchase one at pet stores or at the dog shows. The crate should be 18 inches high, 18 inches wide and 24 inches long. This provides a safe haven for the Pug puppy. Line the front half of the crate with newspaper and put a turkish towel in the back half of the crate for the puppy to sleep on with his favorite toy. This crate is also useful for housebreaking the puppy and traveling in the car. Put the puppy in his crate next to your bed. Many puppies will cry the first few nights because they miss their mother and littermates. If your puppy cries during the night, just reach your hand down to reassure him and let him know you care. By doing this it will not be necessary for you to get out of bed and run downstairs. Devote the first week to your puppy. In this period he will learn to adjust to your lifestyle, discipline and training. The puppy will be more attentive to you and forever grateful for it.

A Pug puppy cannot be shut up in a shed, tied up in the backyard or left down in the basement. It is not in his temperament. He is part of your family and should be treated as such. He may want to share your lap or the pillow on your bed. Remember, the time you put into the puppy now can be a rewarding experience and will pay off later. It is entirely up to you how well the puppy adjusts. During the first month you will be playing with him, feeding him, taking him for walks and picking up after him. Most of all you are trying to teach him who is the boss. The Pug puppy is inquisitive and he will be going around checking out the whole house. Never leave the puppy off lead unless confined to an area where he cannot get out. Your Pug puppy is a Toy breed, and moving vehicles may not see him if he runs into the street; or, he could be killed by a large stray dog. Teach him his name and tell the puppy you love him. The sooner he is comfortable with you the sooner he'll respond to your commands.

An Ivanwold puppy playing with his teddy bear. Owners: Dr. and Mrs. Edward Patterson.

Your Puppy's Diet

When you purchased your Pug puppy, you should have been sent home with a supply of the puppy's diet and schedule with enough food for a few days. Do not try to change the puppy's diet too fast. This could result in diarrhea.

Do not worry if the puppy refuses to eat some of his food. The puppy may decide not to eat anything. If this happens, try to bribe him with some liverwurst. This always gets them going. You must remember it takes a few days for the puppy to adjust to his new home. When you wish to introduce particular foods into the puppy's diet, make the changes slowly. This will give the puppy time to become accustomed to different foods presented to him.

Nutrition plays an important role in the development of your puppy. The main requirements are proteins, fats, carbohydrates and vitamins A, B complex, D and E. I also feel that calcium and iron are essential. Dicalcium phosphate, cod-liver oil and wheat germ oil are absolute musts.

I always start my puppies on formula as soon as their eyes are open and continue until they are six months of age. I feed my puppies five times a day.

This is my simple formula for feeding a Pug puppy. It is suitable for a pet or show dog.

Place all the following ingredients into a blender:

- 1 large can evaporated milk
- 1 raw egg yolk or hard-boiled egg yolk (do not use the whites of the eggs)
- 2 tablespoons honey
- 1 envelope unflavored gelatin

Fill the blender with whole milk, approximately 2 cups. Blend the mixture, place in a container and store in the refrigerator. This should be enough for a few days.

Pick up a box of baby oatmeal or mixed cereal, one bottle of Poly-Vi-Sol baby drops, a bottle of 250-milligram dicalcium phosphate tablets, cod liver oil and wheat germ oil as supplements.

The puppy formula should be given three times a day when he is three months old. It is to his advantage to try to keep him on the formula as long as possible.

Feed him chopped beef twice a day. The meat is cooked fresh every day.

For one puppy simmer ¼ pound of chopped beef, ¼ cup chopped vegetables, ¼ cup water and ½ teaspoon corn oil. When the beef is ready, add ¼ cup cooked rice and let the mixture cool. Then add ¼ cup of a commercial dog kibble, which is available at pet stores and in most supermarkets. Let the kibble soak in the mixture to soften. This is enough for 2 feedings.

Do not feed the puppy cold food or food that is too hot. You do not want the food to be soggy but it should be firm enough so the puppy can pick it up and is easier to digest. It is also better to feed your Pug out of a flat dish, such as a pie pan.

Various combinations may be used in the above formulation; chicken, boned fish and mutton are adequate substitutes for chopped beef. Feed the puppy liver in small amounts added to his food. Cottage cheese or canned tuna fish makes a great supplement for one of the puppy's meals.

Celery, asparagus, peas, carrots and tomatoes all supply important proteins, vitamins and minerals. Chop the vegetables or run them through your food processor. Puppies also like fruit, so give him a little piece of yours. Ice cream is also great as a treat. They love it.

The following feeding schedule will give you some idea of what the average puppy will need at twelve weeks of age:

> *Morning breakfast:* Give ¼ cup formula, mixed with some baby cereal. Add 6 drops of Poly-Vi-Sol baby drops and feed warm.
> *Afternoon* (two meals): Give one-half of the meat mixture, then add ½ crushed dicalcium phosphate pill, ¼ teaspoon cod-liver oil and ⅛ teaspoon wheat germ oil to the puppy's food. At 4:00 P.M. give ¼ cup formula mixed with the cereal.
> *Evening meal:* At 7:00 P.M. give the balance of the meat mixture.
> *Bedtime:* At 10:00 P.M. or later, give ¼ cup formula mixed with the cereal.

Bones help to keep the puppy's teeth clean and strong, but only give him large beef knuckle bones that cannot splinter.

Fresh water is essential and should be available to the puppy twenty-four hours a day. In hot weather give the puppy fresh water or ice cubes often.

It is important to gradually increase the amount of food the puppy will consume. Let the puppy eat all he wants—puppies are supposed to be a little on the fat side. By five months the puppy will reduce his food intake down to four meals a day. Eliminate his bedtime feeding. Some puppies between five and six months refuse their formula. Just give them another meat meal instead. Between six and eight months the puppy should be cut back to three meals a day, but make sure you have compressed the four meals into three. By the time he is one year old the puppy will be down to two meals a day.

If you are feeding a show dog, increase his meat meal to ½ pound per day, broken down into two feedings at a year of age. At one year of age your meat mixture should consist of ½ pound meat, ½ cup rice, 1 cup kibble, ½ cup vegetables and 1 tablespoon cooking oil. Feed one-half in the morning and add ½ dropper of Poly-Vi-Sol baby drops; one dicalcium phosphate pill, which is 250 milligrams; ½ teaspoon cod-liver oil and ⅛ teaspoon wheat germ oil. Leave the vitamins out of the evening meal.

The food should be warm, never cold, for easier digestion when you feed the Pug.

Watch your show dog's weight carefully. You want him chunky but not fat. Never cut back on his meat intake or vegetables. You can reduce or increase the amount of kibble or rice in his diet as needed to regulate his weight. Make sure he is getting plenty of exercise so the food is developing into muscles.

How to Lead Train Your Puppy

Training requires a lot of time, love and patience. Pug puppies are not usually lead broken when you take them home. Put a collar on the puppy for one hour and let him run around the room with it. Some puppies may scratch at the collar. If so, distract him. Now it is time to attach the lead to the puppy's collar. Sit on the floor and call the puppy to you, using his name. When he comes, give the puppy a treat and a lot of praise. The puppy will enjoy this game because he is getting something out of it.

Now take the puppy outside and just stand still. The Pug, being a curious little fellow, will want to investigate the surroundings. Follow the puppy for a while, then call the puppy to come to you. Keep the lead loose while calling him and you will notice that the little guy will be walking next to you on the lead.

It is important to keep the lead in your left hand so you can train the puppy to walk only on your left side. Make sure that you give the puppy a treat everytime he obeys your wishes. Do not pull or yank the puppy. I cannot stress this enough. If you do, he is going to rebel and you will have a difficult time training him.

Disciplining Your Puppy

The Pug is a Toy dog. Do not slap a Pug puppy. There is certainly no need to abuse the puppy in this manner. You are dealing with a very intelligent puppy who is eager to learn. Say, "No!" in a disapproving loud voice. This is enough to correct him.

Never hit a Pug puppy with a rolled-up newspaper or chase him around the room. Never punish the puppy after you call him to you. You must reprimand the Pug puppy only when caught in the act. The puppy will not remember why you are punishing him a few seconds after the act. This can confuse the puppy and make him shy. Always reward the puppy when he responds to your wishes and commands and, on the flip side, verbally reprimand him when he doesn't.

Housebreaking Your Puppy

The first rule of thumb for housebreaking is to keep your puppy confined to a small area. A wire crate is the best method. Pug puppies are not physically mature enough to be completely trained until they are over four months of age. This is another reason why you do not purchase a Pug puppy under twelve weeks of age.

My puppies start their training in the whelping box. Cover half of the whelping box with carpet and the other half with newspaper. The babies will crawl off the carpet to the newspaper to eliminate. The normal healthy puppy is very clean and doesn't want to soil his bed. Using a cat litter tray also works great. Your puppy will think it is fun to dig in the soft kitty litter or shredded newspapers.

Pug puppies have to relieve themselves about every two hours: when they wake up, after each meal, if they play too hard or get excited and just before they go to bed.

You must keep an eye on the puppy. Sometimes the puppy will sniff the floor or he may run around in circles or whimper. When you see this, immediately pick up the puppy and take him to his newspaper or litter tray. Make sure you praise the puppy and give him a treat after he completes his chores.

You should set a regular schedule for outdoor training. Make sure you take the puppy out each morning and to the same spot. The puppy learns quickly from a steady routine. Pick up the Pug puppy, put on his collar and lead, then carry him out. The first few times it is a good idea to take a piece of soiled paper outside with you. Don't forget to praise the puppy and give him a treat.

If the puppy refuses to empty, pick up a jar of baby suppositories. Cut the suppository into three parts. Take the thinnest end and insert it into the puppy's rectum, hold it in for a minute and place the Pug puppy on the ground. Wait until he eliminates. You may have to use the suppositories a few times until the puppy gets the idea.

If the puppy makes a mistake in the house, immediately clean it up with ammonia, soap and water. If you are going out for more than three hours, remember that a Pug puppy under one year of age will need to relieve himself. Make sure he has access to his paper or litter tray. You are the one who will be setting a pattern that will produce healthy, clean habits for your puppy. It takes time and patience and some puppies may take a little longer to housebreak, but it all works out in the end.

9

How to Groom
the Pug

THERE IS nothing more appealing than a clean, healthy and happy Pug. The Pug is an accommodating little guy who learns to love the attention bestowed upon him while groomed. You will need to set aside one hour a week to attend to his needs, whether he is a pet or show dog.

It is much easier to start his grooming procedure on a small table. You can use a sturdy snack table or the kitchen table with a bath math placed on top of it. Place the Pug on the table for a short time. Make the dog feel comfortable and relaxed, give him a treat, praise and pat effusively. Caution should be exercised that the Pug is not left on the table alone. He may try to jump off and can be seriously injured. It is absolutely necessary to keep his collar and lead on for the first few grooming sessions. Proper techniques can achieve better control and quick results.

You will need the following equipment for grooming your Pug for pet or show purposes:

- Pair of rounded-end scissors (pet, show)
- Natural bristle brush (pet, show)
- Thinning shears (show)
- Pair of straight scissors (show)
- Nail file or nail clipper (pet, show)
- Electric nail grinder (show)
- Electric hair trimmer (show)

- Comb (pet, show)
- Jar of vaseline (pet, show)
- Tube of Clairol Vitapointe cream hairdressing and conditioner (show)
- Cotton swabs (pet, show)
- Cotton balls (pet, show)
- Quality dog shampoo and hair conditioner (pet, show)
- Baby toothbrush and toothpaste (pet, show)
- Baby talcum powder (show)

All the above items can be purchased at a pet store, drug store or at a dog show.

The first step is to teach the Pug what brushing is all about. Place the Pug on the grooming table and tell him to stay. Do not use force. He has to learn to stand quietly while being groomed. By giving him a few treats he will be happy to do this for you. When the Pug appears to be accustomed to the table, show him the brush and gently brush his coat and praise him while you are doing this. Try to brush out all the loose and dead hair. This will stimulate the natural oils in the coat and bring back life and shine to the hair. After brushing, rub your palms over the dog's coat a few times from head to tail. The natural oil in your skin will impart sheen to the dog's coat. You will notice that your Pug will look forward to being brushed.

The Pug's anal glands should be checked regularly to prevent infection. The anal glands are situated on either side of the anus. If the glands are not naturally discharged, they will become enlarged and contaminated. You will see two hard lumps and the Pug may drag himself around the floor on his rear end. The glands will discharge an unpleasant odor and liquid, so make sure you have some tissue. Hold his tail with your left hand, encircling its base with the thumb and forefinger of the right hand and gently squeeze each lump up and outward.

We are now ready to try a bath. I find putting the dog in my kitchen sink is much easier for me than the bathtub. I place a rubber mat in the bottom of the sink so the Pug does not slip. Take a cotton ball and break it in half. Place one half into each ear. This is to prevent water from getting into his ears. Be careful you do not push the cotton in too far. Place a drop or two of mineral oil or cod liver oil into the Pug's eyes to prevent the soap from irritating his eyes.

Check the temperature of the water and make sure it is not too hot. Stand him in the sink and shampoo and scrub all of his body thoroughly. Rinse him lightly with warm water and scrub him again. Use only a warm washcloth without soap to wash his head and face. Use a bath spray and rinse all the soap off him. At this point I brush his teeth and cup my hand to catch some water and rinse his mouth. The next step is to check the Pug's nose wrinkle and clean under it with the washcloth. Now use the hair conditioner on the dog and then the final rinse. Remove the cotton from the Pug's ears and clean them with the washcloth over your finger.

Wrap him in a bath towel and dry him well. Then take your hair dryer and, starting with his chest, make sure he is completely dry. Do not place the Pug in a draft while drying.

Your pet Pug only needs a bath four times a year if you brush him every week. The show dog must have a bath before every show to look his best for the judge.

One of the most important parts of grooming a Pug is trimming his toenails. A show Pug's nails especially must be kept short or you can force his toes outward, splay his feet and break down his pasterns. An excellent guide to see if the Pug's nails are short enough is to make sure that they are not touching the floor. It is a good idea to ask the breeder or your veterinarian to show you how to cut his nails. For show, rub some vaseline on the nails to make them shine.

The nails must be kept as short as possible, because the Pug uses his front feet as hands and can scratch his eyes. Nail-trimming is a difficult task; they do not like having their toenails cut.

Take a nail file and sit your Pug in your lap. When you first begin to file you will have to bear down to break the hard polished surface of the nail. File in one direction only, from the top to the bottom in a round stroke. This *must* be done every week, and you cannot put it off. A good time to do the Pug's nails is while you are watching television. The Pug may allow you to lay him on his back. Eventually he will endure this procedure and it will not be a big chore.

On the other hand, you can use a nail clipper. Be careful not to cut the quick. It is the line inside of the nail where the vein begins and it is easy to see. If you accidentally cut the quick apply a styptic pencil or Kwick-stop, a styptic powder you use by inserting his nail into the powder while applying pressure to stop the bleeding. (This is obtained at the pet shop or dog show and it is important to always have some on hand.) The final step after cutting the nails is to take the nail file and finish off the clipping job with one or two strokes, just to remove any sharp edges; I prefer to use the electric nail grinder.

Now let's put the Pug back onto the grooming table. It is time to go back to his nose wrinkle. Take a cotton ball and put some baby oil on it. Use your thumb and pull the skin up above the nose wrinkle, clean inside with the oil and rub some Vaseline inside. For the show dog also rub a little on his nose. If the nose wrinkle is sore, rub some Panalog on the area. You must purchase this from your veterinarian.

Many veterinarians advise leaving your Pug's ears alone. If they are dirty and full of wax, you can clean them gently with a cotton-tipped swab dipped in a little peroxide. Then you must wipe them out with a dry cotton ball. Do not dig deeply into the ear, only go as far as your finger will go. If the Pug's ears are lacerated from scratching, Panalog will help.

The Pug's ears must fold correctly for a show dog. This is an important feature. When the Pug is teething his ears will fly, so we must glue or tape his ears. I feel glueing is the easier method for correcting the Pug's ears. Open the ear flat and apply some eyelash glue to the outside edge of the ear only. The

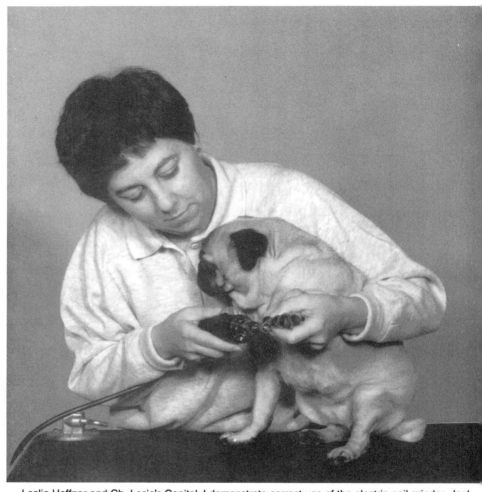

Leslie Heffner and Ch. Lesjo's Capital J demonstrate correct use of the electric nail grinder. *Joel Heffner*

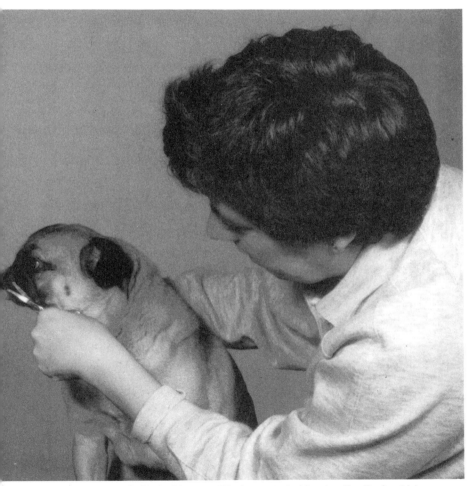

Leslie Heffner and Lesjo's Sweet Mystery, CD, demonstrate trimming the Pug's whiskers.

area you will glue is the V you will see when the ear is open. Glue ¼ inch on each side of the V. Fold the ear over into its normal position, and just above the V press the edges together. Hold between the thumb and index finger until the glue is set (approximately 3 to 5 minutes). You must keep the show Pug's ears glued until the teething period is over. This does not have to be done for a pet Pug puppy, but I always suggest that you do this because it gives the Pug a nicer finished look to the head.

Trimming your Pug is only necessary for the show dog. Let's start with his head. Using the rounded scissors, trim the whiskers off at the base of his mask and under the jaw. Next, cut off the three hairs above each eye. You will also find three hairs in each of the Pug's five black moles, on each side and under the jaw. Cut them off. I personally use the hair clipper for the whiskers on the Pug's mask and underjaw. Do not use the clippers until someone shows you how.

While the Pug is still standing on the table, look at the front of the dog's chest. Take your thinning scissors and trim only the few hairs that stick out. This will give the Pug a clean line. Comb the hairs that form a line behind the Pug's ears and go down the side of the dog's neck. Pick up your thinning scissors and carefully trim the hairs that are out of place. With the straight scissors trim the little hairs that form a straight line at the back of the Pug's front legs.

If you are showing a male Pug, take the electric clipper and trim the hair off his penis. Look at the Pug's loin area and trim any hair that hangs down.

The Pug's pants and tail must be trimmed. This is done with both the straight and thinning scissors. Using the straight scissors, trim the hair around his anus and tail to give the Pug a clean look. Change to the thinning scissors and trim his pants, getting rid of all the long hairs. It will give the Pug a smooth outline. Sprinkle some baby talcum powder on his pants and penis and brush it all out the morning of the show.

We must not forget his eyes. Make sure they are clean. You can put a few drops of Eye Brite into each eye.

Now you are ready for the final touches the morning of the show. Put a small amount of Vitapointe in the palm of your hand, rub your hands together and rub throughout the Pug's coat, on the ears and on the face. Go back over his coat a few times. Take a tiny bit of Vaseline and go over the Pug's trace, nose and toenails. Your Pug is now groomed for the show ring.

The basic grooming for the pet Pug is brushing, cutting his toenails, cleaning his ears, checking anal glands, cleaning the nose wrinkle, bathing and brushing his teeth. Don't forget to wipe out the matter in the corner of the dog's eyes. This will keep your Pug happy.

One other bit of advice: The Pug loves a bath, so when you run a bath for yourself, be careful to close the bathroom door or you may find a Pug in your tub!

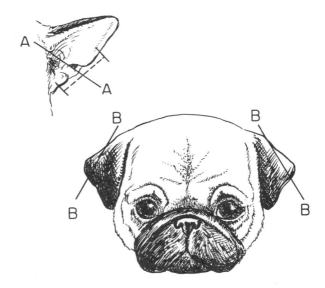

Setting puppy ears. To assure a good ear set in a mature Pug, it is recommended that when he begins to cut his second teeth and his ears start to "fly" (fall back into a "rose" position) his ears be kept glued in the correct position. This will train his muscles to hold the ear correctly. The method described is a simple, painless way to train the Pug puppy's ear muscles. The adhesive is the cement used to apply false eyelashes ("Duo eyelash adhesive"). It is not likely to irritate the skin and is easily removed.

Step 1. Open ear flat and apply adhesive to outside edge of ear only.

Step 2. Fold ear along line marked "A."

Step 3. Press ear together along line marked "B" and hold between thumb and index finger until glue is set (approximately three to five minutes).

The puppy's ears should be kept glued until he has completely finished teething.

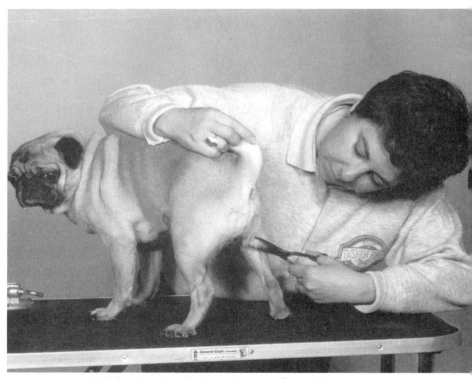

Leslie Heffner is using thinning scissors on Sweet Mystery's hindquarters.

10

How to Show
a Pug

SHOWING A PUG is a lot of fun if you can be a good sport. You must be able to win or lose graciously, as you will be competing with experienced Pug breeders and agents. You must learn how to evaluate the breed standard. You must know your Pug's strong points as well as your Pug's faults to properly evaluate on what you are being judged.

It is important to listen to the judge and try to see what an individual judge is looking for in a Pug. Your Pug will be judged on breed type, soundness, appearance, temperament, condition, on how he covers ground and his examination on the table. The judge will be doing all of this with the breed standard in his or her mind on the given day. The judge cannot anticipate how this particular Pug might develop as he matures. As we know, the Pug standard allows for some variances in breed type, which represents the ideal Pug.

The experienced agent and breeder can cover up many of the Pug's faults and is able to show off their finer points. It takes time and experience to accomplish this.

If you have a quality Pug, you will get your share of wins. Do not brag about your Pug or criticize a losing or winning dog. All dogs have faults. If you can't say something nice, do not say anything at all. All today's Pugs descend from the same lines, but not the same mold. If you hear someone tearing a Pug apart, they are also inadvertently criticizing their own lines.

The first step in training a Pug for the show ring should start in the whelping box at three weeks of age. Train the puppies to learn and accept treats from your hand. I also pick up my puppies and hold them on a table for a few minutes each day. By the time they are three months of age stacking on the table will be familiar and fun.

At three weeks I place a ¼-inch ribbon loosely around their necks. Make sure that you can get two fingers in and that the ribbon cannot slip off the puppy's neck. Leave one inch of ribbon on one end so that the puppies can pull on the end of the ribbon. This serves two purposes: Your puppies will be leash trained when they come out of the whelping box, and the ribbon serves as a show lead while you are stacking them on the table. Reward them with a treat and praise them.

Now lift the upper lip of each puppy to show his bite. It is important for them to feel comfortable with this examination, as it will be done by a judge later on. Once the Pug adjusts to being stacked on the table, rotate the puppy so that he faces in all directions. I say this because I had a Pug who would only face to the right. A Pug can be stubborn. After the puppy learns to be comfortable on the table, try stacking him on the floor. Teach the Pug to stack on the floor by just baiting him.

The next step is to teach the Pug to move properly on a loose lead. Correct procedure is to keep him at your left side. Make sure that the end of the show lead is gathered up in your left hand. Try to move at the Pug's natural gait. Keep a loose lead and practice taking him around in a circle, in a triangle, straight forward and back, in a T and in a reversed L. In this way the dog will become familiar with any type of ring procedure that the judge will ask you to perform. In the show ring you are always striving for perfection.

Spend only a short time working your Pug. If he is overworked he will get bored and refuse to show for you. You should practice this procedure at least once a day, however.

If your Pug drops his head or lags behind while moving on lead, all that is needed are a few quick tugs on the lead. If he veers to the left, a quick pull will bring him back in line. If he moves too close, an outward jerk will set him straight. Don't forget to talk to your Pug and give him a treat when he responds to your commands.

Always keep your Pug in front of you. Never step between the judge and the Pug. If you do not understand the directions, ask the judge to repeat them. You should not carry on a conversation with the judge, however, while in the show ring.

Handling classes can be helpful but you must be careful that you don't subject your Pug to a class with only large breeds of dogs. This can spook him, and it may take months before he'll be comfortable showing again. Also, make sure the teacher of the class is familiar with Toy breeds or the class can do more damage than good. Your best bet is join one of the local Pug clubs in your area. The members will help you. Attend the Pug Specialty Match shows and the Pug Specialty shows in your area. Enter your Pug and see how he stacks up with the others.

Make sure you crate train your puppy and get him used to riding crated in your car. If your Pug is going to be a show dog, he must be comfortable

Ch. Shirrayne's Music Man has a record of over eighty-five Bests of Breed and many Group placements. Owners: Shirrayne Kennels and Carol and Fred Schmidt.

Ch. Ivanwold Pistol Pete of Rontu and some of his laurels. Owners: Dr. and Mrs. Edward N. K. Patterson.

in a crate. You should also take the puppy out to public areas with you to socialize.

Exercising a show dog requires a little more work. A Pug must be conditioned and his muscles must be hard. He must be walked every day. Start the puppy off with one-half mile each day. At six months you should be up to one mile a day. At eighteen months the Pug should be walked three miles a day. When you walk your Pug, be sure that you use his show lead. Keep him on your left side, moving at a controlled pace. At the end of his walk stop and stack him. Keep in mind that exercise and play are important in the development of the show dog's health.

A puppy's first show must be fun, regardless of what he does in the ring. When the judge puts his hands on the puppy, he must be in top condition and outgoing. That's what makes a worthy show dog.

11

Special Care and Training of a Pug

ONE ADVANTAGE of owning a Pug is that the dog requires only a small amount of exercise. Playing with his toys and romping around the house will provide ample exercise for your pet Pug.

Pugs love stuffed toys. If you buy the Pug toys, be careful of the rubber toys; make sure that they cannot pull apart. Buy only nylon bones because rawhide bones can break up and lodge in the throat.

Sunshine and fresh air are vitally important for a Pug. You must remember that a Pug is a brachycephalic breed—*short-nosed*. They can react to heat on a humid day and have a difficult time breathing. It is advisable to schedule all walks early in the morning or after the sun goes down.

Pugs must be watched carefully in hot and humid weather. This is to prevent heat prostration. The earliest signs of trouble are heavy panting, snorting or gasping. If you see any of the above symptoms immediately wet the Pug down with cold water. If ice water is available, use it. Lie the Pug down flat on his side and continue to pour the ice water over him. If possible, turn on an electric fan and continue to cool the Pug with ice water as necessary. You may have to give the Pug a cold-water enema if his temperature is over 104 degrees. At temperatures of 106 degrees you can lose the dog. Rush your Pug to a veterinarian as quickly as possible.

When traveling with your Pug, you must carry a large thermos of ice water, ice cubes and towels. If the dog shows any signs of discomfort, saturate one of the towels with ice water and wrap the Pug in it. Give the dog some of the ice cubes to lick. Never leave your dog locked in a closed car. The windows must always be left open.

If possible, try to purchase a child's throat ice collar or an ice bag. Fill the collar with ice, tie it around your Pug's neck. You can purchase the ice collar or ice bag from any hospital supply company or drugstore. If you can find a #379 child's throat collar made by Davol, purchase it.

If it is above eighty degrees and you plan to be out for the day make sure you leave the air conditioner or the fan on for your Pug, especially if it is humid. Make sure you leave the dog a fresh bowl of ice cubes. It is important to add salt to the Pug's diet in the summertime. This will replace all the sodium they lose from heavy panting.

In the winter, if it is bitter cold outside, put a doggie coat on the Pug. Salt on the sidewalk or road can burn a dog's feet and make them sore, so when the dog comes inside make sure you wash his feet.

You should never let your Pug off lead unless you have a fenced-in yard. If you do, let him romp for a while each day.

The Pug has large, beautiful black eyes. You must prepare for the possibility of an eye injury. In an emergency you can always use Panalog, mineral oil or even cod-liver oil in the Pug's eyes if an ulceration or an injury occurs. Take your Pug to your veterinarian as soon as possible for the proper medication. A neglected ulcer can rupture, and the Pug would be left with partial or complete loss of sight.

You should always keep a tube of Atropine Sulfate Ophthalmic eye ointment in the house for the Pug. It is effective on injuries and ulcers. Chlorasone Ophthalmic eye ointment should also be on hand, but do not use it until the infection is under control and corneal regeneration is well under way. I have found this works great on the treatment of corneal ulcers. However, I usually use the Atropine Sulfate for about fourteen days and then use the Chlorasone Ophthalmic eye ointment. The eyes have healed, leaving no scars or marks that can be seen. Please check with your veterinarian before you use it.

Care and Diet of Older Pugs

The diet for the older Pug should be well planned. Do not overfeed, but rather try to keep him on the thin side. Make sure you provide a well-balanced diet. Fresh meat, vegetables and rice, plus calcium, cod liver oil and ½ teaspoon of corn oil should do the trick. Use other dietary supplements only on the advice of your veterinarian. If your older Pug has no teeth, put his food through the food processor so he can digest it properly.

Have your veterinarian check your dog or bitch if the Pug starts to drink excessive amounts of water. This is a sign of kidney disease or even diabetes. As your Pug approaches the age of eight, it is recommended that you have your veterinarian give him a thorough physical yearly. He may be developing geriatric problems.

You must be careful with the old Pug to avoid temperature changes from

Ch. Candy's Almond Joy was the top-rated Pug dam and the #1 Dam among all Toy breeds for 1975, according to the *Kennel Review* magazine system. Owner: Shirrayne Kennels.

Ch. Donaldson's Sylvester, bred and owned by Marie Donaldson

extreme heat to extreme cold. If you have to give the Pug a bath, make sure that it isn't in a draft. You must use your hair dryer on them and dry their chest first. Try brushing your Pug every day to keep them clean. It will also help in keeping Pug hair loss under control.

It is common for older Pugs to come down with arthritis. Do not give them any home remedies that you would use; obtain medication only from your veterinarian. If you have a vibrator you can give the Pug a light massage. The Pug will love it. Sometimes a heating pad for them to sleep on helps, but I have found that a heated water bed works great.

Loss of sight and hearing will encumber old Pugs. Please give them special attention and be patient. Keep the Pug in a familiar area. It will surprise you how well they will manage. They only need reassurance.

The Pug is a lap dog and demands a lot of attention and love. During his old age he will need your companionship and love more than ever before. Don't turn your back on him.

Just one last bit of advice, and the most difficult. You must never let your old boy or girl be in pain. If there is no hope for recovery, you must speak to your veterinarian and put the little fellow or gal to rest.

Pug Teeth

Many breeders and owners do not realize how important the Pug's teeth and bite are. The Pug is a slightly undershot dog. If they do not have a proper bite they cannot digest their food properly, and this can impede the Pug's weight and growth. The average Pug puppy has twenty-eight baby teeth. They first appear between four and five weeks. Pug puppies start to acquire their permanent teeth at about four to five months of age. They also start to fly their ears at this time. Between three and six months of age you must check the puppy's teeth to make sure that he has not retained his baby teeth as the adult teeth come in. You may have to have any baby teeth removed by your veterinarian if they are still present. This is quite common in Pugs.

The normal number of adult teeth is forty-two. Due to the fact that the Pug is a short-faced breed, they sometimes have fewer teeth.

Most bad bites are inherited, and the wry mouth is the worst. This occurs as a result of one side of the jaw growing faster than the other. It gives a twisted appearance, and it is difficult for the Pug to eat. A Pug with a wry mouth should never be used for breeding.

Periodontal disease is also common in Pugs. Food is trapped in the pockets along the sides of the teeth and the gums start to recede. You may see some pus come out of the gums when you press on the sides of them. If this problem appears, take your Pug to your veterinarian so he or she can give you the proper oral antibiotic.

Pugs are also prone to tumors in their mouth. Better than 50 percent are malignant cancers. If you see any bleeding in your Pug's mouth, rush him to your veterinarian.

Make sure your Pug is fed milk bones and large knuckle bones, which

I find are the best; these all help to keep teeth clean and are excellent as teething pacifiers. Try to keep the tartar from building up on his teeth. If you cannot do it have your veterinarian remove it for you at least once a year. Don't forget to brush your Pug's teeth. Purchase a C.E.T. toothbrush and Novaldent toothpaste from your veterinarian or an Oral B-20 soft children's toothbrush. Brushing twice a week will be a great help in keeping your Pug's gums and teeth healthy and clean. Oral hygiene is important to health and condition.

Int./Am./Braz. Ch. Shirrayne's Golddigger with handler Jayme Martinilli; owner, Tracy Williams. "Diggy" was in the top ten for 1975, and in four months of showing in Brazil won four Bests in Show and six Group firsts. His American record stands at thirty-four Bests of Breed, one Group first, nine Group thirds and four Group fourths. At the Pug Dog Club of America on September 13, 1974, "Diggy" went Best of Winners and Best Junior Puppy. Breeder: Shirrayne Kennels.

12

Breeding, Motherhood and Whelping a Pug

As A NOVICE you should remember that it is very important that you start with the best Pug bitch you can obtain that is true breed type, being from a line of sound stock. Remember she will not be without faults. Your aim will be to correct these deficiencies in her progeny, and to accomplish this you must also know the characteristics of her sire, dam and ancestors.

To do all this, learn the breed standard and apply the standard to the bitch. Attend many dog shows and discuss the dogs' and bitches' good points with the breeders. It is also important to watch the judging and form your own conclusion as to the merits of the competing dogs and bitches. Most Pug breeders are eager to help the novice with sound advice, as you try to develop an eye for a dog. However, what you learn at shows is not always gospel. You must be able to distinguish between opinion and faults. Many successful breeders have years of experience in their breed, and these are the people you should seek out.

If you are devoted to the Pug, you should aim to improve on the stock you begin with—to produce puppies that are better than their parents. To do this, you must be able to choose a stud dog who will correct the faults of the female's line and yet retain the virtues she already has. You must plan each step thoughtfully and work your breeding program out on paper for at least ten years ahead. Any improvement in the breed will continue on into future generations.

When choosing a stud dog for your bitch, you must find the proper match. The dog that is the latest champion or the biggest Best in Show winner or the dog next door may or may not be the right stud dog for your bitch.

The study of genetics—the laws and principles of heredity—govern the inheritance of every characteristic: coat color, eye color, length of leg, nose, black mask, trace, tail, body, wry mouth and so on.

Check out the potential stud dog's pedigree. Speak or write to the owner of the stud dog and ask what the dog's dominant and recessive genes are and what characteristics show up in his puppies—both the desirable and undesirable points. Also check the family tree from which he is derived and go as far back as possible in his ancestral line. There is a constant struggle to consolidate good points and eradicate bad ones.

Much can be learned by reading books, including a study of club yearbooks and show catalogs. Heredity affects not only structural and other physical characteristics, but also such things as temperament and even behavior patterns. However, in considering any proposed mating one should remember that the sex of a parent does not decide the strength of the hereditary effect he or she will have on any offspring. This will be determined by ancestry, by what genes the parents themselves inherited.

Linebreeding

In my opinion the best method of breeding is linebreeding, which usually results in uniform litters. There is far less risk attached to it than other methods, but it takes a little longer to establish a pure strain. Linebreeding includes the following crosses: grandfather to granddaughter, grandmother to grandson, cousin to cousin, uncle to niece or aunt to nephew.

A pedigree can help us to learn from which of the dog's parents he derived his merits or his faults. In choosing a mate for her or for him, one seeks to reinforce the merits and to avoid the faults. Let us assume that one of the dog's grandmothers was straight in shoulder instead of having a correct forty-five-degree angle, which forms the proper layback. We would avoid breeding this dog to a bitch with a tendency to straight shoulders or one whose dam, sire, grandfather or grandmother had straight shoulders. The same principle would apply to a dog carrying a light eye, bad bite, cowhocks, bad topline, wry mouth, color or any other inherited fault. On the other hand, if the dog has good shoulders and straight front legs, and his parents and all his grandparents have nice shoulders and straight front legs, but the bitch or some of her ancestors have poor shoulders and bowed front legs, then one *would* breed this bitch to the dog and hope that the good shoulders and straight front legs inherited from his ancestors will correct her fault.

For another example in planning your breeding, you will hear it said that if a bitch is high on leg, she should be bred to a dog low on leg. This is entirely wrong. You will be breeding one fault to another. Some of the puppies will be too high on leg or some too short. Out of this breeding you may have a puppy with the correct length of leg, and this puppy would carry both his parents'

Ch. Shirrayne's Pert Prima Donna,
owned by Dan and Ann Fischetti

Ch. Gramigna's Samson, owned by Nell Gramigna, shown in a win under the author

Ch. Scullin's Saucy Samson, multiple BIS and Specialty winner, owned by Blanche Roberts

faults to his progeny. Such a bitch should be bred to a dog with the proper length of leg, making sure he is reproducing his own correct type.

There are hereditary malformations that can make a dog a cripple. Patella luxation, often called "slipping stifle," is common among Pugs. This is a defect in the knee joint of the back legs. You should avoid breeding a dog or bitch that has luxation. The same goes for a wry mouth. As a breeder you will obviously want to avoid such things in your line. You can only hope to correct one problem at a time. It is impossible to correct head, front, rear and topline all in one breeding. Select your puppies carefully. If you are breeding for good shoulders, make sure that you keep the one with the best shoulders. Continue to breed the future progeny to good shoulders so that this becomes a dominant gene in your line. Once this gene is dominant in your line, then you can go on to correct the topline, head, hindquarters or whatever you need to reproduce better type.

Inbreeding

Inbreeding is the mating of close Pug relatives, such as father to daughter, mother to son, half-brother to half-sister or the closest inbreeding of all—sister to brother. Inbreeding concentrates both good features and faults. This should only be attempted by extremely knowledgeable Pug breeders who want to establish some particular attribute in their line. Inbreeding has great dangers. All the good points are doubled through such matings, and all the bad points may be so strongly established in a line that it may make it impossible to breed them out.

Selection of the stud and bitch is always important, regardless of which breeding procedure is used, but when inbreeding it becomes imperative! It should only be tried when the Pugs used are outstanding in quality—and outstanding dogs and bitches are few and far between in any breed.

Some breeders advocate brother-to-sister inbreeding for five or six generations to establish "genetic purity" in breeding stock. Some geneticists say that such close matings for a number of generations will eventually produce Pugs that would breed true for most of the qualities desired. Rigid culling must be done, and only the best progeny retained for further breeding. Close breeding such as this may be responsible for infertility, monorchidism and crytorchidism, and you can expect a decrease in the size and vigor of the offspring. Many breeders who experiment with inbreeding, invariably do it with the larger breeds who are more prolific than Pugs. Large litters permit more of a selection and more room for expression of inherited traits passed from sire and dam.

After five or six generations of inbreeding, the next mating should be an outcross to gain what is known as "hybrid vigor" and counteract infertility and size problems. At this point it would appear that the Pug breeder would be back where he started, with an outcross. Some genetic experiments with other animals have shown that when two intensely inbred lines of consecutive brother-and-sister-matings are crossed, the resultant progeny are larger than the original heterozygous stock and possess hybrid vigor. Heterozygous is a hybrid containing genes for two unlike characteristics; it is an organism that will not breed true to type.

Has such a concentrated inbreeding been attempted successfully in Pugs? As far as I know, it has never been tried. The time and money required to keep two or more lines progressing by direct brother-and-sister inbreeding, to cull and destroy Pugs and keep only the best pair as breeding partners to accomplish such a program of inbreeding is much too costly, therefore unsuitable for most breeders. With Pugs certain lines may reveal organic weaknesses that result in decreased vitality, abnormalities both physical and mental or lethal or crippling factors that would terminate such a program before completion.

It is essential that as a Pug breeder you have a complete understanding of the merits of inbreeding and have the ability to be entirely objective in evaluating your Pugs. *Inbreeding is not for the novice breeder.* You must remember that Pugs were inbred to start with, so take the time to examine the pedigrees of dogs bred in the early days; you should only inbreed when you have a great deal of knowledge about the Pug ancestors of the breeding partners.

Another type of inbreeding is backcrossing. This involves finding a superior male Pug who excels in the breed type that we want to perpetuate and reproduce. You should breed this male to the best Pug bitch you can find. Select the best Pug puppy bitch who is similar to her sire's type, and breed her back to her sire. Continue to breed the best Pug puppy bitch out of each litter back to her sire as long as the male can reproduce, or until you lose some soundness. You must continue to make sure that you carefully select the best bitch puppy out of each litter.

This method of breeding is useful to the knowledgeable breeder who wishes to ascertain the breeding worth of an outstanding stud dog. This will enable the breeder to identify some of the genes carried by this particular stud dog. If this outstanding male seems to have acquired his excellent traits through the genetic influences of his mother, the first breeding made could possibly be the breeding of son to mother, and then breed the best bitch puppy back to her sire.

We must remember that inbreeding does not correct faults. It only makes them recognizable so they can be eliminated.

Outcrossing

Outcrossing is the breeding of a Pug bitch to a Pug dog that is completely outside the partner's lines, with no common ancestors. To outcross completely it would be necessary to use a dog of another breed as one of the breeding partners—this is called complete heterozygosity.

Outcrossing is generally considered to be the breeding of Pugs that have no common ancestor within five or six generations. This procedure is used in connection with linebreeding or inbreeding. In order to have some control over the progeny of an outcross mating, the Pug must immediately return to his own line after using the outcross.

Outcrossing will bring in a completely new genetic pattern, and will bring in new faults as well as new virtues. It can be as dangerous as inbreeding for the novice Pug breeder to try.

For the knowledgeable Pug breeder who has been linebreeding for several generations and wishes to correct a fault that has been recurring in his lines, an outcross can be successful. Outcrossing generally produces an uneven litter, however. Unless you have a definite purpose, I do not recommend it. You may not see any results in the first generation and the good points that are required may not become apparent until the second generation, in the grandchildren. Remember when you use an outcross mating the stud should show, in himself and his progeny when bred to other bitches, that he is *dominant* in the needed virtues you wish to incorporate into your line—this is the reason for the outcross.

An outcross will also bring new and needed characteristics into your line. By carefully choosing a stud of similar type you can also achieve better uniformity in an outcross breeding. This method of breeding has produced some excellent Pugs, but it also tends to conceal recessive genes carrying faults as well as virtues.

The stud dog chosen for the outcross must be without the fault you plan to correct and you must be careful not to introduce too many undesirable genes. The ideal Pug to use can be found in a distantly related strain that has good common ancestors.

I have found that by keeping four or five separate but related lines going in my breeding program I have sufficient outcrossings available without going too much outside of my line and I do not have to introduce too varied a genetic pattern. I also like to outcross approximately every five or six years to bring another new line into my breeding program and to correct any fault that has occurred. But the Pug bitch must be an excellent specimen. Just using a good brood bitch, lacking in serious faults and one without outstanding virtues, will only reproduce a line of average Pugs, never one that is outstanding.

It is important to remember that when you outcross, it is for the purpose of utilizing the outcross progeny for further breeding. This should only be done by a knowledgeable Pug breeder who has a large breeding kennel. It must be dealt with skillfully because it can introduce faults that will take a long time to breed out.

From the results of an outcross mating I immediately return to my own lines, breeding the best puppy from the outcross litter back into my strongest strain. This litter will not be sold for six months so I can watch their progress, and I keep the best dog and bitch to further my breeding program. Remember, outcrossing will result in wide variations of type even within a single litter, and they may transmit their own characteristics through their progeny. The more you outcross the less you will be able to recognize your line and you will be relying on a bit of luck. Outcrossing is not for the novice breeder.

It is quite difficult for the novice Pug breeder to obtain the sort of knowledge he needs. If advised by a breeder who is not objective, the novice will gain a very distorted view of different lines. All bloodlines have some virtues and some faults. It is altogether too easy to run into the Pug breeder who has bred two or three litters and "knows all the answers" better than the experienced breeder with many years of knowledge. There are also those who are "kennel blind," or incapable of making a correct evaluation of their own Pugs even though they may have many years of experience.

The novice breeder who is trying to learn should go to as many shows as he can, and look as well as listen, being very critical in their appraisal of the Pugs. Read as much as possible on the Pug breed and start your breeding program by only linebreeding with the best possible Pug bitch that you can obtain. She will be the foundation of your line. The novice breeder who is fortunate enough to have obtained advice and all sorts of information on bloodlines, ancestors, virtues and faults from a knowledgeable, objective and experienced Pug breeder will do well with linebreeding. But he must be able to apply the knowledge of the standard and pedigree and be very selective in choosing his puppies for breeding stock. It will take many generations to approach his goal.

Inbreeding should be tried at least once by the knowledgeable Pug breeder, so he can ascertain the breeding worth of his lines and make his faults recognizable so they can be eliminated.

Remember: *Outcrossing should only be done by the knowledgeable Pug breeder who wishes to correct a fault in his line.*

Have patience. No one has bred a perfect Pug—but we can all try. We must all work together to preserve true Pug type—*multum in parvo* (much in little).

Breeding Black Pugs

Never breed black Pugs to fawns. Nothing is ever accomplished from these breedings. Crossing colors will not improve the pigment of a fawn, head or substance on black dogs or coat and color on either.

The color genes behind fawn and black Pugs are blue, black, liver, yellow, brown, white, silver fawn, tan and apricot-fawn. Quite a combination, isn't it? Everyone considering breeding Pugs should study the basic coat color genes in dogs to learn how indiscriminate breeding can destroy the color genes in Pugs. Improper breeding has just about wiped out our silvers: which color is next?

It is not the intention of this book to go into an elaborate discussion of all these genes or all the symbols that will come into play. A couple of examples to illustrate my point are below. In Pugs the following color genes are present;

$$A_s \quad B \quad C \quad D \quad E^m \quad g \quad m \quad S \quad t$$
$$a^y \quad b \quad c^{ch} \quad Bb$$

Black Pugs are solid-colored dogs, but they are carry SS, which is the white gene. The B gene produces black coat color. Its alternative and recessive form b produces liver and brown. The silver-fawn, on the other hand, shows a dullness and paling of the nonblack and does not carry the black gene. They carry the c^{ch}, which is of chinchilla animal's pigment. The apricot-fawns are in the group a^y and also carry the black gene E^m, and they are fully pigmented by the C gene. Black Pugs also carry the Bb gene, which is also a diluted black gene that produces blue. Fawn Pugs also carry the SS white gene.

We know that there were chestnut and white, black and white, all white and blue Pugs imported into America from England and China. In 1905 interbreeding took place between black and fawn Pugs and whatever else the English threw in back then. The Chinese were known for the array of colors, and bred for the white markings on the Pugs.

If you breed your fawn to black you can luck out and have two clear black puppies, but what about the rest of the litter? Would you just sell them off to someone for a pet? Or—heaven forbid—use the dye bottle on the Pugs and then hide them after you are through showing them. Breeding them will certainly make things even worse. Over the last thirty years I have seen Zebra striped puppies out of a fawn to black cross. While judging out West I excused a Pug for improper coat color. I did not know what color it was. It was half black and half fawn with a brown mask and ears and a white chest with white feet. Is this what we want our Pugs to look like?

I have seen Pugs that were black and white, all brown and even two blues out of black-to-black breeding. In England, from a fawn-to-fawn breeding black Pugs were produced. I have also heard of three different fawn-to-fawn breedings in the last five years that reproduced blacks. Over the years I have seen fawns with white legs and white blazes on their chest. I have seen fawns with black heads, legs and white around the anus. I have seen a totally white Pug out of two fawns.

Is this why people are breeding blacks to fawns? These crosses obviously will not improve the quality of blacks, but will reduce the strength of both black and fawn lines. Coat and pigment color will also be diluted, or smutty Pugs will result. By breeding a fawn Pug to a black dog you will see a washed-out coat that is extremely light, white toenails and a mask that will not be as black as you would like—that is, if you have a clean coat. Most of the time the coats will be smutty, and the blacks will have fawn or rusty hairs running through theirs.

A Pug should be doubled-coated, but we are seeing too many Pugs with single coats. This is due to black and fawn crosses. Most black Pugs are single-coated—blacks have fewer hair follicles to the inch than fawns—and due to these crosses we are starting to see fawns with single coats. Should we accept a single-coated dog? No, we must still try to maintain our beautiful double coats.

What happens on an outcross? It is like playing Russian roulette. Don't people realize that when they interbreed black and fawn Pugs it is the same as an outcross? Remember, outcrossing will result in wide variations of type even within a single litter, and they may not transmit their own characteristics through their progeny. So what has been accomplished by the fawn-to-black breeding? Nothing at all.

A breeder develops a pure, sound black line by breeding black to black.

If you must cross a black to a fawn, only make your cross to the black once in every five generations. You must breed the black puppies on the outcross to black for five more generations and do the same with your fawns from the outcross. Our best black Pugs over the years came out of black-to-black breedings.

I love a beautiful black Pug. We must all work together to protect the quality of our fawns and keep on improving our blacks.

Motherhood

Now that you have a Pug bitch, the idea of breeding her comes to mind. You may think this is a good way to make money (it's not), for your children to learn about sex, or it might be you would like to get into showing or breeding. Whatever the reason, you must be aware of certain things.

You must be prepared to give up eight weeks of your time to be with the puppies constantly. Pugs are not like other breeds of dogs. You must never leave them alone because a Pug cannot whelp without help.

It is also costly to breed Pugs. The stud fee usually starts at $250 and up. What if you need a caesarean section? It can run anywhere from $250 to as much as $600 in some areas. This is only the beginning of the cost. You will have advertising, food and shots. What about the time off from work? It could run as much as $2,500 to have one litter of Pugs.

Your Pug bitch should be carefully checked by your veterinarian for breathing disorders, patella luxation, internal parasites, hip dysplasia, skin diseases and to make sure her vaginal orifice is the correct size. Most important, check her for canine brucellosis. The bitch should have her booster shots for distemper and hepatitis and whatever else she may need. I for one will not breed a bitch until the owner brings me the above checklist okayed by the veterinarian *in writing*.

Another factor to consider is the quality of the bitch. You must consider conformation, disposition and what qualities she will pass along to her puppies. The Pug bitch should never be mated before her third season. Only then is she mature physically and emotionally.

Your bitch's diet plays an important role in the development of her puppies. You are dealing with a Toy dog. A diet of meat, fish, chicken, liver, carbohydrates and fats is essential. She should receive a well-balanced diet from the day she is born. After she has been bred, the pregnancy diet consists of ¼ pound meat, one carrot or other vegetables, ¼ cup rice and ½ cup kibble, which is similar to a crumbled dog biscuit. Add a slice of liver to her food twice a week. She should receive the following vitamins in her morning meal: ½ teaspoon cod liver oil, ⅛ teaspoon wheat germ oil, one half dropper of Poly-Vi-Sol baby drops and one 250 milligram tablet of dicalcium phosphate, and vitamins C and E are important. You should mix 1 teaspoon of cooking oil into her food, occasionally include some cottage cheese plus one egg yolk in her diet. Feed her twice a day, and *never* feed cold food.

Breeding a Pug bitch should be taken seriously. You must plan your

204

breeding program. The bitch normally comes into season every six months, except for a few who come in once a year. You can plan your bitch's first breeding around eighteen months of age, which should be her third season. The heat season normally lasts twenty-one days. This is called the "estrus cycle." The normal breeding pattern is to breed once and then skip the next season. It takes a year for your Pug to build back her strength so that she can produce quality puppies once more.

Before you breed your bitch, she should be well muscled up. You do not want her fat or she will have trouble delivering her puppies. Keep your Pug bitch in top condition at all times. Sunshine, fresh air and taking her for long walks twice a day would be a tremendous help.

You have spent several months or longer checking pedigrees and searching for the right stud dog within your lines to complement your bitch. It isn't easy to do. As you know, the male determines the sex of the puppies; the bitch determines the amount of puppies she will produce. When your bitch is due to come into her third season, watch her carefully. You will notice that her vagina will look a little puffy, and within a few days you will see a dark bloody discharge. This is the time that you should notify the owner of the stud dog. Make sure you mark the date on your calendar. If you are traveling a long distance, I suggest that you bring your bitch to the owner of the stud a few days early. This gives your bitch enough time to adjust and settle down after her trip. This will also save you a wasted trip because you will not miss her ovulation. On the ninth day, when she ovulates, her color will change to pink. The appropriate breeding cycle is between the tenth and the fifteenth day of her season. I have successfully bred a bitch on her third day and one on her seventeenth day, but this is rare. I prefer to breed my bitches only once, either on the tenth or the eleventh day. This lets me know more accurately when they are due. If someone wants two breedings, it is no problem. The breedings should be made within a forty-eight-hour period. Make sure you always witness the mating. Once in a while you can run across an unethical breeder who will try to switch the stud dogs.

A bitch may have what is called a silent heat, which is not noticed because only the swelling of the vulva will occur; you may not pick up any staining. Some bitches can be in and out of season in a few days or they lick themselves clean. If this condition occurs, have your veterinarian check your bitch for a thyroid problem.

The best place to breed a Pug is on a table, although you may find a few studs that will work only on the floor. Make sure you place a piece of carpet under them for good footing. If you have a big bitch, place a large book under the carpet to raise the stud higher so he can reach the bitch. You must have two people or possibly three if the stud is a virgin. Send everyone out of the room so as not to distract the stud. Place the Pug bitch on the table, then, using a lubricated surgical glove, examine inside the vulva to see if she is open enough for the stud to penetrate. You may have to break the membrane. Don't be alarmed if she cries out. This is normal.

When the bitch is ready to receive the stud, she will flag her tail to one side. Secure the lead in one hand and hold both of her front legs. You must hold the bitch tightly. Occasionally a few may try to turn and bite the stud dog. The owner of the stud will support the bitch with his left hand under her pelvis between her legs, lifting the vulva. Sometimes you may have to help the male by holding his penis near the back of the shaft and guide him in. You have to be careful that you do not get the virgin stud too excited while helping him. This is where you may need the third hand to help to hold the virgin stud on top of the bitch so you can guide him in.

When the stud penetrates the bitch, he will grasp her with his two front legs around the loin. When the bulbus gland swells and is held by the vulva it produces a tie. They cannot be separated at this point. I do not let my males turn until they have been tied for about ten minutes. When they turn, they will be facing tail to tail. They can stay tied for over thirty minutes. Bitches may cry during the tie, but you must be careful that they don't try to struggle or pull away. This can injure the stud dog. If you have a prolonged tie, turn the male back on top of the bitch and push on his rump. This will release the vaginal ring so that the dog can slide out. Never try pulling them apart. Once the mating is complete, check the stud dog to be sure that the penis has returned inside the sheath.

After your Pug bitch has been bred, call your veterinarian and give him the due date so he or she can be on call if needed. It is not uncommon for a Pug bitch to whelp as early as the fifty-seventh day, but gestation is normally sixty-three days.

I have had bitches that suffered from morning sickness around the third week. They appeared depressed and would vomit, and some would refuse their food and be picky. My veterinarian suggested giving vitamin B and C and small amounts of food four or five times a day, as the upset is due to hormonal changes.

At four weeks the fetus grows rapidly. This is when I start to boost the bitch's food intake by feeding her three times a day. Some breeds start to show they are in whelp at four weeks after breeding, but because of the large rib cage of the Pug they do not usually show until the fifth or sixth week.

Make sure your bitch is getting enough exercise.

By the end of the sixth week the bitch's food consumption should have doubled. This is when I double her calcium phosphate and cod-liver oil and start her on a piece of liver—a good source of vitamin K—every day. The liver helps prevent the placentas from breaking away from the puppies too early and helps avoid internal hemorrhaging during whelping or just after; a lack of vitamin K in the bitch causes puppies at three or four days old to have a tendency to bleed because the blood is not clotting properly. Some symptoms to watch for are a minor trauma or bleeding from the body openings.

Between five and six weeks the bitch's nipples start to get dark and her breasts start to enlarge. Sometimes when a Pug has only one or two puppies you may notice that the nipples may be only a shade darker in color but her appetite will increase. One clue that might help you to know if your bitch is in whelp is to check her vulva and see if it stays swollen.

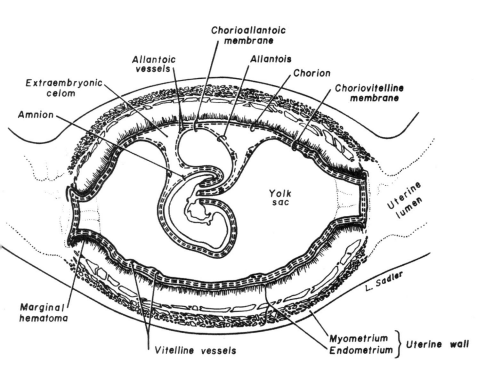

Schematic longitudinal section of uterus with early limb-bud dog embryo, 5mm, 23 days

I have had some bitches who would continue to eat right up until the time they started to whelp their puppies, while others would lose their appetite a week before they whelped. Most of my bitches will not touch any food the night before they whelp. If she is having a large litter, you may have to feed her four small meals a day. This is because the puppies are crowding her abdomen.

Contact your veterinarian at the end of six weeks to let him know your bitch is in whelp, so he can make arrangements to be on hand if you need him. In the meantime, try to discourage your bitch from jumping up on the bed or chair or going up or down stairs. Pick her up by putting your arm through her back legs under her belly to support her. Do not pick her up by her front legs. During the last two or three weeks make sure you take her out for her daily walks, as this will help to make her delivery easier.

There are some important rules to follow after your Pug bitch has been bred concerning when to and when not to take her to visit the veterinarian. The first rule of thumb is not to go around running to different veterinarians to find out if your bitch is in whelp. Doing this will expose your Pug bitch to diseases or infections and put her puppies in danger. Very few veterinarians can tell you if your Pug bitch is in whelp until the fifth or sixth week of her pregnancy because Pug bitches carry their puppies well up into the rib cage.

You should only have an X-ray if necessary, as this can damage the puppies. Sometimes the X-ray will not show anything anyway. I remember when my Ch. Greentubs Busy Bee was overdue and showed no normal signs of labor. I had a feeling that she had one puppy. I took her to my veterinarian and he X-rayed her. He told me she did not have any puppies. I still wanted him to do a caesarean section on her, but he would not. He told me to take her home. One week after I returned her to the kennel she whelped one puppy.

If you notice a purplish discharge a few weeks before the puppies are due to be born, your Pug bitch may be starting to abort her puppies. Call your veterinarian immediately.

If, several weeks before she is due to whelp, you see spots of blood, this may indicate that your bitch is starting to have a miscarriage. Confine your bitch to a crate to keep her quiet and call your veterinarian at once.

Do not give any drugs to your bitch during her pregnancy. You must check with your veterinarian before giving any medication.

Whelping Your Pug

After your Pug bitch has been bred, you should be prepared to make a whelping box. The ideal material to use is formica, which is easy to keep clean. The box for the Pug bitch should be 36 inches long, 24 inches wide and 23½ inches high. Layers of newspaper on the floor of the whelping box make excellent bedding for the puppies. A heated dog waterbed is also available from Between the Sheets, Box 1086, Addison, Ill. 60101. The following sizes are available: Small—20 × 24 inches, Medium—24 × 32 inches, Large—32 × 44 inches.

Throughout her pregnancy, place her in the whelping box for a few minutes each day. Otherwise your Pug may want to have her puppies in your bed. Two weeks before my bitches whelp I put them into the whelping box to sleep. From the fifty-sixth day I keep them in the whelping box. I will only take them out for their walks and to do their chores. I also feed them in the whelping box. By doing this I never have a problem with my bitches staying or taking care of their puppies. The best place for her whelping box is next to your bed, draftfree and warm.

The whelping accessories that you must have are:

1. A towel-covered heating pad, hot water bottle or heating lamp, to keep the puppies warm.
2. Blunt scissors, placed in a bottle of alcohol, to cut the umbilical cord.
3. Clean laundered towels or worn washcloths, to dry the puppies.
4. A baby bulb syringe, to aspirate the substance from the puppies' noses or mouths.
5. Forceps, to clamp the umbilical cord.
6. Plenty of newspaper and paper towels, to remove afterbirth and for use in the whelping box.
7. Vaseline, to help deliver the puppies.
8. Rubber gloves and finger-cots, to help deliver the puppies.
9. Cotton balls or large sterile gauze pads, to clean the puppies.
10. Baby oil, to clean the puppies.
11. Rectal thermometer, to check the bitch's temperature.
12. Oxytocin, obtained from your veterinarian, for delivery of the puppies.
13. Kwick-stop or styptic powder, to stop bleeding.
14. Carpet, blanket or doggie waterbed, to put the puppies and mother on after she is finished whelping.

Make sure you have everything in the house before the fifty-sixth day. *Do not leave your bitch alone for one second.* Make sure that someone is home with her at all times. *Your Pug cannot open the membrane around the fetus or sever the umbilical cord on the puppy.* The amniotic sac must be removed within thirty seconds of birth to allow the puppy to breathe. Over the years I have whelped over sixty litters of Pug puppies and I have never seen a Pug bitch open an amniotic sac.

As your Pug bitch approaches the end of her pregnancy, the puppies will drop down into the birth canal. You will be able to see the puppies kicking. Her stomach may also drag the floor. If your Pug bitch has only one puppy, you may not be able to see anything at all until she is ready to deliver. What you should do is take the bitch's temperature every morning and night beginning seven days before she is due to whelp. Her normal temperature runs between 101 and 102 degrees. You will notice that her temperature will fluctuate eight to twelve hours before she is due to deliver. Her rectal temperature will drop to 99 degrees, and I even had some go as low as 96 degrees. This is usually a pretty good sign that she is getting ready to whelp her puppies.

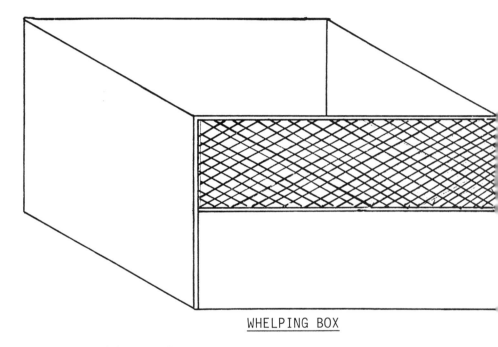

WHELPING BOX

A three-part diagrammatic representation of a practical whelping box

" PLYWOOD 4' X 6' FINISHED BOTH SIDES — CUT AS BELOW
IECE CORNER MOLDING 4'
ALUMINUM STORM WINDOW MOLDING
ORNER CONNECTORS — 1 PIECE STRETCHED METAL 3' X 1'
XY GLUE FOR ALL JOINTS
" FINISHING NAILS — EPOXY PAINT — POUR LEFTOVER PAINT ON FLOOR AND SPREAD.

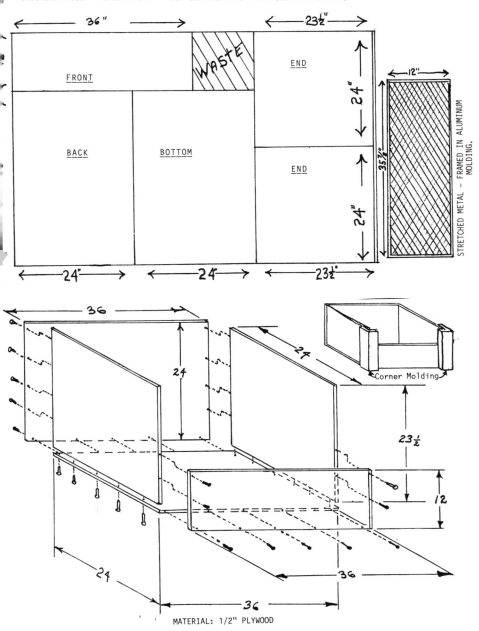

MATERIAL: 1/2" PLYWOOD

On the other hand, I have had a few bitches hold their temperature right up to the time they started to whelp and then it would drop down to 99 degrees. So you can't always count on this.

When the first stage of labor starts, your Pug bitch will tear up paper to make a nest. Some may refuse food and become restless. Others may vomit, which is a normal reflex. I have had some Pug bitches who would quiet down and sleep for hours. You can see the facial expressions change when they go into labor. Your bitch will begin rapid panting. You may see the bitch reach her head up in the air and look like she is stretching her neck. When she starts to strain, you can watch the contractions. She may lie on her side in the whelping box and push her feet against the wall of the box. Occasionally a Pug bitch will not show any of the above signs and just stand up, circle around and deliver a puppy.

A definite sign of labor is when the bitch shows a clear or slightly colored discharge. If your Pug bitch is in labor for over three hours and no puppies arrive, call your veterinarian. If you cannot reach your veterinarian, put on a sterile rubber glove or finger-cot and lubricate your finger with Vaseline. Now stand your bitch up, using your left hand so you do not contaminate your glove, and insert your finger inside the vagina to see if she has dilated at least two fingers or better. Also try to feel for a puppy. It may be breech or lying sideways. Stimulate the bitch by palpating her a few times. This often helps to get them going.

The first thing you should see is the waterbag around the puppy bulging through the vulva. This helps to lubricate the passageway. If it breaks, a straw-colored fluid is passed. Then you should see the puppy's head in a few minutes. The bitch will have another contraction and the rest of the puppy will slide out. Immediately grab the puppy, in a towel, and take your fingers and tear the fetal membranes as quickly as possible. Remember, you only have thirty seconds to get the puppy breathing. Wipe the puppy's mouth and face right away. Grab the bulb syringe and aspirate the fluids from the mouth and nose of the puppy. Rub the puppy vigorously in the towel until it cries. You may also have to hold the puppy in both hands, support its head, then swing the whole puppy in a wide arc from about your shoulder level to about your knee level, stopping abruptly. At the end of the swing the puppy's nose should point toward the ground. This also gets rid of the fluids in the puppy's mouth and prevents them from entering the lungs. Cut the umbilical cord with the scissors one inch from the navel and squeeze it hard for a minute. Make sure you have the puppy breathing before you cut the cord. Throw the placenta away and continue to dry the puppy, then place the puppy on the covered heating pad next to its mother's breast to nurse. Make sure you write down the time and sex, and note whether or not you had a placenta. It is a good idea to weigh the puppy if you have a scale and include the weight on your birth record. This is a nice normal birth.

You can always use forceps to clamp the umbilical cord before you cut it. Some even tie the cord with silk thread. I feel this takes too much time. Others use a scissors to cut the fetal membranes around the puppy. I personally find it faster to tear it open with my fingers. You may cut the puppy if you are not extremely careful.

The temperature in the room must be 80 degrees. Keep your heating pad on 85 degrees. I use two heating pads—one in the whelping box and one in a small separate box. When the bitch gets ready to have the next puppy, I have a warm place to move the first puppy. Make sure you cover part of the box so the puppy gets no drafts.

While you are waiting for the next puppy, check the first puppy for deformities. The first thing to look for is the cleft palate. Open the puppy's mouth and look at the roof of the mouth. If you see an opening from the oral to the nasal cavity, the puppy cannot nurse. A cleft palate may look like a thin opening running from the back of the puppy's throat to his nose in the roof of his mouth. You must tube feed the puppy to keep him alive (have your veterinarian show you how to tube feed). Check and see if the puppy has all his toes and that he is formed properly.

Breech Presentation

I have had more breech presentations in the delivery of Pug puppies than anything else. By this we mean the rump and hind feet are delivered first. If a Pug puppy is still in the fetal membrane or sac the delivery will not be difficult. If the sac ruptures you have thirty seconds to get the Pug puppy out, so you have to work fast.

Put on a sterile glove and lubricate your finger with Vaseline. Put your left hand under the abdomen and feel the puppy. Raise the puppy up and try to align it with the birth canal. Then enter the vagina with your finger, try to hook and ease out one leg and then the other and work the puppy down over the narrow area in the pelvis until the legs appear at the vulva. As the puppy reaches the lower part of the birth canal, gently stretch the vaginal opening to stimulate a push by the mother. I have found that a washcloth or paper towel works better than a big towel when you try to get a Pug puppy out. They won't slip from your hand.

You have another breech and the sac is broken because you can see the rear foot sticking out of the sac. Take your lubricated finger and go around the Pug puppy while you are easing one foot out at a time. Try to grab the puppy's body with a washcloth or paper towel and get it out fast so you can get the puppy breathing. Don't forget to cut the umbilical cord.

Usually when you have a big Pug puppy, the sac will break and the puppy will get stuck in the birth canal. So again take your gloved finger, make sure you put a lot of Vaseline on it, go into the vagina and feel for the head, tail or leg. If the head will not pass through the pelvis, try to insert your finger into the puppy's mouth and carefully try to turn the puppy's head and guide it into the birth canal.

Sometimes you will see a Pug puppy appear then slip back inside the bitch when she relaxes. As the puppy appears, apply pressure just below the bitch's anus and push down to keep the puppy from slipping back into the bitch. Slip the lip of the vulva over the Pug puppy's head. Get a grip on the puppy, with a washcloth or paper towel, behind his neck or back and draw him out carefully. Do not use force or put pressure on his head and legs; you can injure the puppy. Rotating the puppy helps make it easier to get him out. Don't forget to cut the cord and keep track of the placentas. You may have to squeeze the puppy's chest gently from side to side and then from front to back to get the puppy breathing. Sometimes I place my mouth over the puppy's mouth and breathe out carefully until I see its chest expand and let the puppy exhale. I will continue this until the puppy starts to breathe.

If you cannot reach your veterinarian, the puppy must come out. You may have to dislocate a puppy's shoulders to free him; you may also have to use instruments to reach him. But I must caution you to be very careful, because if you do not know what you are doing, you can rupture the uterus. Your bitch is more important than the puppy. Do not try any of these procedures unless you have been checked out by your veterinarian.

Normally you have an afterbirth with each puppy. But if the afterbirth breaks away from the puppy and remains in the bitch, it can slow down the delivery of the next puppy. If this happens, try to hook the placenta with your finger and grab it with some sterile gauze. Pull gently until you get it out of the vagina. Sometimes when I cannot reach the afterbirth I will give the bitch ½ cc of oxytocin into the muscle of the rear leg.

I keep oxytocin on hand because labor can stop. If the bitch has not delivered a puppy after one hour, I will stimulate her. If that does not get her going I will give her a shot of oxytocin. Sometimes labor stops due to emotional upset. This is called "uterine inertia," which is a deficiency of oxytocin or calcium or both. If there is a blockage and you give a shot of oxytocin, you can rupture the uterus. So only use oxytocin if instructed by your vet. You must never use it until after the first puppy is born unless advised to by your vet.

When to Call Your Veterinarian

Prolonged Labor: Never let your Pug bitch be in labor for over two hours between puppies. Puppies should be born about fifteen minutes apart and not longer than two hours apart. Call your vet.

Prolongation of Labor: This is called dystocia, which is due to the birth canal being too narrow. Sometimes the uterus doesn't have enough strength to deliver a puppy. If you see your Pug bitch doing a lot of straining after she is in labor, call your vet. This could mean that there is a Pug puppy partly in the birth canal. A normal delivery may not be possible.

If your Pug bitch has passed some dark green fluid before she has delivered the first puppy, this tells us that the placenta has broken away and the puppy has not been getting any oxygen from its mother. Call your vet.

When your Pug bitch starts to whelp, occasionally what you will see is a waterbag. This is very thin and small and you can feel the water in it. *Do not break this water bag.* What you might be seeing is a prolapsed vagina or even a prolapsed uterus. The uterus is thick and slightly red in color. This waterbag is the size of a small egg, and it normally breaks before you see it, lubricating the passage for the puppy. But once in a while this little water bag will pop out. Just wait. If you are not sure call your veterinarian. Do not call another Pug breeder; they may think you are talking about the water sac around the puppy. It is imperative to call your veterinarian before you risk your Pug's life.

Unless you are an experienced breeder you may find it difficult to determine if your Pug bitch is through whelping. Take her outside and exercise her before you check her. If her bladder is full, you may think there is still a puppy in her. I also give my bitches ½ cc of oxytocin, which helps contract the uterus and bring her into milk. But as a novice, I suggest you have your Pug bitch checked by your vet. Don't forget to count the afterbirths. Make sure you had one for each puppy delivered.

As soon as your bitch is finished whelping, clean her whelping box. Line your box with carpet and place some large beach towels over the carpet. Make sure you place the covered heating pad in the box so the puppies will be on it. Do not forget to keep the puppies on the mother to nurse. Do not leave the mother and her puppies alone. Make sure that you feed your Pug bitch some hot chicken broth and some chicken and rice after she is finished whelping. Then feed her three times a day. She needs a lot of food to take care of her babies. Don't forget her vitamins and liver.

Care of Mother and Puppies

Pug puppies must never be left alone. Arrange to have someone stay with you so you can get a few hours sleep until they are three weeks old. I never leave my puppies alone until they are weaned from their mother.

Watch your bitch's temperature carefully during the first three weeks. If it goes above 102 degrees, call your veterinarian. Some Pugs do not have enough calcium levels and vitamin D in their blood. This leads to "milk fever" or eclampsia. This often occurs in the first three weeks of lactation. The Pug bitch will become restless, will not want to stay with her puppies and will start to pace in the whelping box. Some will also have spasms. The bitch's temperature can go up to 106 degrees. Rush your bitch to your veterinarian at once. The puppies must be taken away from the bitch, as she may need an intravenous calcium solution.

For the first few days, until the umbilical cord falls off, watch your bitch carefully. Some bitches want to pull the umbilical cord, and this can cause a hernia. Umbilical hernia is quite common in Pug puppies, so have your vet check them. Before the Pug puppies are one week old you will also need to have the veterinarian remove the puppies' dewclaws.

Most Pug mothers will not clean their newborn puppies, so you must do the job for them. Put some baby oil on a cotton ball and stimulate the puppies so they eliminate after each feeding.

You will also have to keep an eye on your bitch to make sure her breasts don't cake. This is called "mastitis." The bitch may have too much milk. The affected glands are swollen, hard and painful and may sometimes feel warm to the touch. I have found hot compresses help to soften the caked breast. You can also massage it with camphorated oil twice a day. It also helps to drain the milk from the caked breast.

To avoid another potential breast problem, you must keep your puppies' nails short so they do not scratch their mother's breast; this can cause an infection in the mammary glands that is both painful to the bitch and can make the puppies sick because the milk is infected. You can test the bitch's milk with pH paper; between 6.0 to 6.5 is normal, at pH 7.0 it is infected. If you do not know how to do this, have your veterinarian do it for you. Reducing the bitch's food often helps in such cases. Do not let your puppies nurse on the infected breast. I have taken some sterile gauze and tape and covered the infected breast so the puppies could not nurse on it.

Pug bitches can give you a hard time when they are nursing their puppies. They not only do not want their regular foods, but they know you will go out of your way to keep them eating. Some will only eat turkey, fruit, chicken, vegetables or steak; they will not even look at chopped beef. They may crave all sorts of crazy things—like pickles and ice cream. Make sure you double her vitamins and give her a small piece of liver or vitamin K every day. You may have to try different foods. I have found that few can resist french toast with syrup!

Make sure you keep the puppies with the mother. If you have five or more puppies, rotate them. Put three on to nurse, and when they are full and fall asleep on the nipple, put the other two puppies on. Pug puppies will nurse for about ten to fifteen minutes and each day nurse a little longer as they grow. Their stomachs should be firm and round when they are full. Puppies should gain one to one and one-half grams of weight per day. I weigh my puppies every twelve hours on a gram scale. They should double their weight in about ten days. If the puppies do not gain properly, I supplement their feedings. I only tube feed two or three times with my formula to give them an extra boost.

Above all, you must keep the puppies warm. Cold puppies are dead puppies.

As soon as their eyes open, start the puppies on the formula of evaporated milk, egg yolk, honey, gelatin, milk and baby cereal (page 173). Make sure it is warm. Hold a puppy on your lap, and using a demitasse spoon, feed the puppy 1 to 3 demitasse spoonfuls of formula and cereal. Add 3 drops of the Poly-Vi-Sol baby drops on top of the puppy's first spoonful once a day. Feed each puppy five times a day. Buy a jar of baby beef and give each puppy 1 demitasse spoonful twice a day. At the end of the first week each puppy should be up to 10 demitasse spoonfuls of formula three times a day and 3 to 5 demitasse spoonfuls of beef twice a day. Continue to increase the amount of food you are feeding each day. At five weeks add fresh top-choice beef braised in a little butter, mixed with 1 tablespoon of mashed carrots and the same amount of cooked rice. It breaks down to ¼ cup formula and ¼ cup meat mixture per puppy per day. Introduce some cottage cheese or tuna fish into their diet twice a week in place of one of the meat meals. Don't forget to increase their food every few days.

Between four and five weeks of age I worm my puppies with 4 drops of Pyrantel pamoite. The puppies have no after effects and they can be fed. Ask your vet about it. My older dogs get ½ cc in the mouth for each twenty pounds of body weight. It takes care of everything except tapeworms.

By the time my puppies are six or seven weeks old, the mother can be taken away. Before you do this make sure the puppies are doing well on their own.

As soon as the puppies are permanently separated, I give the dam a heaping tablespoon of Epsom salts followed with one tablespoon of water. I give her no food or water for twenty-four hours; this breaks the milk cycle. It will dry her up faster, yet does not give her diarrhea. Your bitch will dry up so nice and tight you will not even know she had puppies.

Do not take your bitch out of the whelping box until the puppies are weaned. Do not let the puppies go in and out or permit anyone to see or pick up the puppies until after they have had their first shot. Some mothers will try to protect their puppies by covering them with their bodies. In trying to protect her puppies the mother may smother, injure and even kill the puppies. If you do not stay with your puppies you may lose them. When they are nursing, Pug puppies can get milk into their noses and choke. If you are not there to monitor a litter, puppies can smother.

It is extremely important to keep the temperature in the whelping box between 85 and 90 degrees during the first two weeks. Make sure your puppies are not in a draft and get chilled. There are a few things that you should watch for in newborn puppies. The babies don't cry much, and they pile on top of one another. When you pick them up they are warm and wiggle in your hands. This is a healthy puppy.

Let me relate a story about the need for warmth. I had a puppy that felt cold who would not nurse. He would not stay with his littermates. He started to cry as if he was in pain. I could see that his breathing was much slower than that of his littermates and that he had diarrhea. I wrapped the puppy in a baby receiving blanket and tucked him under my sweater for about six hours. This was done to stop him from crying and to raise his temperature to a normal level. I also tube fed the puppy, giving him some honey and water because he would not nurse. I put one drop of ampicillin and one drop of Biosol-M in the honey and water. Two hours later I gave the puppy more of the honey and water. When I pinched his skin it stayed up instead of springing back. I knew I had a sick puppy. I guess it was about six hours later that I felt the puppy starting to move around under my sweater. I took him out and he felt warm, so I put him on his mother's breast and to my surprise he started to nurse again. The puppy was fine after that. Another way to warm a chilled puppy is to wrap the entire body of the puppy in plastic wrap: this works like an incubator.

One way of knowing if your puppy is getting enough food is by examining his stool. It should be firm and yellowish. If it is loose and yellowish you are feeding a little too much. Cut back on the formula. If you see the color green in the puppy's stool, check with your vet. My vet suggested I give the puppy one or two ccs of milk of magnesia every three hours, and cut back on his food. If you see a grayish diarrhea stool, your puppy is in trouble and is becoming dehydrated. Call your veterinarian at once. If you cannot reach him, dilute the formula by one-third by adding water and give the puppy milk of magnesia until your vet can be contacted.

Remember, what you put into the mother before and after she is bred will show up in your puppies.

Caesarean Sections

In all the years that I have been breeding Pugs, I have had three caesarean sections. Each of these Pug bitches had one large puppy. Some breeders automatically have their bitches sectioned whether they need it or not. Pug bitches should never be sectioned more than twice.

I have found that exercise, proper diet and vitamins are the key to a normal whelping. But most important of all is the calcium, phosphorus and cod liver oil in their diet. And a Pug must have fresh beef and vegetables every day with the rest of her food.

If you need a caesarean section on your Pug bitch, caution your veterinarian not to give her penicillin after the C-section. Some Pugs are allergic to it.

If the puppies are allergic, they will stop nursing and red blotches will appear on their stomachs. If you see this, immediately take the puppies off the mother and bottle feed. Give them a few drops of yogurt on their tongues. This seems to stimulate "friendly" stomach bacteria and the blotches should disappear. Do not put the puppies back on the bitch, or they will die.

False Pregnancy

False pregnancy is quite common in Pugs. It occurs about six weeks after the Pug bitch is out of heat. She will gain weight. Her breasts will enlarge and she may have milk. I had one bitch who went into labor, another who tore paper and made a nest. You will also have to watch her so that her breasts won't cake. If the breast cakes or they come into milk, don't forget to give her Epsom salts. Some bitches will vomit, some are depressed and some have cramps.

Due to the false pregnancy a few bitches will break out in pustules. They are little pimples, like prickly heat. If this happens, give her a bath in Phisohex shampoo. Then take a cup of water and $1/8$ cup of olive oil. Warm the water and oil and rub it into the bitch's coat. Make sure you cover the area where the pustules are, then place her into a large plastic bag—leaving her head out, of course. Insert the hair dryer into the plastic bag until she is dry. The oil will penetrate her skin and in a few days the pustules will go away. You may have to repeat the process once more if she has a bad case.

13

Problems in the Pug Breed

$\mathbf{A}$S PUG BREEDERS we must work together and educate the novice breeder if we are to eliminate hereditary defects in Pugs. We are striving to educate ourselves by properly interpreting the breed standard, attending seminars, reading books and articles. Sharing information among ourselves and other Pug breeders can be a big help. That is, if the information is not filled with inaccuracies or comes from prejudiced sources.

It is a shame that there are a few Pug breeders who are eager to point a finger. They make hasty conclusions, without the facts, that create nasty rumors. Think twice and get your facts straight before you make disparaging remarks about other Pug breeders and their bloodlines. You must learn the difference between isolated incidents at birth and true genetic defects.

It amazes me when I hear new Pug breeders comment that someone's breeding produces congenital defects. It may be wise for that individual to do some studying. Pugs, being so inbred to begin with, all go back to essentially the same dogs in every pedigree. You must look for frequent occurrences within lines before you decide to eliminate them from your breeding program.

Cleft Lip and Palate

Cleft palate is a median fissure due to nonclosure of bones. Environmental or genetic factors may be involved.

Did you know that there are several environmental influences that can cause defects in Pugs? That's right—they have nothing to do with the genetic inheritance of the sire and dam in Pugs. For instance, excessive use of steroids, abnormal levels of vitamin A or severe stress in a pregnant bitch can cause cleft palates in Pug puppies.

Canine Intersexuality

Intersexuality in Pugs can be either hereditary or induced by nonhereditary factors. Environmental influences that can affect the developing fetuses include illness, worm medications, exposure to insecticide or flea sprays, vaccinations, treatment with any drugs or hormones during gestation or the use of steroids at any time. All of these can cause intersexuality in Pugs, a condition where both male and female sexual characteristics are displayed.

Progesterone administered to pregnant bitches to prevent abortion has been reported to induce female pseudohermaphroditism in Pugs. Intersexuality is categorized as either true hermaphroditism or pseudohermaphroditism. If both ovaries and testes are present, the condition is known as true hermaphroditism. Pseudohermaphrodites have either testes or ovaries and are further classified as either male or female depending on the gonads present. Intersexuality in Pugs is a problem in the breed and we must all try to do something about it. An afflicted Pug will show a fleshy, fingerlike structure that will protrude from the vulva of a dog that appears to be a female. You should report all cases to the University of Pennsylvania, Philadelphia, Pennsylvania, Attention of Dr. Patterson, who is working on the project.

Through much research it has been found that intersexuality in Pugs *may* have been brought into this country by Ch. Philwil Cherub of Glenva (E). He is the only common link in the pedigrees of all the affected dogs researched. Although there is no conclusive proof of a genetic transmission in this case, I mention it here to illustrate the possible extent of contamination in the breed by a single dog.

Patella Luxation

Having a patella luxation, or dislocating kneecap, can be inherited or acquired through an injury. There is a small movable bone in front of the knee, which is anchored in place by ligaments and slides in and out of the femur, the heavy bone of the thigh. Inherited conditions are a shallow groove, weak ligaments and/or improper alignment of the tendons and muscles. It is an undesirable disorder due to recessive genes. Do not breed any Pug dog or bitch exhibiting this problem, as we must try to eliminate this condition.

Canine Hip Dysplasia

What is hip dysplasia? It is the degeneration of the hip joint, a ball-and-socket joint formed by the reception of the globular head of the femur or thighbone into the socket of the acetabulum. When a Pug has hip dysplasia

Hip dysplasia

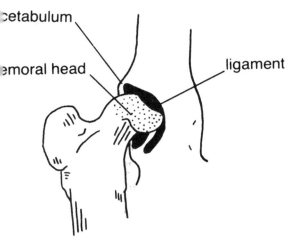

cetabulum

emoral head

ligament

Normal hip joint

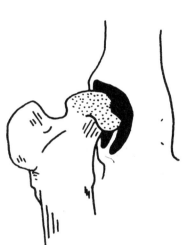

Mild dysplasia

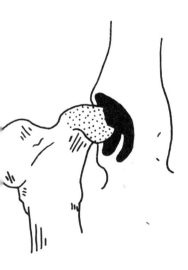

Severe dysplasia

Sketch showing the normal hip, mild dysplasia and severe dysplasia the ball does not fit into the socket joint properly. This allows for excessive movement of the femur head. The effect is damage and eventual weakening to the hip joint. This condition develops in growing puppies and can show up in the Pug breed as early as four to ten months of age.

Recent evidence suggests that the shoulder and stifle joints, and the joints between individual vertebrae, often have similar abnormalities.

Some of the early signs of hip dysplasia in young Pugs are a swaying and unsteady gait. Afflicted Pugs will often run with both hind legs moving together. This is called "bunny-hopping."

Walking, swimming or slow running is beneficial, but jumping and intense activity aggravates the condition. A small dose of buffered aspirin can help to relieve the pain.

Studies suggest that more than one gene is involved with hip dysplasia, yet they do not know how many. We can help to reduce this problem by selecting for breeding only Pugs that have disease-free hips. The cause of hip dysplasia is still unknown. They are also looking into the amount of food a young puppy eats to substantiate the dietary effect on the development of hip dysplasia. There is, however, a theory that links trauma to the early appearance of the abnormality.

We should not ignore this condition and every effort should be made to eliminate this from our bloodlines.

Legg-Perthes

Legg-Perthes is more common in Pugs than hip dysplasia. While symptomatically similar to hip dysplasia, it differs in that it is a breakdown of the femoral head rather than the hip joint. Deterioration or decay of the bone occurs, the affected bone often resembling Swiss cheese. Some of the possible causes are trauma, bacteria in the bloodstream, endocrine disorders and nutritional deficiencies or congenital hip dysplasia. Heredity factors have not been ruled out. This condition occurs primarily in the developing puppy between three and ten months of age.

Pug Dog Encephalitis

This has become a serious problem in the Pug breed today. The following text is a report on the subject by Alexander de Lahunta, DVM, Ph.D., of Cornell University, New York State College of Veterinary Medicine.

> An encephalitis was first recognized in the Pug in the 1960's in California. It now has been diagnosed throughout the United States, in Australia and in Europe. The microscopic features of this encephalitis differ from all the other known encephalitides of the dog. This makes it unique for this breed and the reason for the name: *Pug Dog Encephalitis.* There is no scientific journal publication of this disease. In 1983 I described this disease in the second edition of my textbook *Veterinary Neuroanatomy and Clinical Neurology.* Those of us involved in veterinary neuropathology have shared our pathologic material and from this and our

personal experience, we are all agreed that this is a unique disease in this breed of dogs. Although the disease has features that you would expect an infectious agent to cause, none has yet been identified.

What clinical signs do you expect to see in these dogs and where do they occur? Our collective experience to date shows a range of onset of clinical signs from 9 months to 4 years. These signs can come on suddenly and progress rapidly to death in a few days or be more subtle and slowly progress over weeks and months. The most common sign is that of a seizure or convulsion. These vary in their form but most dogs will suddenly act strange, lose consciousness, have muscle tremors or spasms that rapidly spread over the body causing their limbs to stiffen, be unable to move, and the dog loses its balance and falls over. It often thrashes, sometimes violently for a few seconds, chews vigorously and salivates excessively. Sometimes it will defecate and urinate. All of this violent, uncontrolled activity usually lasts less than a minute and the dog will slowly or occasionally rapidly return to normal. Usually the dog is very depressed and sometimes blind for one to a few hours after the seizure before full recovery. Occasionally recovery does not occur and the dog will continue to seizure or have rapidly recurring seizures.

The dog with the slowly progressive form of the disease will return to normal but will continue to have seizures at varying intervals from a few days to a few weeks. The dog with the acute, rapidly progressive form of the disease will usually have an abnormal gait and posture that persists between seizures. The dog will have difficulty walking and be weak and uncoordinated. It will often lose its balance and fall and may have its head tilted to one side. It will usually act depressed and bewildered. Sometimes partial blindness is evident. These same signs may occur with the slow form of this disease but at a slower rate of development and late in the course of the disease.

Ultimately, with either form, the dog will become recumbent, be unable to ambulate, become comatose and die. Usually owners elect euthanasia before these terminal signs occur. There is no specific treatment for this disease. The seizures can sometimes be controlled initially by the anticonvulsant drug phenobarbitol but eventually, as the disease progresses, this will be ineffective.

Many of us have had the experience of recognizing this disease in more than one animal in a litter. Usually the onset of signs is weeks to months apart in these littermates. This observation, plus the breed specification, makes a genetic predisposition a significant consideration. This may involve a genetically determined abnormality of their immune system that makes these dogs susceptible to an infectious agent such as a virus that normally does not cause disease or the agent may be an altered form of a known canine viral disease to which these dogs are especially susceptible. These are speculations that remain to be proven or disproven.

The only way to better determine the possible genetic basis for this disease is to carefully document all the suspected cases and study their pedigrees. The breed association should appoint an individual or group of individuals to be responsible for the pedigree studies. The only way to make a definitive diagnosis of this disease is by autopsy and microscopic examination of the nervous system. This must be done by individuals experienced in veterinary neuropathology, which usually means at a College of Veterinary Medicine.

I am willing to provide this service at the New York State College of Veterinary Medicine at Cornell University and will accept donations of sick dogs or the formalin-preserved nervous system of dogs who have been autopsied. The most can be gained by the opportunity to study the living, affected dog prior to euthanasia. Any donated animal will be cared for like all other hospitalized patients in the Teaching Hospital for the clinical examination. At the time of humane euthanasia, tissues can be obtained for possible isolation of an infectious agent. To make arrangements for this service, please call Mrs. Muriel Keller at 607-253-3547.

I urge all Pug breeders and owners to take advantage of this service. We must make every effort to eliminate this killing disease.

PRA—Progressive Retinal Atrophy

The retina, a layer of cells sensitive to light, is the innermost coat of the back part of the eyeball. The image formed by the lens on the retina is carried to the brain by the optic nerve. In PRA the retinal vessels become thin and eventually waste away. This affects young dogs first by night blindness and then progresses to blindness.

PRA is caused by simple autosomal recessive trait—incomplete penetrance. Penetrance, however, is high—probably over 80 percent. In a pure dominant every dog carrying the gene will show the effects, which will be passed on by the effective dog to half of its offspring. However, a dominant gene does not show up in all dogs carrying it, meaning that it is not fully penetrated. This means that there is a proportion of carriers of the gene that do not show the disease but will transmit it. A transmitting dog can transmit the actual disease to less than one-half of its progeny.

It is important that breeders and owners do everything in their power to contribute to the eradication and prevention of PRA before it becomes widespread and involves all our lines.

Occasionally PRA may be due to trauma, infection or a vitamin deficiency. Make sure you have this checked by a qualified specialist.

There have been a few reported cases, one in a Pug in Canada that had been purchased from New England on breeder's terms. Upon discovery of PRA in his lines a Long Island breeder had his veterinarian spay all his Pug bitches so as to contain the spread of the disease. A few cases were also reported in California. If this problem exists in your own lines, remove all affected dogs from your breeding program.

We must bring this out into the open. It is a very serious problem and breeders knowingly ignoring it should be publicly identified. Only ophthalmoscopic examinations by an expert can determine whether a dog is free from PRA. Age of onset varies among breeds, and stud dogs should be checked annually.

Trichiasis

This is an abnormal condition in which hairs, especially the eyelashes, grow inward. This irritates the transparent tissue forming the outer coat of the

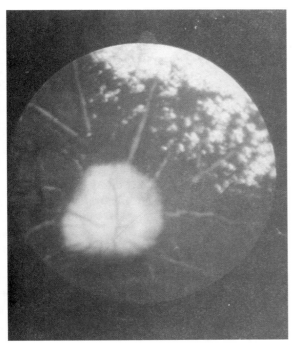

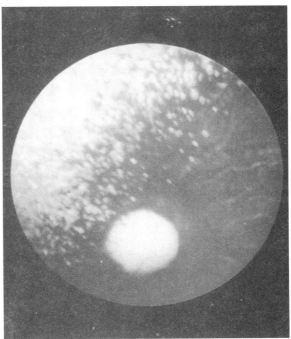

Advanced progressive retinal atrophy

eyeball, i.e. the cornea. It also affects the mucous membrane lining the inner surface of the eyelids and covering the front part of the eyeball. We do not know the mode of inheritance.

This condition causes severe squinting. The hairs roll against the eyeball, causing pain. This condition may require surgical correction.

Entropion

Entropion is the inversion of the eyelid, usually affecting the lower lid. The lid turns inward, affecting the eye. In the past few years this has become a common clinical entity in Pugs. It is detected in young Pugs and is considered to be an inherited defect. Entropion causes superficial irritation of the cornea, caused by the lashes of the eyelid abrading the cornea. If there is any abnormal positioning of the eyelid, have your Pug checked by your veterinarian.

Do not breed your Pug if this problem exists.

Elongated Palate

The elongated palate affects the voice box of the Pug. This is a birth defect in Pugs and the mode of inheritance has not been determined. The opening to the voice box is quite small, and an elongated soft palate will partially block it. The Pug will have difficulty breathing. If the Pug gets excited or needs more air, he will hyperventilate and may collapse. This condition may be corrected surgically.

Collapsed Trachea

The collapsed trachea is also a birth defect. This is caused by the collapse of the cartilage rings in the windpipe. Some of the signs are a honking cough and abnormal respiratory sounds, like croupy breathing. You must be careful to keep your Pug's weight under control with this condition.

Anyone who has had the experience of having any of the above problems will understand how important it is for all of us to work closely together to solve the genetic problems in our Pug breed. You must remember that an affected Pug is severely handicapped, and by perpetuating these conditions you are depriving the dog of a healthy and enjoyable life.

Ch. Vandonna's Diggy of Shirrayne, owned by and shown with the author

Playtime for the Yorkshires and Pugs at the home of Helen Stern

Austin and Leslie Heffner sharing a happy moment with Ch. Shirrayne's Eligible Felix

14

Character of the Pug

THE PERFECT little house dog, a bundle of love is the Pug. The Pug is not a dog that you can keep kenneled outside. He must be part of your family and always be close to you. Since the early Shang Dynasty of his Chinese origin, he was bred to be a lap dog. We know the Pug has been favored by all the emperors of China for their loyalty, stamina and courage.

Children and Pugs have a special bond. Just watch them play together. Pugs are born comedians and cannot do enough to please you.

The Pug has a beautiful, soft, plush coat that is easy to care for. But watch out for Pug hairs; they are always on you. No question about it, Pugs shed. But it is a small price to pay for such an adorable creature. He is exceptionally clean and does not drool. However, he snores. Not all the time, only when he is overtired or plays too hard.

If you live in an apartment or house, the Pug is an ideal dog for you. He will bark if someone rings the doorbell but will settle down right away. He will also try to protect you. Other breeds of dogs are his friends. He will certainly defend himself if challenged.

Some say there is a streak of obstinacy in the Pug; there are certainly a few who have to be coaxed, and they are amusing—just like my Tiger. He would take Daddy to the refrigerator when he was hungry. He would wait for Daddy to get his food ready in his dish. Then Tiger would make a mad dash for the living room and jump into my lap. Daddy would have to bring his food to me. I would have to hand feed him each bite. Tiger had me well trained.

If you are looking for an intelligent little dog, the Pug fits the bill. He is always going to be one step ahead of you, and you will love him for it.

When he gets into mischief, he will show you what he did wrong. He will give you a big kiss. There is no way you are going to scold him. He loves sleeping in bed on the pillow or on top of you. Your lap will do if the right television program is on. He loves to run in the yard and play with you and his toys.

The Pug is also a gentle and understanding companion for the senior citizen. He is the best medicine for someone who is ill. He is full of personality and the most affectionate, terrific, stubborn, perfect companion anybody would want to own. This is a Pug.

15

The Pug
in Obedience

IN THIS CHAPTER I shall present to you some of the high-
lights of our prestigious obedience Pugs and information regarding obedience.

In England and Germany dogs were used in connection with police and
guard work. They were tested on agility, strength and courage. In 1933 Mrs.
Whitehouse returned from England and three years later persuaded the American Kennel Club to approve organized obedience competition. She introduced
the sport of obedience in the United States and convinced the American
Kennel Club to assume jurisdiction over obedience regulations.

Obedience competition is suitable for all pet Pugs and show dogs and
enables them to function effectively as exceptional companions. It is a sport
for which the average Pug owner, young or old, can train his dog to achieve
proper behavior in his home and community. Obedience offers an excellent
way to lengthen the show career of a retired champion. It allows a person who
can't, doesn't want to or doesn't enjoy showing in the breed ring to participate
in the sport of dogs. Obedience training opens up new scopes of enjoyment for
the Pug and his owner. Trained Pugs look forward to modeling and movie
careers, visiting nursing homes, schools and care centers, bringing joy to all
involved.

Each individual Pug is scored on a point rating system. The Pug is judged
on his response to certain commands. He must achieve a minimum of 170
points out of a total of 200 and must receive over 50 percent of the available
points in each exercise. This most be done in three successive trials under

Gale's My Gal Sal, CDX, owned by Debby J. Limon

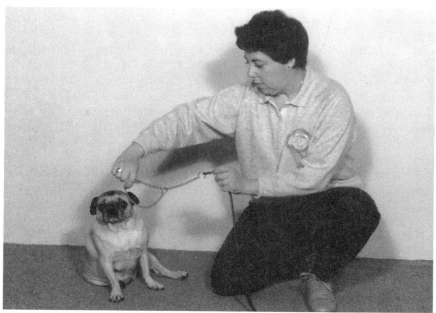

Leslie Heffner demonstrates the correct way of putting the obedience chain-link collar on Ch. Shirrayne's Ornery Pandora, CD. *Joel Heffner*

different judges to receive an obedience degree. This is referred to as a "leg," with three legs being required per degree. The degrees awarded are CD (Companion Dog), CDX (Companion Dog Excellent) and UD (Utility Dog). The two tracking degrees that are issued are the TD (Tracking Dog) and the TDX (Tracking Dog Excellent). An OT Ch (Obedience Trail Champion) has a UD title and has accumulated 100 points in first and second place wins in Open B and the Utility class competition.

Books containing rules and regulations governing obedience and tracking competition and information on obedience training clubs are available upon request from the American Kennel Club, 51 Madison Avenue, New York, NY 10010. Should you also want to show in another country, obtain a copy of their clubs' rules and regulations. Some of the rules may vary in other countries.

Novice Class is the first obedience class and is the one in which the CD is earned. The Novice Class A division is reserved for people who have never trained a dog and obtained a CD degree. There is no difference in exercises or scoring in the A or B division. Basically, a dog needs to be able to heel on and off lead, stand for examination off lead, come when called, go to heel position, sit and stay in place with a group of dogs for one minute and remain in a down position with a group of dogs for three minutes.

The Open Class, where the CDX is earned, refines and adds to the exercises learned for the novice. It is in this class that the dog adds retrieving and jumping to his repertoire. He must be able to broad jump. In addition, he needs to drop on command when he is coming, and stay in a sit and down position with the handler out of sight for three and five minutes respectively.

The Utility Class incorporates all that is learned in the first two classes and adds even more difficult exercises. Success here means the award of the coveted UD degree. At this point, the dog must be able to heel, stand, sit, come and go to finish (the heel position) on signal alone—no verbal commands. Scent discrimination is now added. This means he must be able to distinguish an article with his owner's scent from a group of identical and similar articles. This is done twice, using identical leather and identical metal objects mixed together. One of each must be found. (The first UD Pugs were also required to find a wooden scent article; this is still true in Canada today.) The dog must be able to take a line from his handler and retrieve the designated glove, which is one of three gloves placed across the end of the ring. He must also, on command from the handler, go away from the handler, sit on command and go over the designated jumps on command and signal. The stand for examination also becomes more involved.

Pugs are a great breed for obedience. Their spirit, intelligence and devilish attitude all come through to enthrall all who are watching. There are many who still think Pugs do not have any potential for learning obedience training or advanced work. It just takes a lot of love and a little patience on the owner's part. You will be nicely surprised to see how well the Pug adapts to the training program. Patience and repetition are the key words. Informal obedience train-

Leslie Heffner with Ch. Shirrayne's Ornery Pandora, CD, demonstrates the proper "Sit" after recall.

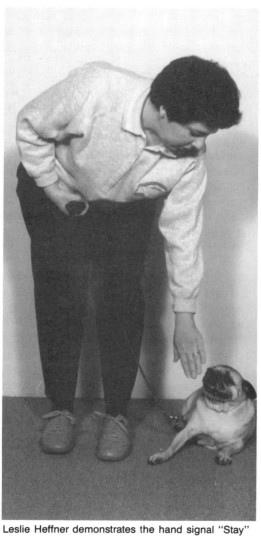

Leslie Heffner demonstrates the hand signal "Stay" with Pandora.

ing should start at six months of age, with the Pug on lead, as he learns a new task.

The collar, a metal chain-link variety, and the snap bolt lead should be the lightest weight possible; these can be found in pet supply stores and at dog shows. Tiny snap bolts can be purchased separately and used to replace the bolts that are found on the commercial leashes. The lighter weights ease the transition from on lead work to off lead.

Baiting is an accepted practice in conformation but is a major no-no in obedience. There is nothing wrong, however, with using treats during the training process. Slowly the treats are replaced by happy voice sounds as the Pug begins to perform the exercises properly. The basic commands are heel, sit, stand stay, down stay and come.

Going into the obedience ring with a Pug automatically sets you apart from the crowd. There are few Pug fanciers in this sport, yet the breed has proven that it can compete with the superlative.

One of the most outstanding obedience Pugs in the 1960s was Lord Percival Wessex, belonging to Patricia Scully, of Suffern, New York. He is the only Pug to hold the CDX title in the United States, Canada, Bermuda and Mexico. Pat is the president of the Pug Dog Club of America and has been an obedience judge for many years.

The Weavers, of Portland, Oregon, and their daughter Pamela have been active in obedience for many years. One of their accomplishments was when Pamela began training Dorken's Irish Colleen, UD. She became the first bitch (the second Pug) to earn her UD title. When Pamela Weaver appeared at obedience school with this six-year-old, grossly overweight Pug, it was believed by some that the dog wouldn't even finish the ten-week class. "Nobody trains Pugs; she's too old and too fat." Not only did Cuddles place first in her class, but went on to complete her CD, CDX and UD degrees with a number of first-place class placements. She completed her UD June 23, 1963 at the age of almost ten years. At that time there was only one other UD Pug in the United States, Ch. Kelly Boy of Man.

Another one of the Weaver's Pugs went on to correct some more misconceptions and set some new records. This was owner-bred, trained and handled, Ch. Weavers' Wrinkled Valentine, UD (the third UD in the breed). "Casey," as he was known, was shown simultaneously in breed and obedience. He completed his CD while winning the *Dog World* award for outstanding obedience work. In order to win this award a dog must complete his degree in three consecutive shows with scores of 195 or above out of a possible 200 points. Casey's scores were 198, 198 and 195 and included two first place wins. He continued garnering wins in both breed and obedience. The coup came on September 28, 1963, at the Tacoma Kennel Club show, when he won the Toy Group and placed third in Open B with a score of 197. This is an accomplishment attained by few of any breed.

Pamela is approved by the American Kennel Club to judge obedience and breed conformation.

In 1964 at the Pug Dog Club of America show, Little Lottie, owned by

Patrick Hallagan, age thirteen, with Ch. Hallagan's Hoosier Tara. Tara was trained in obedience by Patrick and won awards in both Junior Showmanship and Obedience at both the county and state fairs two years in a row.

Ch. Limon's Klondike Joe, CDX, pictured with Patty Ricketts winning High in Match at the Kachina Kennel Club with a score of 198½.

Mrs. Bonham B. Barton, won the club's obedience award for attaining the highest average score of 194½ while earning her UD title.

Barbara Burr, Donald O. Burr and Debby Limon are the proud owners of Int., Mex. & Am. Ch. Fringe Benefit, CD. He received both titles before the age of two on November 2, 1985. Debby teaches obedience classes and writes the obedience column for *Pug Talk*, along with her friend Patty Ricketts. An exciting day for Debby was when she received a High in Trial, CD and the *Dog World* award all on the same day with Gales My Gal Sally, CDX. She later received her CDX by finishing in four shows.

It is too big a task to list all the Pugs who have obedience titles. It is also inspiring to know that so many Pugs qualify as dual champions. Some of our recent winners are New Moon's Domna Digger, CDX, owned by Pam Ortel; Ch. Limon's Klondike Joe, CDX, owned by Patty Ricketts and Debby Limon; Ch. Snowcrest Mighty Simpson, CD, owned by Janet and Mike Zniewski; Ch. Virgo's Tangled Webb, CD, owned by Owen and Virginia Proctor; Mr. Extra Terrific Munch-Kin, CD, owned by Thelma Calman and Hy Calman; and Ch. Harper's As I Bee, CD, owned by Christine Dresser.

There are a number of good books available on training, as well as classes and seminars. Keep in mind that a lot of the common training methods may have been used successfully on the breeds seen more frequently in obedience, but they might not be as successful on the Pug or other lesser known breeds. That is no reason to be discouraged, as Pugs can excel in obedience competition.

The Pug in Trials

A tracking test is an event that is always held outdoors. The Pug must follow a scent trail that is two hours old and 440 to 500 yards in length. The Pug must locate a glove or wallet that is a scent article left by a stranger who has laid the track. A Pug that passes a tracking test receives a Tracking Dog (TD) certificate. If the dog has a UD title, he is designated as a Utility Dog Tracker (UDT). The Tracking Dog Excellent (TDX) test is from 800 to 1,000 yards in length and involves four articles and cross tracks. The scent on the track is from three to four hours old.

Over twenty Pugs have obtained the UD title, with several being breed champions as well. We have on record that Tora John, UDT, owned by Ruth Minge, is the only Pug who has captured the Tracking Dog and Utility Dog degrees. There have been no OT champions or TDX Pugs, but hopefully in the near future this goal will be achieved.

Ch. Harper's Barnum Bailey—no couch potato—owned by Virginia M. Warner

16

The Pug as
a Hunting Dog

IN THE CHOU DYNASTY the Pug was brought to the hunting place and used to flush out and catch small game. Although a Pug cannot compete with a Labrador Retriever or a Pointer in retrieving, he surely will participate in the hunt. Abby Fox, who lives in New Jersey, let her Pugs out one morning to romp in the yard. To Abby's surprise one of her boys caught a white rabbit. You must remember the Pug is inquisitive and curious and he will take part in any activity if just given the chance.

Patty, a Pug bitch owned by Cecilia Geary, thought she was a herding dog. When Cecilia visited friends who owned a farm, Patty would herd the flock of geese into the pond and patrol the shore to be certain they stayed in the water. She also would go out into the pasture and herd the cow back to the barn. She felt geese belonged in the water, and cows belonged in the barn.

This beautiful handmade quilt, c. 1888, features a Pug in its design. This treasured, valuable artifact is owned by Helen Pittinger.

A few favorite pieces of Juanita Benninger's Pug memorabilia

17

The Pug
in Modern Culture

THROUGH THE YEARS the Pug has reached the hearts of many and became the favorite of Queen Victoria. They graced the palaces of kings and queens around the world. Pugs were the household pets of the Duke and Duchess of Windsor. Her Royal Highness, the Duchess of Windsor, was the honorary chairwoman of a Pug art collection held at the J. Edward Zollinger Gallery in the Swen Library at the College of William and Mary in Williamsburg, Virginia. This exhibition was dedicated to His Royal Highness, the Duke of Windsor. We were also honored when the Duke and Duchess of Windsor attended our dog shows.

As the Pug became popular in this country, many famous people became charmed by the breed. Prince Rainier and Princess Grace of Monaco; Cornelia Otis Skinner; Marguerite Tyson, sister of Perle Mesta; Erica Rhodes; Rex Harrison; Jan Miner; Luther Adler; Lena Horne; Mrs. John F. Kennedy; Edward Kennedy; Amanda and Carter Burden; Joan Blondell; Andy Warhol; Senator Lowell Weicker; and Nobel Prize–winner Patrick White all owned Pugs.

Four of the Goodchance Pugs, owned by Mrs. E. S. Brown in Middlesex, England, appeared on television. They appeared with Richard Burton in *The Gathering Storm;* in *Jenny,* the story of the life of Sir Winston Churchill's mother; in *The Great Gatsby* and in the play *The Snares of Death.*

Ch. Shirrayne's Victorious Vance, owned by the author, appeared on the *Looking East* television program.

The celebrated actor Richard Thomas is also an avid dog fancier. He is pictured here with veteran Pug authority John Marsh.

PUG MOVIE INTERVIEWS

PUG MOVIE INTERVIEWS

Some of Mary De Camp's amusing pen-and-ink drawings

Ch. Nazrep Rare Bear, owned by Diana Gardner

Valentino (Garavani), the Italian dress designer, travels all over the world with his Shirrayne Pugs, and they are pictured in the fashion magazine with his models.

Alice Austen, a well-known photojournalist, was devoted to Pugs. The Alice Austin House and Gardens are now a designated National Landmark bordering the Narrows, the entrance to the great port of New York City in Staten Island. The Pug Dog Club of Greater New York holds their match shows on her grounds in honor of Alice Austin for the benefit of the museum.

Pugs were painted by many famous artists around the world, and one of my favorite paintings is the *La Marquesa de Pontejos,* by Goya (1785). The paintings by Spanish artist Francisco Ubeda Marin of my Ch. Shirrayne's Golddigger and the other showing my two boys, Am. & Can. Ch. Bitterwell Broth of a Boy and Bda. & Am. Ch. Shirrayne's Earthquake Earl, are two of my prized possessions. These two paintings were gifts to the author from Shirley and Tracy Williams, São Paulo, Brazil.

Pugs were popular on advertising cards during the late 1800s and these have become collector's items.

Mary De Camp's first oil painting was of my Ch. Bitterwell Broth of a Boy. Mary has been commissioned by Joan Perry, Michael Weisman, Jim Moran and others to do individual paintings of their Pugs. She and her husband Jack, who is a retired airline pilot, live in California. Mary has distinguished herself by her cartoon pen-and-ink drawings of Pugs. Her drawings and poems by Mary and Margaret Cameron are featured in a book entitled *Pugs and Poems.* It is a wonderful book to have and is published by *Pug Talk,* 223 W. Louisiana, Dallas, Texas 75224.

Pug Talk is a bi-monthly publication that was founded by Jack and Mimi Keller. Anna Marie Wilson is the current editor. The Kellers have supplied us with documentation of our Pug breed. The magazine is informative and instrumental in further promoting and disseminating important information about Pugs.

The Duke and Duchess of Windsor had an extensive collection of Pug memorabilia. James Cavallaro, Helen Bortner, Marianne Johnson, Diana and Ken Mulhern, James Moran, Bob and Ann White, Sylvia Sidney, the author and many other Pug fanciers have important collections.

The first book about Pugs was published in 1905 and is entitled *Hints on the Management of Black Pugs,* by L. J. F. Pughe (Northgate, England: Times Printing Works). The second book published on Pugs is the paperback book *The Truth About the Pug Dog,* by Wilhelmine Swainston Goodger (Bradford and London: Watmoughs Limited Idle). Another book is *The Oracle Dog and the Sages,* by Colin and Hurry. These are all in the author's collection and have become collector's items.

Paintings, literature and art all have played an important role in the history and development of our present and future Pugs. They will continue to be educational tools in the breeding of quality Pugs.

18

The Pug Parent
and Regional Clubs

WHAT ARE PUG DOG CLUBS all about? They are to protect and carry on the development of the Pug breed. Also, they maintain the quality of the Pug's breed type and are the watchdogs of the breed standard. Dog clubs are there to help the individual pet owners, breeders and exhibitors. One of their functions is to hold dog shows under the rules of the American Kennel Club so that fanciers can exhibit and show off their breeding stock in a sportsmanlike manner. They are there to educate the pet owners and their Pugs to be responsible citizens in their community, and to teach children what good sportsmanship is all about and how to treat and care for the Pug. These are big responsibilities and clubs cannot function properly without everyone's support. Therefore, it is important that all Pug fanciers join their local Pug dog club and participate in their activities. This will ensure that our Pugs will always be here for future generations to love and enjoy.

A list of the secretaries of the following breed clubs can be obtained by writing the American Kennel Club, 51 Madison Avenue, New York, NY 10010.

Pug Dog Club of America, Inc.
Pug Dog Club of Greater New York, Inc.
Tampa Bay Pug Club, Inc.
Greater Atlanta Pug Club
Puget Sound Pug Dog Club

Members of the Pug Club of Greater New York presenting an educational symposium on Pugs at the Monmouth County (New Jersey) Fair Grounds. *From left:* June Lysandrou, Shirley Thomas, Cecilia Geary, and Joel and Leslie Heffner demonstrating obedience.

John Marsh and Lena Horne pictured at the 1958 Pug Dog Club of America Specialty show held in New York City

Actress Sylvia Sidney shown judging the Pug Dog Club of Greater
New York's 1972 match show with the author and Shirrayne's
Doodlebug

Vandonna's Matchmaker being awarded Grand Prize in Sweepstakes by judge Dennis
B. Sprung, at the Pug Dog Club of Greater New York Specialty show, February 1987.
Owners: Lloyd Alton (handling) and Bill Gorodner.

Yankee Pug Dog Club
Central Indiana Pug Dog Club, Inc.
Pug Dog Club of Maryland, Inc.
Great Lakes Pug Dog Club, Inc.
Pug Dog Club of Greater Cincinnati
City of Angels Pug Dog Club, Inc.
Bluebonnet Pug Dog Club
Missouri Valley Pug Fanciers
Pug Dog Club of Greater San Antonio

Nonmember Clubs:
Columbine Pug Dog Club of Denver, Colorado
Mid-Michigan Pug Dog Club, Inc.
Greater Milwaukee Pug Dog Club
Pug Dog Club of Northern California

The Pug Dog Club of America was first recognized by the American Kennel Club in 1931. Their first specialty show was held in conjunction with the Morris & Essex show in 1938.

In 1950, in a plush hotel room at the McAlpin hotel in New York City, Filomena Doherty, Sis Sewall, Mr. and Mrs. Arthur Cassler, Mr. and Mrs. Fred Greenly, Mr. and Mrs. John Marsh, Mrs. Don Smith, Harriett Smith, Mr. and Mrs. Walter Foster and Dr. Nancy Riser gathered together to pick up the pieces of a broken-down club. The first specialty show was held in New York City in 1957 at the McAlpin Hotel and reported the attendance of 79 Pugs in 94 entries. Dorothy Wagstaff chose Ch. Tarralong Philip (Belcrest Kennels) as Best of Breed.

The Pug Dog Club of America has come a long way since that time. Their specialty show entries are over 300 dogs today. There are now more than 368 members of the parent club with seventeen chapter clubs.

19

What a Pedigree
Is All About

WHAT IS a pedigree? A pedigree is a record of known lines in a Pug's ancestry. It is also a Pug's family tree.

Being able to use these pedigrees will enable you to breed quality Pugs, which will enhance the development of the breed.

As you go through the following pedigrees you will see that the name of the sire, or father, appears above the name of the dam, or mother, in each generation. You will also see abbreviations used in some of the Pugs' pedigrees. "Ch.," which appears before the name, means "champion." Sometimes you will see an "(E)" after the dog's name; this means that he is an English import. If you see "Eng. & Am. Ch." before the Pug's name it means he is an English and American champion.

Some pedigrees will also include notations about characteristics. After the Pug's name you may see "(blk)" or just a "(B)"; this means the Pug's color is black. You may see "fn/blk msk," which means the Pug is fawn with a black mask.

Following the Pug's name you may see "CD" (Companion Dog), "CDX" (Companion Dog Excellent) or "UD" (Utility Dog). These are a few of the obedience titles.

The majority of the Pug pedigrees that follow will show you that all Pugs come out of the same gene pool, if you trace back far enough. While studying the enclosed pedigrees try to trace all the dogs back to an English import, Ch. Philwil Cherub of Glenva (E). Trace the Pugs in your pedigree back by looking at pictures or speaking to knowledgeable breeders to find out your dog's good or bad traits. In this way you can learn what has been passed down into your line, like a lovely head or maybe a rear that is too straight.

This knowledge can help us all in breeding quality, soundness and most of all true Pug breed type.

```
                    Ch. Wall's Warrior of Paramin
                Ch. Sheffield's Sunday Punch
                    Ch. Serenade of Sheffield
            Ch. Shep's Sassafras Coca
                    Ch. Wolf's Li'l Joe
                Shep's Li'l Tamu of Dunroamin
                    Dunroamin Dyna Might
        Ch. Shep's Rising Sun
                    Ch. Merrimaker Tawny Tokay
                Ch. Shep's Li'l Golden Rooster
                    Ch. Li'l Golden Tilei of Shangra-La
            Ch. Shep's Highfalutin Floozy
                    Ch. Shep's Major Tom Cat
                Ch. Shep's Afternoon Delite
                    Ch. Shep's Peach Puddin
CH. ROWELL'S SOLO MOON RISING
                    Gais Rufty Tufty (E)
                Ch. Broughcastl Balladeer
                    Ch. Bonjor's Susan B. Anthony
            Ch. Terytam Taskmaster
                    Ch. Wolf's Li'l Joe
                Ch. Terytam's Tallyho of Patagon
                    Ch. Sheffield's Sally Sunshine
        Ch. Rowell's Sassy Scruples
                    Ch. Prelly's Rolly Roister
                Ch. Chen's a Favorite of the Gods
                    Ch. Alexander's Village Idiot
            Ch. Rowell's Dhandy Gypsy Rose
                    Ch. Sheffield's Dancing Tiger
                Ch. Dhandy's Skylark
                    Dhandy's Bleuridge Robin
```

Auwil Heron of Paramin (E)
Phirefly of Paramin (E)
Philippa of Paramin (E)
Ch. Samet Paul of Paramin (E)
Ch. Paramin Dillypin of Pantaloon (E)
Paramin Paulette (E)
Ch. Dillypin Delightful Doreen of Dobray
Ch. Sheffield's Stuff 'N' Nonsense
Ch. Cheerio of Even So
Ch. Wolf's Li'l Joe
Ch. Wolf's Kauffee Royal Rose
Ch. Sheffield's Sweeter Than Wine
Ch. Sheffield's Sunday Punch
Ch. Sheffield's Sure-Fire
Ch. Sheffield's Lucy Locket Shogo
CH. IVANWOLD HONEYSUCKLE ROSE
Gais Rufty Tufty (E)
Ch. Broughcastl Balladeer
Ch. Bonjor's Susan B. Anthony
Ch. Terytam Taskmaster
Ch. Wolf's Li'l Joe
Ch. Terytam's Tallyho of Patagon
Ch. Sheffield's Sally Sunshine
Ivanwold Autumn Rose
Ch. Ivanwold Johnny Appleseed
Ch. Ivanwold Apple Jack
Ch. Ivanwold High Barbary
Ch. Ivanwold Mighty Lak a Rose
Ch. Ivanwold High Tor
Ch. Ivanwold Gayberry Carolina
Ch. Gayberry Victoria of Gore

<pre>
                    Ch. Sheffield's Tuff Stuff
              Ch. Sheffield's Kendoric Hot Stuff
                    Ch. Sheffield's Shasta
        Ch. Kendoric's Pipin' Hot
                    Cobby's Jeremy Fisher of Martlesham
              Brentchase Daisychain
                    Brentchase the Dollybird
     Ch. Kendoric's Hot Connection
                    Phirefly of Paramin (E)
              Ch. Samet Paul of Paramin (E)
                    Paramin Paulette (E)
        Ch. Kendoric's French Connection
                    Ch. Ravencrofts Kendoric Gambler
              Kendoric Double Play
                    Al Tora Peanut Girl
CH. KENDORIC'S ANGEL ON A STRING
                    Phirefly of Paramin (E)
              Ch. Samet Paul of Paramin (E)
                    Paramin Paulette (E)
        Ch. Sheffield's Stuff 'N' Nonsense
                    Ch. Wolf's Li'l Joe
              Ch. Sheffield's Sweeter Than Wine
                    Ch. Sheffield's Sure-Fire
     Ch. Pelshire's Magic Phantasy
                    Jenalees Kauffee Royal Joe
              Kendoric's Triple Trouble
                    Ch. Kendoric's Li'l China Star, CD
        Ch. Pelshire's Magic Kristal
                    Carol's Bobbie
              Bruso's Little TJ
                    Polly Anna Libby
</pre>

<pre>
                              Ch. Winna Canadian Capers
                   Ch. Winna Sir Robin
                      Sweet Nancy of Swainston
          Ch. Winna Sir Walter
                              Ch. Winna John Peel
                   Winna Lady Clementine
                              Ch. Winna Lady Pamela
     Ch. Velvet Tubby
                              Ch. Winna John Peel
                   Ch. Winna Tuppence
                              Ch. Tricolour Queen
          Ch. Bilby's Debby-Dee
                      Winna Ark Royal
                   Ch. Bilby's Little Dutchess
                      Peggy of Holly Lodge
CH. BLAYLOCK'S MAR-MA-DUKE
                              Ch. Winna John Bull
                   Ch. Melcroft Music Maker
                      Tailspin Q.T. Belle
          Ch. Melcroft Melancholy Manderin
                              Ch. Apollo of Green Gables
                   Winna Polly-Anna of Melcroft
                              Ch. Winna Lady Jennifer
     Blaylock's Cheata
                              Ch. Winna Sir Robin
                   Ch. Winna Sir Walter
                      Winna Lady Clementine
          Blaylock's Toi-Len
                              Ch. Philwil Cherub of Glenva (E)
                   Velvet Winkie
                              Madam Jinrikisha
</pre>

Philwil Abbot (E)
Ch. Philwil Cherub of Glenva (E)
Philwil Candy (E)
Ch. Short Snort of Even So
Ch. Harloo Philip (E)
Ch. Pine Echo's See See
Ch. Philwil Garnet (E)
Ch. Cheerio of Even So
Ch. Philwil Cherub of Glenva (E)
Ch. Blondo Hill Happy Birthday
Ch. Melcroft Maid O' Mist
Dilly Dally of Even So
Ch. Kobby Knoll Himself
Floradora of Even So
Ch. Pine Echo's Ving Ling

CH. WOLF'S LI'L JOE
Ch. Philwil Cherub of Glenva (E)
Ch. Short Snort of Even So
Ch. Pine Echo's See See
Ch. Wolf's Li'l Short Snort
Ch. Blondo Hill Tom Fool
Wolf's Lulu Belle
Missie Toy
Ch. Wolf's Kauffee Royal Rose
Sammey
Ch. Furst's Jack
Adair's Tiffany
Ch. Furst's Princess
Hazelbridge Hercules
Furst's Sunday Girl
Petsie

                        Crispin of Pugholm
                Harloo Dandino
                        Harloo Black Magic
        Ch. Doc
                        Ch. Velvet Tubby
                Velvet Betsy
                        Blaylock's Cheata
    Ch. Pug Haven's Cactus Jim
                        Ch. Carduff's Prince Charlie
                Ch. Car-Mac Golden Prince C
                        Ch. Car-Mac Golden Lass
        Ch. Velvet Tracey
                        Ch. Philwil Cherub of Glenva (E)
                Ch. Velvet Jetty
                        Bilby's Debby Dee
CH. LITTLE VICKIE GRAMIGNA
                        Ch. Philwil Cherub of Glenva (E)
                Ch. Short Snort of Even So
                        Ch. Pine Echo's See See
        Ch. Wolf's Li'l Short Snort
                        Ch. Blondo Hill Tom Fool
                Wolf's Lulu Belle
                        Missie Toy
    Litl Jewel Fahey
                        Ch. Philwil Cherub of Glenva (E)
                Ch. Allen's Tom Thumb
                        Swainston Thumbelina (E)
        Ch. Fahey's Jewel Box
                        Ch. Melcroft Mountain Music
                Ch. Melcroft Miss Marlene
                        Melcroft Marva

Ciello's Spring Froliic (E)

Fahey's Filbert
           Ch. Philwil Cherub of Glenva (E)
      Ch. Allen's Tom Thumb
           Swainston Thumbelina (E)
    Ch. Fahey's Jewel Box
           Ch. Melcroft Mountain Music
      Ch. Melcroft Miss Marlene
           Melcroft Marva
CH. FOR SURE FAHEY
           Ch. Philwil Cherub of Glenva (E)
      Ch. Streeter's Madcap Harry
           Allen's Linda Lou
    Ch. Woodlou's Hallmark
           Ch. Philwil Cherub of Glenva (E)
      Allen's Linda Lou
           Swainston Thumbelina (E)
Phanney Fahey

    Philwil Hermit (E)

Ch. Raydium Little Susie of Harloo (E)

    Raydium Plucky Tiggy (E)

Bluedoor Tituson (E)

Ch. Tarralong Tony

Antoinette of Chetrose (E)

Ch. Star Jade of North Boro
                His Honor of Swainston (E)
            Ch. Harloo Philip (E)
            Harloo Beauty (E)
        Ch. Tarralong Star of India
                Tarralong Gay Blade
            Ch. Tarralong More Mischief
                Ch. Melcroft Mischief
CH. SABBADAY ECHO
                Philwil Abbot (E)
            Ch. Philwil Cherub of Glenva (E)
            Philwil Candy (E)
        Ch. Allen's Mighty Mo

Mimma Bella of Swainston (E)

Allen's Susie Q

Benjamin of Gladwyn

Ch. Shella

Allen's Miss Maryville

258

```
                        Black John of Longlands
                Crispin of Pugholm
                        Goldengleam Inkspot
        Harloo Dandino
                        Philwil Cloister
                Harloo Black Magic
                        Jemima of Littlefoxes
    Ch. Doc
                        Ch. Winna Sir Walter
                Ch. Velvet Tubby
                        Ch. Bilby's Debby-Dee
        Velvet Betsy
                        Ch. Melcroft's Melancholy Manderin
                Blaylock's Cheata
                        Blaylock's Toi-Len
CH. PUG HAVEN'S CACTUS JIM
                        _____
                Ch. Carduff's Prince Charlie
                        _____
        Ch. Car-Mac Golden Prince C
                        _____
                Ch. Car-Mac Golden Lass
                        _____
    Ch. Velvet Tracey
                        Philwil Abbot (E)
                Ch. Philwil Cherub of Glenva (E)
                        Philwil Candy (E)
        Ch. Velvet Jetty
                        _____
                Bilby's Debby Dee
                        _____
```

                    Tito of Masberk
            Black John of Longlands
                    Blackberry of Longlands
        Crispin of Pugholm
                    Jester of Le Taysll
            Goldengleam Inkspot
                    Lindylou of Goldengleam
    Harloo Dandino
                    Philwil Abbot
            Philwil Cloister
                    Philwil Candy
        Harloo Black Magic
                    Black John of Longlands
            Jemima of Littlefoxes
                    Tresa of Longlands
CH. DOC
                    Ch. Winna Sir Robbin
            Ch. Winna Sir Walter
                    Winna Lady Clementine
        Ch. Velvet Tubby
                    Ch. Winna Tuppence
            Ch. Bilby's Debby-Dee
                    Ch. Bilby's Little Dutchess
    Velvet Betsy
                    Ch. Melcroft's Music Maker
            Ch. Melcroft's Melancholy Manderin
                    Winna Pollyanna of Melcroft
        Blaylock's Cheata
                    Ch. Winna Sir Walter
            Blaylock's Toi-Len
                    Velvet Winkie

260

Ch. Heisler's Tom Tully
Ch. Heisler's Elite Eros
Hazelbridge Maid Marion
Ch. Heritage Tom Cat of Gore
Ch. Mickey Flynn Fahey
Gore's Dutchess of Watson
Ch. Susie Needham
Ch. Shep's Major Top Cat
Ch. Cheerio of Even So
Ch. Wolf's Li'l Joe
Ch. Wolf's Kauffee Royal Rose
Shep's Li'l Tamu of Dun
Ch. Kauffee Royal Li'l Mr. Satchmo
Dunroamin Dyna Might
Rosalie's Becky Lou
CH. SHEP'S BUTCH CASSIDY
Ch. Cheerio of Even So
Ch. Wolf's Li'l Joe
Ch. Wolf's Kauffee Royal Rose
Ch. Sheffield's Dancing Tiger
Ch. Sheffield's Sunday Punch
Ch. Sheffield's Sure-Fire
Ch. Sheffield's Lucy Locket Shogo
Shep's Miss Georgia Peach
Ch. Heisler's Elite Eros
Ch. Heritage Tom Cat of Gore
Gore's Dutchess of Watson
Ch. Shep's Miss Tom Girl
Ch. Wolf's Li'l Joe
Shep's Li'l Tamu of Dun
Dunroamin Dyna Might

Ch. Edger's Koko Bennie's Hibred
Ch. Hoyle's Sir Beand
Bryant's Q.T. Babette
Ch. Prelly's Rolly Roister
Ch. Edger's Koko Bennie's Hibred
Prelly's Fair Dinkum
Ch. Hoyle's Franella
Ch. Chen's a Favorite of the Gods
Ch. Cheerio of Even So
Ch. Wolf's Li'l Joe
Ch. Wolf's Kauffee Royal Rose
Ch. Alexander's Village Idiot
Ch. Blaylock's Mar-Ma-Duke
Ch. Sylin's Kuku Koolie
Sylin's Puddin Surprise
CH. DHANDY'S FAVORITE WOODCHUCK
Ch. Cheerio of Even So
Ch. Wolf's Li'l Joe
Ch. Wolf's Kauffee Royal Rose
Ch. Sheffield's Dancing Tiger
Ch. Sheffield's Sunday Punch
Ch. Sheffield's Sure-Fire
Ch. Sheffield's Lucy Locket Shogo
Ch. Heritage Wicket Witch
Ch. Prelly's Rolly Roister
Ch. Bleuridge's Tuffy Boy
Gore's Tammy
Bleuridge's Natasha
Ch. Heritage Tom Cat of Gore
Bleuridge's Image
Ch. Bleuridge's Tuffy's Button

Ch. Robertson's Buc-O Nunnally
Ch. Robertson's Bourbon Prince
Nunnally's Derby Doll
Ch. Gore's Up'N Adam
Ch. Ivanwold High Tor
Ch. Robertson's Goldelle
Ch. Reinitz Babe Doll of Gore
Ch. Paulmar's Trace of Antiquity
Ch. Prelly's Rolly Roister
Rosened's Oriental Tobi Tong
Rosened's Sweet Peg
Ch. Rosened's Lovin Abby
Ch. Rosened's Buddy
Rosened's Jumping Judy
Ch. Rosened's Cinnamon Patch
CH. PAULMAR'S LITTLE LUKE
Ch. Prelly's Rolly Roister
Ch. Chen's a Favorite of the Gods
Ch. Alexander's Village Idiot
Ch. Dhandy's Favorite Woodchuck
Ch. Sheffield's Dancing Tiger
Ch. Heritage Wicket Witch
Bleuridge's Natasha
Paulmar's Favorite Dolly
Ch. Rosened's Buddy
Ch. Rosened's Tomac
Rosened's Dainty Gem
Ch. Paulmar's Luk-E Lollipop
Ch. Rosened's Buddy
Velvet's Precious Penelope
Rosened's Velvet Button

263

                    Phirefly of Paramin (E)
            Ch. Samet Paul of Paramin (E)
                    Paramin Paulette (E)
        Ch. Sheffield's Sneaky Pete
                    Ch. Wolf's Li'l Joe
            Ch. Sheffield's Constant Comment
                    Ch. Sheffield's Sally Sunshine
    Ch. Sheffield's Rose Tatoo
                    Ch. Cheerio of Even So
            Ch. Wolf's Li'l Joe
                    Ch. Wolf's Kauffee Royal Rose
        Ch. Sheffield's Second Hand Rose
                    Ch. Sheffield's Sunday Punch
            Ch. Sheffield's Sure Fire
                    Ch. Sheffield's Lucy Locket Shogo
CH. SHEFFIELD'S LITTLE RED WAGON
                    Auwil Heron of Paramin (E)
            Phirefly of Paramin (E)
                    Philippa of Paramin (E)
        Ch. Samet Paul of Paramin (E)
                    Ch. Paramin Dillypin of Pantaloon (E)
            Paramin Paulette (E)
                    Ch. Dillypin Delightful Doreen of Dobray
    Ch. Sheffield's Country Cousin
                    Ch. Cheerio of Even So
            Ch. Wolf's Li'l Joe
                    Ch. Wolf's Kauffee Royal Rose
        Ch. Sheffield's Constant Comment
                    Ch. Wall's Warrior of Paramin
            Ch. Sheffield's Sally Sunshine
                    Ch. Serenade of Sheffield

```
                    Ch. Carolyn's Jiminy Cricket
              Ch. Carolyn's Chocolate Chip
                    Blaylock's Bonnie Belle
        Ch. Charlamar's Billy Joe Black
                    Ch. Ellis Lucifer
              Ch. Broughcastl Licorice Stick
                    Black Puff of Happiness
  Ch. Charlamar's J. Randall Brown
                    Reinitz Gore Noir of Lucas
              Nunnally's Blackmail
                    Nunnally's Derby Doll
        Ch. Nunnally's Witch Hazel
                    Ch. Mitchell's Goliath
              Whiteman's Miss Sapphire
                    Little Velvet Beulah
CH. CHARLAMAR'S ANCIENT DREAMER
                    Ch. Buster of Rydens (E)
              Ch. What Oh of Rydens (E)
                    Polly Flinders of Rydens (E)
        Ch. Hazelbridge Black Eros (E)
                    Hazelbridge Black Frinnie (E)
              Hazelbridge Black Ann (E)
                    Hazelbridge Cinders (E)
   Charlamar's Alpha Omega
                    Ch. Tick Tock of Letasyll (E)
              Ch. May's Pepper
                    Ch. May's Dina Mite
        Black Puff of Happiness
                    Ch. Gore's Jack Tarr
              Gore's Debutante
                    Gore's Midge
```

                    Ch. Philwil Cherub of Glenva (E)
            Ch. Short Snort of Even So
                    Ch. Pine Echo's See See
        Ch. Cheerio of Even So
                    Ch. Blondo Hill Happy Birthday
            Dilly Dally of Even So
                    Floradora of Even So
    Ch. Wolf's Li'l Joe
                    Ch. Short Snort of Even So
            Ch. Wolf's Li'l Short Snort
                    Wolf's Lulu Belle
        Ch. Wolf's Kauffee Royal Rose
                    Ch. Furst's Jack
            Ch. Furst's Princess
                    Furst's Sunday Girl
CH. SHIRRAYNE'S BRASH BUFFI
                    Ch. Mickey Flynn Fahey
            Ch. Gore's Royal Mick
                    Ch. Susie Needham
        Ch. Gore's Line Backer
                    Gore's Mr. Flipper
            Gore's Sunny Imp of St. John
                    Velvet Queen
    Pugtowne's Barbarella of Gore
                    Ch. Velvet Tubby
            Ch. Blaylock's Mar-Ma-Duke
                    Blaylock's Cheata
        Ch. Gore's Summer Night
                    Green Blinkum
            Gore's Summer Tan
                    Ginger Louise Need

                    Peeugee Family Solicitor (E)
            Ch. Buster of Rydens (E)
                    Jill of Rydens (E)
        Ch. What Oh of Rydens (E)
                    Sam of Rydens (E)
            Polly Flinders of Rydens (E)
                    Anna of Rydens (E)
    Ch. Hazelbridge Black Eros (E)
                        Ch. Edenderry Barney Campbell (E)
                    Hazelbridge Black Frinnie (E)
                        Hazelbridge Chin-Chin (E)
            Hazelbridge Black Ann (E)
                        Hazelbridge Black Fury (E)
                    Hazelbridge Cinders (E)
                        Raygay Roundabout (E)
CHARLAMAR'S ALPHA OMEGA
                    Ch. Buster of Rydens (E)
            Ch. Tick Tock of Letasyll (E)
                        Hazelbridge Little Toy of Letasyll (E)
        Ch. May's Pepper
                    Ch. Vickiri Little Black Sambo
            Ch. May's Dina Mite
                    May's Shady Lady
    Black Puff of Happiness
                    Ch. Satan of Rydens (E)
            Ch. Gore's Jack Tarr
                    Gore's Miss Quipper
        Gore's Debutante
                    Ch. Gore's Jolly Joker
            Gore's Midge
                    Gore's Bit of Starlight

Ch. Winna Sir Walter
Ch. Velvet Tubby
Ch. Bilby's Debby-Dee
Ch. Blaylock's Mar-Ma-Duke
Ch. Melcroft Melancoly Manderin
Blaylock's Cheata
Blaylock's Toi-Len
Ch. Mickey Flynn Fahey
Ciello's Spring Froliic (E)
Fahey's Filbert
Ch. Fahey's Jewel Box
Ch. Fahey's Vampire

Fahey's Sugapud

GORE'S DUTCHESS OF WATSON
Ch. Runnaways Trumpeter
Green Blinkum
Ch. Caprice Claytonia
Ch. Gore's Sir Flip
Gore's Atlas
Ginger Louise Need
Princess Penny Need
Ch. Susie Needham
Ch. Blondo Hill Happy Birthday
Tempest of Even So
Ch. Pine Echo's Ving Ling
Green Silk
Ch. Carduff's Prince Charlie
Ch. Caprice Claytonia
Ch. Venus of Valiview

Martlesham Rust of Pendorey (E)
Ch. Stormie of Martlesham (E)
Smartie of Martlesham (E)
Ch. Martlesham Galahad of Bournie (E)
Ch. Justatwerp of Cedarwood (E)
Olive Beaute of Bournle (E)
Ophelia of Bournle (E)
Ch. Ivanwold High Tor
Ch. Runnaways Topper
Ch. Walhaven Acrobat
Ch. Wispering Lane's Chloe
Ch. Ivanwold Portia's Pride
Le-Mar's Mystery Man
Ivanwold Pugable
Heisler's Miss America
CH. IVANWOLD GAYBERRY CAROLINA
Ch. Blaylock's Mar-Ma-Duke
Ch. Mickey Flynn Fahey
Ch. Fahey's Vampire
Ch. Gore's Royal Mick
Ch. Gore's Sir Flip
Ch. Susie Needham
Green Silk
Ch. Gayberry Victoria of Gore
Ch. Gore's Sir Flip
Gore's Mr. Flipper
Ch. Gore's Merry Quip
Gore's Sunny Imp of St. John
Green Blinkum
Velvet Queen
Ginger XIII

Ch. Sabbaday Captain's Kidd
Ch. Sabbaday Kidd's Capricorn
Ch. Sabbaday Sabrina
Ch. Silvertown Capricorn's Caper
Ch. Sabbaday Titus
Ch. Sabbaday Sabrina
Ch. Sabbaday Favor
Ch. Silvertown Grand Slam
Ch. Pug Pen's Captain Midnight
Ch. Sabbaday Captain's Kidd
Sabbaday Silver Lace
Ch. Silvertown Surprise Package
Ch. Sabbaday Bonanza
Ch. Sabbaday Favor
Sabbaday Amanda
CH. SILVERTOWN SEQUEL
Ch. Candy's Mr. Teddy Bear
Sabbaday Saboteur
Ch. Sabbaday Solitaire
Ch. Sabbaday Titus
Ch. Sabbaday Captain's Kidd
Sabbaday Fantasy
Ch. Sabbaday Favor
Ch. Sabbaday Sabrina
Ch. Sabbaday Opus
Ch. Sabbaday Bonanza
Sabbaday Firecracker
Ch. Sabbaday Favor
Ch. Sabbaday By Request
Sabbaday Amanda
Sabbaday Angel Face

                              Ch. Phidgity Phircone (E)
                  Ch. Auburndale Aquarius
                              Ch. Wheatland's Little Sue
              Anchorage Killer Joe
                              Drumbeat of Doms
                  Mar Mil's Call Me Wrinkles
                              Ch. Mar Mil's Hey Look Me Over
  Ch. Shirrayne's Earthquake Earl
                              Ch. Heisler's Elite Eros
                  Ch. Gore's Jolly Joker
                              Gore's Dutchess of Watson
              Ch. Candy's Almond Joy
                              Ch. Sabbaday Bonanza
                  Ch. Sabbaday Cinnamon Candy
                              Sabbaday Jane Fahey
CH. SHIRRAYNE'S JOLLY KID
                              Ch. Anchorage Matthew
                  Shirrayne's Notable Nimrod
                              Ch. Shirrayne's Brash Buffi
              Ch. Shirrayne's Victorious Vance
                              Ch. Shirrayne's Golden Gaymark
                  Ch. Shirrayne's Lotsa Lovin
                              Ch. Greentubs Busy Bee (E)
      Shirrayne's Adorable Bambi
                              Ch. Bitterwell Broth of a Boy (E)
                  Ch. Shirrayne's Cool Cappy
                              Ch. Candy's Almond Joy
              Haedricks Glamour Girl
                              Ch. Wolf's Li'l Joe
                  Shirrayne's Baby Barby
                              Pugtowne's Barbarella of Gore

Stars Top Jewel of Nortboro

Ch. Heisler's Tom Tully

Sheltons Scenic Paint Topaz

Ch. Heisler's Elite Eros
    Ch. Phidgety Philbert (E)
   Ch. Hazelbridge Paul (E)
    Sugar Plum of Ttiweh (E)
  Hazelbridge Maid Marion

Hazelbridge Carol (E)

CH. GORE'S JOLLY JOKER
    Ch. Velvet Tubby
   Ch. Blaylock's Mar-Ma-Duke
    Blaylock's Cheata
  Ch. Mickey Flynn Fahey
    Fahey's Filbert
   Ch. Fahey's Vampire
    Fahey's Sugapud
 Gore's Dutchess of Watson
    Green Blinkum
   Ch. Gore's Sir Flip
    Ginger Louise Need
  Ch. Susie Needham
    Tempest of Even So
   Green Silk
    Ch. Caprice Claytonia

                    Ch. Auburndale Aquarius
              Anchorage Killer Joe
                    Mar Mil's Call Me Wrinkles
        Ch. Shirrayne's Earthquake Earl
                    Ch. Gore's Jolly Joker
              Ch. Candy's Almond Joy
                    Ch. Sabbaday Cinnamon Candy
  Ch. Shirrayne's Golddigger
                    Ch. Cheerio of Even So
              Ch. Wolf's Li'l Joe
                    Ch. Wolf's Kauffee Royal Rose
        Ch. Shirrayne's Brash Buffi
                    Ch. Gore's Line Backer
              Pugtowne's Barbarella of Gore
                    Ch. Gore's Summer Night
CH. VANDONNA'S DIGGY OF SHIRRAYNE
                    Ch. Auburndale Aquarius
              Ch. Anchorage Matthew
                    Anchorage Angela of Pugtowne
        Shirrayne's Notable Nimrod
                    Ch. Wolf's Li'l Joe
              Ch. Shirrayne's Brash Buffi
                    Pugtowne's Barbarella of Gore
  Ch. Shirrayne's Vivid Vanessa
                    Ch. Shirrayne's Earthquake Earl
              Ch. Shirrayne's Golden Gaymark
                    Ch. Shirrayne's Brash Buffi
        Ch. Shirrayne's Lotsa Lovin
                    Ch. Adoram Cinderfella of Pallas (E)
              Ch. Greentubs Busy Bee (E)
                    Hattie of Greentubs (E)

Glossary of Dog Terms

Achilles tendon: The large tendon attaching the muscle of the calf in the second thigh to the bone below the hock; the hamstring.

A.K.C.: The American Kennel Club.

Albino: An animal having a congenital deficiency of pigment in the skin, hair, and eyes.

American Kennel Club: A federation of member show-giving and specialty clubs which maintains a stud book, and formulates and enforces rules under which dog shows and other canine activities in the United States are conducted. Its address is 51 Madison Ave., New York, N. Y. 10010.

Angulation: The angles of the bony structure at the joints, particularly of the shoulder with the upper arm (front angulation), or the angles at the stifle and the hock (rear angulation).

Anus: The posterior opening of the alimentary canal through which the feces are discharged.

Apple head: A rounded or domed skull.

Balance: A nice adjustment of the parts one to another; no part too big or too small for the whole organism; symmetry.

Barrel: The ribs and body.

Bitch: The female of the dog species.

Blaze: A white line or marking extending from the top of the skull (often from the occiput), between the eyes, and over the muzzle.

Brisket: The breast or lower part of the chest in front of and between the forelegs, sometimes including the part extending back some distance behind the forelegs.

Burr: The visible, irregular inside formation of the ear.

Butterfly nose: A nose spotted or speckled with flesh color.

Canine: (Noun) Any animal of the family *Canidae*, including dogs, wolves, jackals, and foxes.
(Adjective) Of or pertaining to such animals; having the nature and qualities of a dog.

Canine tooth: The long tooth next behind the incisors in each side of each jaw; the fang.

Castrate: (Verb) Surgically to remove the gonads of either sex, usually said of the testes of the male.

Character: A combination of points of appearance, behavior, and disposition contributing to the whole dog and distinctive of the individual dog or of its particular breed.

Cheeky: Having rounded muscular padding on sides of the skull.

Chiseled: (Said of the muzzle) modeled or delicately cut away in front of the eyes to conform to breed type.

Chops: The mouth, jaws, lips, and cushion.

Close-coupled: Short in the loins.

Cobby: Stout, stocky, short-bodied; compactly made; like a cob (horse).

Coupling: The part of the body joining the hindquarters to the parts of the body in front; the loin; the flank.

Cowhocks: Hocks turned inward and converging like the presumed hocks of a cow.

Croup: The rear of the back above the hind limbs; the line from the pelvis to the set-on of the tail.

Cryptorchid: A male animal in which the testicles are not externally apparent, having failed to descend normally, not to be confused with a castrated dog.

Dentition: The number, kind, form, and arrangement of the teeth.

Dewclaws: Additional toes on the inside of the leg above the foot; the ones on the rear legs usually removed in puppyhood in most breeds.

Dewlap: The pendulous fold of skin under the neck.

Distemper teeth: The discolored and pitted teeth which result from some febrile disease.

Down in (or on) pastern: With forelegs more or less bent at the pastern joint.

Dry: Free from surplus skin or flesh about mouth, lips, or throat.

Dudley nose: A brown or flesh-colored nose, usually accompanied by eye-rims of the same shade and light eyes.

Ewe-neck: A thin sheep-like neck, having insufficient, faulty, or concave arch.

Expression: The combination of various features of the head and face, particularly the size, shape, placement and color of eyes, to produce a certain impression, the outlook.

Femur: The heavy bone of the true thigh.

Fetlock or Fetlock joint: The joint between the pastern and the lower arm; sometimes called the "knee," although it does not correspond to the human knee.

Fiddle front: A crooked front with bandy legs, out at elbow, converging at pastern joints, and turned out pasterns and feet, with or without bent bones of forearms.

Flews: The chops; pendulous lateral parts of the upper lips.

Forearm: The part of the front leg between the elbow and pastern.

Front: The entire aspect of a dog, except the head, when seen from the front; the forehand.

Guard hairs: The longer, smoother, stiffer hairs which grow through the undercoat and normally conceal it.

Hackney action: The high lifting of the front feet, like that of a Hackney horse, a waste of effort.

Hare-foot: A long, narrow, and close-toed foot, like that of the hare or rabbit.

Haw: The third eyelid, or nictitating membrane, especially when inflamed.

Height: The vertical distance from withers at top of shoulder blades to floor.

Hock: The lower joint in the hind leg, corresponding to the human ankle; sometimes, incorrectly, the part of the hind leg, from the hock joint to the foot.

Humerus: The bone of the upper arm.

Incisors: The teeth adapted for cutting; specifically, the six small front teeth in each jaw between the canines or fangs.

Knuckling over: Projecting or bulging forward of the front legs at the pastern joint; incorrectly called knuckle knees.

Leather: Pendant ears.

Lippy: With lips longer or fuller than desirable in the breed under consideration.

Loaded: Padded with superfluous muscle (said of such shoulders).

Loins: That part on either side of the spinal column between the hipbone and the false ribs.

Molar tooth: A rear, cheek tooth adapted for grinding food.

Monorchid: A male animal having but one testicle in the scrotum; monorchids may be potent and fertile.

Muzzle: The part of the face in front of the eyes.

Nictitating membrane: A thin membrane at the inner angle of the eye or beneath the lower lid, capable of being drawn across the eyeball. This membrane is frequently surgically excised in some breeds to improve the expression.

Occiput or occiputal protuberance: The bony knob at the top of the skull between the ears.

Occlusion: The bringing together of the opposing surfaces of the two jaws; the relation between those surfaces when in contact.

Olfactory: Of or pertaining to the sense of smell.

Out at elbow: With elbows turned outward from body due to faulty joint and front formation, usually accompanied by pigeon-toes; loose-fronted.

Out at shoulder: With shoulder blades loosely attached to the body, leaving the shoulders jutting out in relief and increasing the breadth of the front.

Overshot: Having the lower jaw so short that the upper and lower incisors fail to meet; pig-jawed.

Pace: A gait in which the legs move in lateral pairs, the animal supported alternatively by the right and left legs.

Pad: The cushion-like, tough sole of the foot.

Pastern: That part of the foreleg between the fetlock or pastern joint and the foot; sometimes incorrectly used for pastern joint or fetlock.

Period of gestation: The duration of pregnancy, about 63 days in the dog.

Puppy: Technically, a dog under a year in age.

Quarters: The two hind legs taken together.

Roach-back: An arched or convex spine, the curvature rising gently behind the withers and carrying over the loins; wheel-back.

Roman nose: The convex curved top line of the muzzle.

Scapula: The shoulder blade.

Scissors bite: A bite in which the incisors of the upper jaw just overlap and play upon those of the lower jaw.

Slab sides: Flat sides with insufficient spring of ribs.

Snipey: Snipe-nosed, said of a muzzle too sharply pointed, narrow, or weak.

Spay: To render a bitch sterile by the surgical removal of her ovaries; to castrate a bitch.

Specialty club: An organization to sponsor and forward the interests of a single breed.

Specialty show: A dog show confined to a single breed.

Spring: The roundness of ribs.

Stifle or stifle joint: The joint next above the hock, and near the flank, in the hind leg; the joint corresponding to the knee in man.

Stop: The depression or step between the forehead and the muzzle between the eyes.

Straight hocks: Hocks lacking bend or angulation.

Straight shoulders: Shoulder formation with blades too upright, with angle greater than 90° with bone of upper arm.

Substance: Strength of skeleton, and weight of solid musculature.

Sway-back: A spine with sagging, concave curvature from withers to pelvis.

Thorax: The part of the body between the neck and the abdomen, and supported by the ribs and sternum.

Throaty: Possessing a superfluous amount of skin under the throat.

Undercoat: A growth of short, fine hair, or pile, partly or entirely concealed by the coarser top coat which grows through it.

Undershot: Having the lower incisor teeth projecting beyond the upper ones when the mouth is closed; the opposite to overshot; prognathous; underhung.

Upper arm: The part of the dog between the elbow and point of shoulder.

Weaving: Crossing the front legs one over the other in action.

Withers: The part between the shoulder bones at the base of the neck; the point from which the height of a dog is usually measured.